Honest to God

Christianity at the Convergence of Tradition, Reason, and Mystery

John Speers

Honest to God

*Christianity at the Convergence of
Tradition, Reason, and Mystery*

John Speers

ISBN 978-0-578-27262-7 (paperback)
ISBN 979-8-88796-260-3 (eBook)

Publisher: John Speers
Publisher Contact: publish@jlspeers.net

Cover design: John Speers.

Scripture quotations designated with RSV are from Revised Standard Version of the Bible, copyright © 1946, 1952, and 1971 National Council of the Churches of Christ in the United States of America. Used by permission. All rights reserved worldwide.

Scripture quotations designated with NRSV are from New Revised Standard Version Bible, copyright © 1989 National Council of the Churches of Christ in the United States of America. Used by permission. All rights reserved worldwide.

*For my wife Louise
and my daughters
Sarah and Laura.*

*In memory of my mother, Margaret,
with whom I often butted heads
in matters of religion.*

Contents

*Much thanks to my daughter Laura
for her help with
copyediting, proofreading,
content feedback, and layout.*

Preface

... you will know the truth, and the truth will make you free.
John 8:32 (NRSV)

This book is the product of a lifetime of seeking both truth and faith. The term *spiritual journey* has become cliché, but it fits my life. It started with a literalist, evangelical upbringing, progressed through a scientific education and decades of spiritual and theological exploration into a liberal, progressive perspective and beyond that into a mystically informed Christianity that is at peace with the modern worldview. I don't think you need to know more about me to understand what follows, but I have included a biographical sketch as an appendix.

I have written this book first and foremost to work things out for myself, always with the idea in the back of my mind that I would publish it if I thought others might find it helpful. The writing process involved more than a decade of pondering the issues, wrestling with them, and allowing ideas to coalesce from many sources, including my own experience, intuition, and what sometimes felt like inspiration. I often found myself revisiting and revising earlier parts. The process could go on forever—but the time has come to let what I have be good enough and to push it out into the world for you, dear reader, to consider.

I have found, strangely enough, that the path to religious truth is truth. By *truth* I mean uncompromising honesty about what one truly knows, what one does not know, and what is unsure. As one seeks from such a posture of personal honesty, things become slowly but ever clearer. As the gospels of Matthew and Luke both report Jesus to have said, "Search, and you will find."

Honesty is sorely lacking in most religion today. Since Christianity is my religion, I will leave the other religions to their adherents and speak primarily to my native tradition. Popular Christianity is rife with lies. It asks people to literally believe things that can be truly believable only to people who don't have the education and/or courage to see beyond the traditional understanding. That being said, I have also come to see that the Christian tradition expresses the most profound, deep, and important of spiritual truths. While I am uncomfortable with what goes on in most churches, I am also entirely unwilling to abandon the amazing truths embedded in Christian tradition.

I have wrestled with this conflict most of my life. The same issues that underly this conflict in me also underly the culture wars that so trouble America and much of our world. The conflict is the result of cultural change and divergence over the past five-hundred years. What traditional Christianity asks us to believe literally was literally believable five-hundred years ago, but, with the rise of science and the mixing of the world's cultures, the Christian narrative and scheme of salvation are no longer literally credible.

Although my journey to the resolution of this conflict has been long and convoluted, the resolution is itself quite simple: **Just be honest!** Stop trying to believe literally what is not literally believable. In other words, accept that Christianity is just one religion among many and that it communicates its meaning through myths that are not literally true, just as the myths of other religions are not literally true.

The only way to do this is to accept that all religion is a product of human evolution rather than a product of special divine revelation in the traditional sense. The entire evolutionary process, including the emergence of religion, is of divine origin, but it is a mistake to regard any scripture as directly inspired by an anthropomorphized deity as imagined by Iron-Age tribes in an obscure region of the Middle East thousands of years ago. That sort of god is far too small and conceptually fragile for the worldview we occupy today. The astounding vastness and mind-blowing nature of Creation that has been exposed by science demands a far greater and more abstract understanding of God, an understanding that I will try to elicit in the chapters that follow.

This is a radical change of perspective. I realize that what I suggest will seem to many ordinary Christians to be a total betrayal and abandonment of the faith, but I tell you that I have found in it a deep sense of truth and peace and a simple and confident spirituality.

What finally matters is faith. Faith is a relationship with the mystery we call God—the mystery represented in Christianity by the doctrine of the Trinity—the mystery from which all things come, including us, and to which all things return. Faith is not a matter of belief if belief is defined as what we understand to be true. Faith is, in fact, quite possible in the absence of any belief whatsoever. Faith is trust in an ultimate reality that exceeds understanding. Faith arises from and rests on divine spirit that is also our deepest self.

But we creatures, while definitely spiritual beings, live in a physical, temporal universe where the objective truth matters. A truthful understanding of how the world works is important for survival and living well, but it is also important for getting in touch with the spiritual side of reality. God, as eternal reality, is the source of temporal reality. The truth as we experience it within this temporal reality points back to the eternal source. Herein lies the connection between truth and faith. Truth is the objective, outward experience of God, and faith is the subjective, inward experience of God. The spiritual journey is about bringing the two into connection and balance.

Institutional Christianity today is tragically out of touch with the paths to real faith, the paths to knowing God. This is so tragic because Christianity has a rich mystical tradition. Christianity has reacted to the Reformation and the scientific revolution by doubling down on theology, dogma, and belief to such an extent that concern for healthy spiritual awareness has been pushed quite far to the margins. Although theology, dogma, and belief are important and very much in need of attention, they can never play anything more than a supporting role. True faith, faith that brings peace of heart and mind, is found elsewhere. It is found in the moments when a deeper or higher (pick your metaphor) level of consciousness breaks into one's experience. If Christianity is to have any hope of survival, it must shift its emphasis much more to the practices that stimulate such experience.

Fundamentalism, biblical literalism, and fearful clinging to traditional understandings are stances that distort both truth and faith. They are fundamentally dishonest and counterproductive to genuine openness. They make it hard to let authentic spiritual experience emerge. This book is mostly about untwisting such conceptual distortions to allow the pursuit of genuine, honest faith.

It was not until after I had settled on the title for this work that I discovered John A. T. Robinson's book from 1963 of the same title. His work was widely read, controversial, and prescient. I appreciate Bishop Robinson's courage and honesty. His book and mine have much in common. Unfortunately, nearly sixty years later, there has been little progress on the concerns he expressed. Christianity seems only to be much farther down the road his book sought to avoid. My offering here has, I hope, benefitted from the perspective of those years. I push some of the issues in ways that might have made the good reverend a bit uncomfortable, but I do so in much the same spirit.

I write this book for the Christian Church. As a one-time active member and leader in a declining local congregation of a mainline Protestant denomination, I am quite familiar with what is going on in that culture: mostly good people very much stuck in an old way of understanding God and their relationship to God, who don't welcome change, and who are bewildered and resentful about the increasing marginalization of the church. To such people and their churches, I say that the biggest part of the problem is to be found, not in the broader culture, but in church culture. The church has lost its way. It dutifully defends what once was but can no longer be accepted as true, and it has forgotten the deeper paths to knowing God that are what really matter. This book is about finding ways out of this predicament, ways that are very much present in the tradition if we look in the right places and in the right ways.

I write this book also for those who have mostly given up on the church after seeking spiritual nourishment there. I hope to show that, despite its considerable problems, Christianity truly is a storehouse of deep spiritual wisdom and insight for the spiritual journey.

My hope is that these two audiences may one day share a more honest, mature, and spiritually attuned Christianity.

September 2022
Saugerties, NY

Introduction

But truly it is the spirit in a mortal, the breath of the Almighty,
that makes for understanding.
Job 32:8 (NRSV)

There are some things I must say—things about deep stuff like God and spirit and religion and human consciousness. These things are at the same time both beautifully simple and awesomely complex. This is paradoxical, for in such deep things paradox abounds, but other things must be said before we delve very far into paradox and mystery.

I consider myself to be a Christian. Being a Christian for me does not in any way involve assent or allegiance to any dogma, doctrine, or set of beliefs. In fact, I believe that traditional Christian belief as traditionally believed is no longer tenable. Rather, I claim the label *Christian* because Christianity is deeply a part of my origins and has become a deep if not always welcome part of me. I was baptized as an infant and raised in the church, so Christianity claimed me before I had anything to say about it. Christianity is the religion of my formative years and of much of my social world. It was the point of departure for my spiritual journey as a young adult. Christian tradition and practice comprise the primary framework on which my personal spirituality and theology hang. Christianity belongs to me and I to it in ways that go beyond choice.

The deepest values I learned in my Christian upbringing were love and honesty. Following these values has led me to distrust other parts of what the church teaches. This presents me with a choice: I can reject Christianity—the good along with the bad— and release Christianity from the claim it placed on me, or I can hold Christianity to its claim and insist that Christianity itself do a better job of fulfilling its own deepest values of love and honesty. I choose the latter.

This position will undoubtedly elicit the charge that I am only a cultural Christian and not a sincere believer. To that I respond: All Christians are cultural Christians. Religion is a cultural phenomenon, and Christianity comes to all Christians from and through culture. Some of us are simply more honest about this than others. Those who claim today to be "true" or "born-again" believers have no more right to the label *Christian* or to shaping the future of Christianity than anyone else who identifies with it.

As Christianity has reacted to the emergence of science, most avowed Christians have come to understand faith to be about believing what, if they are truly honest, is no longer believable. It seems that for most such "true believers" the biggest challenge to faith has come from the theory of biological evolution. Darwin's theory shows that the presence of human life on Earth can be accounted for purely by natural processes without any role for divine intervention. This, in the mind of such believers, unacceptably brings into question the veracity of the Bible and the very identity of God as Creator. Such Christians have taken up opposition to the theory of evolution as a holy crusade. They either refuse to honestly consider the overwhelming weight of scientific evidence or they promulgate sham science to explain it away. In attempting to be true to the faith of their "fathers", these Christians have turned away from the truth of reality. I suggest that ultimately this means they have turned away from the God who stands behind reality. Where religion should be a path to truth, they have made it a cult that twists the truth and brainwashes its adherents, distorting their humanity by demanding that they not trust their own, God-given capacities of reason.

But the sciences are not the only source of challenge to traditional belief. The most threatening challenges have actually arisen mostly from within Christian culture itself. Some Christians have taken their faith so seriously that they have devoted much time and energy to the critical study of its origins, history, and sacred writings. *Critical* here is about *critical reason*. It means that these scholars have tried, with varying degrees of success, to let the evidence speak for itself rather than letting their conclusions be shaped by what they want to be true. In other words, these mostly Christian scholars have turned the scientific lens on religion in general and Christianity in particular. After several hundred years, the evidence they have accumulated strongly suggests that the Bible is a very human product, that the Jesus of history was quite different from what Christians have come to believe about him, and that traditional Christian faith rests far more on myth than on fact.

So—am I saying that Christianity is false?

No. I am saying that much of it is not *literally* true. There are other kinds of truth: metaphorical and symbolic truth, emotional truth, social and relational truth, aesthetic truth, ethical truth, spiritual truth. Religion can be literally false but still be true on other levels. In fact, a very important early Christian theologian named Origen argued that the most valuable scripture passages are those that do not make literal sense because such passages point to deeper truth. The early Christians could be very inventive at squeezing meaning out of such passages, and we might find some of their interpretations rather far-fetched, but the point is that the Judeo-Christian tradition has long recognized different levels of meaning and truth in its stories, scriptures, and theologies.

To be fair, before the scientific revolution Christians did not have to seriously consider the possibility that their scriptures were not, for the most part, literally true. There was simply no other credible perspective to challenge the worldview they had built from the Bible and their cultural past. Although the non-literal truth of scripture has always been most important, prior to about 1500 CE there was little reason for Christians to doubt the literal veracity of the Bible. The rise of disciplined, evidence-based, impartial, rational analysis—which is the basis of science—has handed Christians of recent generations a challenge that was not present in the Christendom (European Christian culture) of the Middle Ages. It has shown us that our religion was not revealed from heaven as a complete, unified, self-consistent whole but, rather, that it developed slowly and messily through the activities of many different people and is far from perfect in the way many Christians like to think. Christian culture remains in turmoil under the pressure of this challenge. The confusion and distress are natural. Unfortunately, Christianity has yet to meet the challenge squarely.

Insistence on the literal truth of scripture is a fool's errand. The truth is that myth is the language of religion, and Christianity is a religion like any other. As with other religions, the core meanings of Christianity are expressed and conveyed through myth. To be sure, there is historical fact mixed into the myths of the Judeo-Christian tradition, but historicity has very little to do with the important content of the faith. In fact, concern to defend the historical veracity of scripture can actually obscure its most important messages. The assertion that the Judeo-Christian tradition is superior to the other religious traditions of the world because it alone is rooted in actual history is entirely bogus; the most important stories in the Bible are not historically accurate reports.

Myth has gotten a bad rap in modernity. Myth is often dismissed as false and of no value, but myth is an ancient, natural, and wonderful form of human expression that frequently bears truly amazing—and I would say even inspired—truth and wisdom. I invite your attention on this topic to the work of Joseph Campbell.[1]

The best myths speak from the collective unconscious of their culture, from the spirit present in all people, expressing deep truth in symbolic form. Myth operates through metaphor and symbol that often carry deeper meaning and truth than even those who originated the myths may have realized. Myths tend to be flexible over time and context because they both invite and require interpretation. The narrative structure and archetypal content of myth resonate in the human psyche, beckoning us to go within ourselves to find its meaning and truth.

Such going within is crucial to healthy religion. When religion loses its capacity to invite us to find living spirit deep within ourselves, it then truly loses its truth and validity. This is the great tragedy of today's fundamentalists and scriptural literalists. They cannot see the forest for the trees. In trying to be loyal to the faith of their ancestors, they have turned their attention to the wrong things. They have lost sight of the inside (spirit) by focusing on the outside (literal meaning). They have turned ignorance, narrow-mindedness, and stubbornness into virtues, thereby failing to recognize the full awesomeness of spirit as it expresses in the real

---

[1] The video series *The Power of Myth with Bill Moyers* is a good place to start.

world, in their own souls, and in the myths they insist are not myths.

I am convinced that religion is not ultimately about belief, obedience, or social conformity, although those things were culturally important in the past and are often emphasized by traditionalists. Rather, religion at its best is about recognizing that all things are permeated by spirit and then resting one's faith (trust) in the eternal nature of that spirit. Such faith cannot be shaken by new objective evidence (science) because such faith rests in the subjective experience of eternity beyond reason and ideas—what is referred to by St. Paul in the New Testament as *the peace that passes understanding.* In other words, true religion is a path to personal awareness of what we call God. That is what the religious categories of spirituality and mysticism are specifically about: seeking to somehow know God directly through prayer, meditation, contemplation, and other practices. Religion that does not emphasize spirituality is hollow, superficial, essentially false, and too often evil.

The most valuable outward forms of religion—the most valuable scriptures, teachings, rituals, practices, and art—are inspired by and intended to remember and re-evoke inward spiritual experience. Religions are founded and perpetuated by people who have had deep personal experiences of God and who hope to somehow bring other people to similar experiences. The problem, as mystics of all religions tell us, is that such experience is ultimately ineffable, ultimately beyond what anyone can adequately express in words or outward forms. This creates a religious dilemma: People new to the faith encounter the religion through its outward forms (words, art, rituals, etc.), but those forms are inherently inadequate to express what the faith is really about. Some people, whether inspired by or despite the outward forms, somehow become consciously aware of the ineffable inward reality that the forms can only point to. Others never get beyond the outward forms but, instead, become fixated on and identify more and more with those forms.

In times of change and crisis, those whose identity and understanding of the faith are entirely wrapped up in the outward forms will feel deeply threatened and tend to vigorously fight any change. On the other hand, those in touch with the ineffable realities that underlie the faith have little trouble letting go of and reshaping the outward forms. In times when tradition breaks down, it is the mystics who remain anchored to the core of the faith and who can authentically inform the reshaping of the outward forms.

Fortunately, Christianity has a deep and rich mystical tradition, even if most Christians today are quite unaware of it. Christian apophatic mysticism is especially profound for moving beyond forms. Apophatic spirituality is often labeled as 'negative' or 'dark' because it finds God even in the darkness and silence that lies beyond all senses, things, and ideas. The Greek roots of the word *apophasis* mean "unsaying" or "speaking away." Apophatic theology insists that whatever is said of God must ultimately be unsaid because of the ultimately ineffable, transcendent, and paradoxical nature of divinity. I must strongly suggest that this apophatic mystical tradition is the greatest resource Christianity has for bridging the gap from its traditional premodern worldview into and beyond the modern perspective.

Broadly speaking, the shift of perspective that needs to happen is from ethno-centric supernatural theism to world-centric evolutionary panentheism and from dogmatic belief to experiential spirituality. This is a shift from perspectives rooted in our human social instincts of dominance and submission (top-down authority) to ones based on reason and experience (inside-out authority). It is a shift from fear-based religion to love-based religion.

This means giving up the idea of the magical, white-bearded old man in the sky who capriciously controls our universe, meting out reward and punishment. It means giving up the idea that God favors only certain people with certain beliefs or behaviors. It means giving up the idea that God is a being at all but instead seeing God as the mysterious source of all being. It means giving up the idea that the historical Jesus was some sort of magical superhero. And it means much more.

In the pages that follow, I suggest a radical reorientation of popular Christian theology and practice. While I applaud the efforts of progressive Christians to move the tradition in a positive direction, it is my experience that the deep problems with some of Christianity's most important tenets—things like substitutionary atonement, Christology, theodicy (the problem of good and evil), and the topics of salvation and afterlife—remain largely unaddressed. I am convinced that only by confronting these issues head-on can Christianity have any hope to survive and mature along with human culture. Mainstream Christianity will continue to wither until it produces and enthusiastically proclaims a straightforward, popularly understandable and embraceable systematic theology that is consistent with the scientifically based worldview shared by well-educated people the world over. Trying to be politely progressive within a system stuck in outdated and uninspiring thinking, language, and ritual simply won't work. Bold change is needed.

This is not about throwing out the past. It is about embracing past tradition, our best understanding of how that tradition came to be, and the best intentions and values of that tradition to grow it forward into the future. The Judeo-Christian tradition has ALWAYS evolved. There is no doubt that it will change further. Even those who are trying so hard to preserve it as they think it was in the past are actually changing it. The question is not whether it will change but how it will change.

It is time for Christianity to finally grow up into the Age of Reason and Science. That means giving up literal belief and letting our myths be myths that point to deeper things. Although this may seem utterly terrifying to many Christians, there is nothing to fear. The God behind our vast, evolving universe is simply much bigger and truer than the God of traditional belief. That older version of God worked for Christians who occupied a premodern worldview, but today we have a very different understanding of reality that requires different religious perspectives.

This is a big change to go through, but it is hardest at the outset. Once you let go of the old religious worldview and trust God to replace it with a more honest one, things soon start to make more sense and to be less troubling. Giving up literal belief in what is not literally true does not mean giving up the other layers of truth. It means seeing God and reality more clearly, and it brings relief from the pressure to hoodwink yourself into thinking you believe what you don't really believe. This starts by seeing religion, not as the final destination, but as a path that leads to something beyond itself. To borrow a Buddhist analogy, religion is the finger pointing at the moon; we must not confuse it for the moon itself. What finally matters is the mystery that is our source, not the various religions that each point to that mystery in their own way.

The long experience of the Judeo-Christian tradition—the ugliness and missteps along with the beauty and inspiration—is too valuable to let slip through our fingers. It is history that we will have to relive if we forget it. What Christianity validly offers, as do all other religions, is the subjective experience and awareness of what it calls *spirit* or *God*. This mystical awareness brings the deep realization that we and all of Creation are entirely of and inseparable from spirit/God. This realization is transformative; it changes everything and makes love and compassion the moving principles of one's life. This is awesome, deeply fulfilling stuff. People should be knocking down church doors to get it. The fact that they are not is an indication that the Church has very much lost its way. The way forward for Christianity is to get back in touch with the awesomeness and find effective ways to share it in contemporary culture.

In what follows I have tried to provide conceptual resources for transitioning beyond the traditional Christian worldview. This path is paved with critical awareness of Christianity itself, but—perhaps more importantly—it also requires that we see ourselves more clearly as human beings: that we begin to recognize how our psychology and patterns of psychosocial development interact with and shape our religious and spiritual perspectives. If we are honest about it, our religion is much more about us than it is about God. Christianity is in crisis, not because God has changed, but because human consciousness has shifted in profound ways over the past five-hundred years. Recognizing the nature of that change and how we all develop psychologically, socially, and spiritually is essential to making sense of what is going on with religion in today's culture.

Few of the basic concepts I offer are new, but I hope I contribute something new in how I connect them, in emphasis, and in directness. Little of the best contemporary theology and religious scholarship ever penetrates down to the laity, down to the Sunday morning sermon at the local church. It gets lost in convoluted, obtuse language and the circumscribed discourses of academia. I shall try to say what I think needs saying without dumbing it down but also in words that I hope ordinary people can understand—if, perhaps, with a bit of effort.

It is not really my goal to prove anything. You must decide for yourself. I will sometimes offer evidence I have found helpful or point you toward other sources for deeper treatment of a topic. I simply express my perspective for you to consider. I hope you find it helpful.

If you identify with the conventional Christianity of today, what follows will likely be a bit of a wild ride for you. I hope you will buckle up, hold on, and see where it goes.

The next four chapters set the table, then I will serve the meal. It's a big meal, so let yourself digest each course before moving on the next one.

A Note on the Gender of God: God has no gender; that is, God is neither male nor female. However, the Judeo-Christian tradition, being the product of patriarchal cultures, has, until very recently, referred to God all but exclusively as male. When I use the male pronouns in discussing the traditional view of God, I shall place them in quotes. Otherwise, I shall avoid using personal pronouns for God or I shall mix genders when I do use them.

The Limitations of Language and Reason

Such knowledge is too wonderful for me;
it is so high that I cannot attain it.
Psalms 139:6 (NRSV)

Our language and reason work pretty well in our ordinary, day-to-day lives in this material, temporal world (space and time continuum). With religion and spirituality, we expand our attention to things beyond the material, temporal world. This *beyond* is not by any means disconnected from our everyday world, but it involves different, more fundamental layers of reality where the logic and understanding we find natural at the level of our physical and social world do not apply so well. The level of reality that holds our attention most of the time is one of duality (difference and separateness), but spirit is rooted in levels where oneness and unity are the greater reality and where paradox (two seemingly opposite things being true at the same time) is commonplace.

The only brains we have for understanding that deeper reality are these brains that have evolved to understand and survive in our dualistic, physical world. The only language we have is language those brains have developed for the same purpose. Although we are connected to the deeper levels and may intuit and even experience them to some extent, our capacity to understand and express what we find to be true there is limited. This is what mystics mean when they say that God and the experience of God are ineffable.

As you proceed into the reflections that follow, please be aware of these linguistic and conceptual limitations. Language can only point to deeper things; it cannot fully capture and convey them.

For example, in this chapter I have used the words *beyond*, *layer*, *level*, and *deeper*. The literal meanings of these words have to do with spatial relationships, but I have used them metaphorically to refer to things that have very little to do with physical space. It is simply the best I can do with the language I know.

When my comments turn to God and spirit and what I call deeper or higher things, please don't get stuck on the words and their literal meanings; try to look through them for the meaning the words can only point to.[2]

You will also find that I use some important words in more than one sense—words like *God, spirit, love,* and *faith*. I both use them in the standard sense in which they tend to be used and understood in traditional Christianity and I redefine them according to the theological perspective I am trying to convey. The context will usually make clear which sense I mean, but sometimes I also allow ambiguity.

---

[2] For an excellent academic discussion of this topic see *Mystical Languages of Unsaying* by Michael A. Sells (University of Chicago Press, 1994).

It's About Consciousness

*God is spirit, and those who worship him
must worship in spirit and truth.*
John 4:24 (NRSV)

What is spirit? What is this spooky, mysterious, obscure stuff spoken of by theologians and mystics?

Well, actually, it is neither spooky nor obscure. Mysterious? Yes—in the sense that it eludes full understanding—but at the same time it is common and entirely familiar.

I will go out on a limb here and assume that because you are reading this you are a self-conscious being. If that is true, then you know spirit from the inside.

As you read these words, you are aware of what you are reading—unless, of course, your mind is elsewhere, but then you would be aware of something else—perhaps a daydream or a memory or something that is troubling you or something you desire. Whatever it is that you are aware of is the object of your awareness, and you are the subject who is having the experience of awareness. Take a moment to let your experience of awareness be the object of your awareness. That is, direct your awareness to your experience of being aware—not to whatever understanding you may have of how awareness happens with neurons and brain centers and whatnot—but to your own, inward, immediate, personal experience of being aware. Look around you and let yourself be aware of the moment and all your senses—the sights, sounds, skin sensations, smells, tastes. Stop reading for a minute and just do that!

What is it in you that is aware of these things?

I don't pretend to completely understand it. In fact, I suspect that its fullness is ultimately beyond understanding. It is not, however, beyond naming, and the Judeo-Christian tradition has named it *spirit*.

Isn't it mind-blowingly amazing that you have a conscious mind that can know it is aware of anything at all? How can it be?

We can understand how sensory neurons are stimulated and how they transmit their input to certain parts of the brain and how those parts of the brain send impulses on to other parts of the brain, but how such objectively observable physical events involving cells and chemicals and electrical impulses become our inward, subjective experience of awareness is a total mystery.

Why are we conscious at all? Why don't our neurological systems just function as they do—receiving sensory input, responding, and otherwise regulating our bodies and behaviors—without our having any subjective awareness of any of it, in the way that machines presumably function without consciousness? If it all happens in the objectively observable, material wet-ware of our bodies and brains, why doesn't it all just stay on the unconscious physical/material level? Why should all that interacting matter result in this non-material, subjective experience of awareness that you are having right now as you read these words?

Mystical religion's answer to these questions is that spirit and consciousness are actually more fundamental than matter. This is the opposite of how science tends to see things.[3] Science takes as its basic input the observable, measurable, material world—the world of sub-atomic particles and atoms and rocks and planets and galaxies and gravity and electromagnetism and time. Science assumes that its fundamental inputs are the fundamental stuff of reality.[4] Science notices that complex consciousness seems to live in complex biological beings, so it tends to conclude that consciousness derives from complex biology. Thus, science tends to see consciousness as being an emergent function of matter.

---

[3] Actually, many of the greatest modern physicists expressed spiritual perspectives. See Ken Wilber's book *Quantum Questions: Mystical Writings of the World's Greatest Physicists* (Shambala, 2001). Science does not rule out spirit but, because spirit is ultimately subjective and science is rooted in objectivity, the routine professional practice of science tends to ignore spirit.

[4] This perspective is not really science but the philosophical perspective of *scientific materialism*. True science limits itself to observable facts and relationships; scientific materialism assumes that the observable, material world where science is valid is the only or fundamental domain of existence—which is finally a subjective commitment rather than objective science.

Mystical religion can agree that, among living creatures, complex consciousness is associated with complex biology, but mystical religion must insist that the fundamental stuff of that consciousness—spirit—is eternal and that matter ultimately derives from spirit.

In other words, matter can be thought of as solidified spirit. Matter is confined within time, but spirit transcends time. Physical beings are all mortal, but the spirit inside them was never born and can never die.

This means that consciousness is not a rare phenomenon that pops up in a few complex animals, but that consciousness is present in some way in everything. It manifests as the invisible interior of all material things. Everything that has an outside (material body) has an inside (spirit, consciousness). To be sure, simple things have simple consciousness, but some level of consciousness resides inside everything.

I would argue, in fact, that consciousness is a fundamental requirement of existence. No thing exists if its existence is entirely unknown; that is, no thing exists if neither itself nor anything else is aware of it. Existence cannot be separated from awareness.

This is like the old conundrum: if a tree falls in the forest and no one is there to hear it, does it make a sound? From a spiritual perspective, the answer is no—if no one is there to hear it, to be aware of it, it does not exist—but that is an impossible condition because the tree itself and everything else in the forest, including the air molecules that vibrate with the sound, are there to "hear" it. They may not hear it in the same way a person would hear it, but it and they are present to its being and its effects. It exists and is known because it is enmeshed in and part of the web of consciousness (spirit) that underlies and constitutes the Kosmos.[5]

Nothing exists in isolation; to exist is to be connected. Everything that exists is a manifestation of spirit, and spirit arises ultimately from and is anchored in the unity of oneness which is also utter emptiness.

---

[5] *Kosmos* derives from the ancient Pythagoreans and has been revived by Ken Wilber to mean "the patterned nature or process of all domains of existence, from matter to math to theos, and not merely the physical universe." Wilber includes in the Kosmos the physiosphere, the biosphere, the noosphere, and the theosphere. (Wilber, Ken. *Sex, Ecology, Spirituality: The Spirit of Evolution.* [Shambala, 2000], 45)

But don't take my word for it!!!!!

The consciousness of which I speak—that arises from spirit rooted in oneness—is present in YOU. Beneath the noise of thought and sensory awareness and self-conscious preoccupation that normally fill your awareness, there is a deep, eternal state of "knowing". Just as the ocean can be stormy and turbulent on the surface but profoundly calm and still in its depths, so does our awareness in and of the world swirl at the surface of spirit which, in its depths, is rooted in unchanging eternity. Under all the noise and commotion there is a loud silence and a bright darkness where you are present to your own infinite, eternal, and connected nature. Enlightenment is simply becoming consciously aware of that reality, the reality that you and all beings are eternally in and of what the Abrahamic religions call God.

In the Christian mystical tradition, the state of that direct awareness is called *contemplation* or *resting in God* or *the cloud of unknowing* or *the dark night*. It is a state of knowing that has no content because it connects to spirit outside the intellect; it does not depend on rational knowledge but is simply there to be recognized. Contemplation happens when the conscious mind quiets enough to let one's attention drop out of ego-centered awareness and into the deeper, primal layer of spirit (nondual consciousness) that is common to all things. Contemplation cannot be forced, but practices like deep prayer, meditation, fasting, and silent retreat create thin places in the stream of one's life where contemplation can sooner or later break through.

I shall not explore contemplative and meditative practices in this book, but I urge you to be deliberate in seeking out and regularly engaging in such practices. They are the most reliable way to access the experiential dimension of spirituality, without which this is all just a hollow head trip. Find what works for you and be patient with the process. Buddhist, Yoga, and Sufi practices can all be quite good. From the Christian tradition, I particularly recommend the regular practice of the Centering Prayer technique developed by Fr. Thomas Keating. Look for information and how-to at contemplativeoutreach.org. There is a helpful brochure at https://www.contemplativeoutreach.org/wp-content/uploads/2012/04/method_cp_eng-2016-06_0.pdf.

For an excellent practical treatment of the topic of mysticism, I also recommend Richard Rohr's book *The Naked Now: Learning to See as the Mystics See* (Crossroads, 2009).

I have dropped a lot on you here that may not seem at all like what you understand Christianity to be. If you are confused, I urge you to stick with me for a while, but my real point is that you don't finally need me or anyone else to show you the truth of spirit. In fact, my advice to you is to not rely too much on any teacher. What you seek, what you most deeply want and need is in you as what the Christian tradition calls the image of God. It is at the roots of your own consciousness. It is the one and only spirit that has given rise to all things and that manifests to us as our universe and the multiplicity of beings in it. That multiplicity is not to be ignored, but the most important answers are to be found within yourself.

Fear Not!

There is no fear in love, but perfect love casts out fear;
for fear has to do with punishment,
and whoever fears has not reached perfection in love.
1 John 4:18 (NRSV)

Fear has played a major role in Christianity. This is partly because of Christianity's origins in Palestine and its roots in the ancient religion of Israel. Palestine lies at what was a crossroads between all the major Iron Age powers of the Mediterranean world: Egypt, Assyria, Babylon, Persia, Greece, and Rome. Various of these nations were at war with one another or engaged in forcefully exercising dominion over less-powerful neighbors throughout the entire history of ancient Israel and into the early years of the Christian period. Israel and Judea were right in the middle of it. They suffered frequent conquest and domination by harsh overlords. Violent death, exploitation, famine, and disease were commonplace. Fear of these things and hope of deliverance from them naturally became a major theme of the Judeo-Christian traditions. In particular, the Kingdom of God that Jesus preached was an expression of such fear and hope.

That is all legitimate. Fear is a powerful part of being human, and it is natural that religion should express it and respond to it. But fear enters Christianity in two other ways: fear of the religious establishment and fear of God.

Fear of the religious establishment has horribly distorted and deformed Christianity. For the first three-hundred years after Jesus, no Christian needed to fear what another Christian might do to them because of what they believed. It was a time of diverse belief about Jesus and the nature of the good news associated with him. There were vehement disagreements, but very little violence. After the conversion of Constantine, the great church councils defined standards of orthodoxy, and the Roman state put its brutal power behind enforcing those standards. Soon a devout Christian could be tortured and put to death by other Christians for her or his sincere beliefs. This naturally squelched the healthy divergence of religious opinion and greatly slowed tendencies of religious development. Doctrinal correctness took precedence over spiritual experience and insight. The spiritually inclined where relegated to religious orders under the strict control of the church hierarchy. Mystics who were not careful about how they expressed their spiritual views could and did come to very unpleasant ends. The church was often influenced as much or more by politics as by the teachings of Jesus and the values of love, compassion, and forgiveness that he taught. Power deeply corrupted many religious leaders and institutions. With the Reformation, religious wars erupted and devastated Europe. It was only in 1648 with the Peace of Westphalia at the end of the Thirty-Years War that the politics of Europe started to untangle itself from religion, a trend that is still working itself out. The separation of church and state enshrined in the American constitution is part of that trend.

We who live in western democracies today can be thankful for our freedom of religion. If we choose to exercise that freedom as Christians, I strongly suggest that we not forget that the doctrines of our faith were shaped for 1500 years under the shadow of coercion. We would do well to maintain a healthy suspicion toward orthodoxy. We should reclaim the right to question, rethink, and innovate that was denied to so many of our forebears in the faith for a millennium and a half. We should revisit the great theological controversies of the past with the attitude that the losers may not have been entirely wrong, and the winners may not have been entirely right. We must allow, embrace, and celebrate diversity of perspective and belief, respecting and loving one another even as we engage in vigorous debate. It is simply essential for the free exploration, expression, and evolution of Christian spirituality that we be able to pursue these ends without fear of one another.

But what then about fear of God? Such fear is based in the logic and mentality of punishment. Punishment was a huge part of life in the ancient world—even more than it is today. You did what you were supposed to do because, if you did not, you would suffer severe punishment. That's how things worked in human interactions, and the ancients projected the same mentality onto their god or gods. The ancients assumed that divine beings controlled their world, and when misfortune or disaster struck, they naturally assumed they had somehow displeased those beings. The Hebrew understanding of covenant was a formalization of this mechanism: the Hebrews pledged loyalty to their god and obedience to their god's laws in exchange for the favor of that god. The understanding was that if they did not hold up their end of the bargain, then they would be punished. The conquest and exile of the northern kingdom of Israel in 721 BCE and of the southern kingdom of Judea in 586 BCE were understood as being their god's judgment on them for not being faithful to the covenant. This way of thinking is sometimes labeled "Deuteronomic theology" because it is most clearly expressed in the book of Deuteronomy in the Torah and in related Old-Testament books of the history of Israel and her kings. It seems to be the theology that dominated among Jews during their exile in Babylon when much of the Hebrew Bible was redacted into more or less its current form, so this theology colors much of the Old Testament.

The important question is, is this how God thinks? I think not. The God I have come to know in my own spiritual life is not a punisher. In my view, the God of most of the Bible who judges and threatens and rewards and punishes is a product of human imagination, an anthropomorphic projection of ourselves onto divinity, a God we have made in our own image. In my view, the thrust of the entire Judeo-Christian tradition, when seen in an evolutionary light, is toward another sort of God, a God of grace. Grace means that this God's love and forgiveness are free, unconditional, and always available.

This newer understanding of God just starts to poke through here and there in the New Testament. Jesus' commandment that we love our enemies is rooted in such an understanding of God.

> But I say to you, Love your enemies and pray for those who persecute you, so that you may be children of your Father in heaven; for he makes his sun rise on the evil and on the good, and sends rain on the righteous and on the unrighteous.
> Matthew 5:44-45 (NRSV)

This newer view of God is most developed in the Johannine tradition (the gospel and epistles of John). The excerpt from the

First Epistle of John at the beginning of this chapter clearly indicates that the Johannine community saw the Christian spiritual path as leading away from fear and the mentality of punishment. In what I consider to be the theological pinnacle of the New Testament and, indeed, of the entire Bible, the authors of First John go so far as to say twice that "God is love." (1 John 4:8, 16 NRSV)

This points to a God of absolute grace, but such a God is never fully declared in the Bible or in mainstream Christian doctrine. We have always put strings on God's grace. Even the Johannine community put requirements on God's love—that we must confess that Jesus is God's son. Nevertheless, the broad trend was clearly toward a God whose grace is unconditional.

The thrust of the Bible has a direction, and that direction is away from Deuteronomic theology toward grace. After the last book of the New Testament was written, the trend continued into the Christian mystical tradition. Unfortunately, the mystics were pretty much always under the scrutiny and power of a doctrinally rigid and coercive religious establishment, so they were rarely free to say how they really came to think of God. We are now free to be more open and direct about such things.

My point here is that on the spiritual journey fear must be left behind. I refer especially to fear that might prevent you from considering new perspectives. It is vital that you know that God will not punish you for what you honestly do or do not believe. If you find yourself bumping into such fear, face it squarely and take it to God in prayer.

Remember that over and over again in the Bible, divine messengers preface their words with some version of "Fear not!"

Truth, Doubt, Honesty, and Intuition

"Everyone then who hears these words of mine and acts on them will be like a wise man who built his house on rock.
The rain fell, the floods came, and the winds blew and beat on that house, but it did not fall, because it had been founded on rock.
And everyone who hears these words of mine and does not act on them will be like a foolish man who built his house on sand.
The rain fell, and the floods came, and the winds blew and beat against that house, and it fell—and great was its fall!"
Matthew 7:24-27 (NRSV)

Religion is very psychological. It happens at the confluence of our hearts (emotions) and our heads (intellect), which are two major components of our psychology. Add a few more psychological components—instinct, social influence, altered states of consciousness, and imagination—and you pretty much have the mechanisms that shape and drive religion. I would argue that there is also an ineffable spiritual dimension that underlies religious experience, but that experience is always brought into the social phenomenon of religion mediated through our minds, our psychology.

To be sure, real-world experience, both positive and negative, that originates outside our minds provides much of the impetus for religion. Experiences of pain and joy grab our attention and send us searching for ways, first, to survive and avoid suffering and, then, to find and hold what we find most fulfilling. In other words, fears and hopes with their roots in the real world drive our religious interest. The Bible is nothing if not a record of how real-world suffering—the captivity in Egypt, the Babylonian exile, the Greek and Roman occupations—drove the Hebrews to reevaluate and adjust their religious understanding over time.

But the religious dimension of our human experience does not happen in the physical "real" world. In fact, religious significance and all other dimensions of meaningfulness are experienced inwardly; they are subjective experiences of our inner selves. We must recognize the difference between our inner and outer worlds and the relationship between the two.

The capacity for understanding our world is an evolutionary adaptation that is more advanced in us humans than any other earthly species. Because the world is always more complicated than we can fully sense or understand, we have developed the capacity to extrapolate beyond what we truly do know to build more complete understandings. In other words, we have a natural drive to understand things, and that drive pushes us to make assumptions in the absence of complete information. Evolution has built us to go with our best guess when we don't fully understand—which is much of the time.

This is a bit of a crap shoot. Some guesses are not as good as others. Good guesses help us survive; bad guesses put us in danger or, at least, create unpleasant doubts and cognitive dissonance. Eventually real-world experience helps us reject the poorer understandings and refine the better ones. Ultimately this comes down to survival. Accurate internal understandings tend to survive because they help the people who hold such understandings to survive better than those who don't. Inaccurate understandings will either be replaced with better ones, or they tend to die out over time because the people who hold them tend not to do as well as those who have more accurate understandings.

This is about worldviews. Worldviews are the models we carry around in our heads of what the world is and how it works. Our worldviews are the inner understandings we use to react to and to try to control our situation in the outward, "real" world.

Worldviews are *very* important. Our sense of identity, our sense of who we are and how we fit into things, is entirely wrapped up in our worldview.

To a significant degree, we live more in our subjective worldview than in the objective, "real" world. To the extent that our worldview is congruent with the objective world, that is not a problem. However, in the areas where our worldview is not accurate, we will, in fact, be living in a false understanding—in illusion.

The point of the passage that introduces this chapter is that it really matters what understandings we take seriously enough to act on. The spiritual journey requires that we be willing to give up our illusions. Because God is ultimate truth, holding on to our illusions prevents us from seeing God better. It also prevents us from seeing ourselves better.

On the spiritual journey it is crucial to be aware that there is always a difference between what is real and what we think is real. Our worldviews are not perfect and never can be, if for no other reason than that our mental capacities are limited. Worldviews are always perspectives on the truth and never fully the truth itself.

Deep spiritual growth requires that we pay attention, not just to God and spirit, but to our understandings of God and spirit, which are not the same thing. To grow, we must be willing to give up old, comfortable ways of thinking.

The process of spiritual growth requires scrupulous honesty. Whereas traditional religion sees doubt to be dangerous weakness that can destroy "faith", doubt is, in fact, a valuable aspect of human psychology that alerts us to weak points in our worldviews. There is simply no harm in following doubt. Following doubt leads eventually to the conclusion either that the doubt is warranted or it is not. Either way, it is a win. Either way, we have grown to see reality a little more accurately.

The idea that faith is a set of beliefs that must be held no matter what is sheer nonsense and the epitome of arrogance. What are the chances that of all the billions of people on Earth, you and your religious group are the only ones who got it right on every point? How is it possible that God chose you over everyone else to know the whole truth?

Such arrogance and dishonesty—both, of course, rooted in fear—make spiritual growth impossible. If you accept that your religious duty is to defend what you have been taught, you will never grow. Faith is not a set of ideas that reside in our brains; faith is the acceptance of relationship with the reality behind reality. Ideas can help open us to the experience of that relationship, but the relationship is entirely independent of any ideas.

Truth matters because truth dissolves illusion, but one bit of truth is that illusion can be comfortable. We find comfort in thinking we know and understand. As I explained above, we have evolved to be uncomfortable with incomplete understandings, so we find comfort in completing our understandings with guesswork, with our imaginations. This behavior has its place; it has helped us survive or it would not exist, but this is a case where we can have too much of a good thing. It has gone too far when we hold onto our imaginary solutions even when more of the truth becomes available. Our guesses must be temporary substitutes for the truth. As more truth becomes available, we must let it displace our imaginings, our illusions.

All of this can be scary, even terrifying sometimes—especially in early stages of the journey. But we are not alone in the process. The reality behind reality that is the subject of faith is in us— always has been and always will be. We are expressions (manifestations, incarnations) of that reality. The divine presence (image of God) in us brings something to the process of spiritual growth. If we dare to be honest with ourselves, there is an intuition, a sense of discernment, a Holy Spirit if you will, that can rise out of our subconscious to nudge us toward the truth. Our task is to learn to recognize which of those nudges come from the deepest, most honest places and to give them honest consideration.

Too many Christians today—and others, too, although my concern is Christianity—have given into fear, ignored their best intuitions, and chosen to cling for dear life to the old and familiar. By so doing they have become liars. They lie to everyone, but especially they lie to themselves—and, deep down, they know they are doing it. This plague of fear-driven dishonestly lies at the root of a great many of the ugly social conflicts that roil our world. We all need to calm down, take a deep breath, and look for the log (illusion) in our own eye before we criticize the speck in our neighbor's eye.[6] We must take responsibility for our own fear and not act it out through belligerence and hostility.

---

[6] Matthew 7:3-5; Luke 6:41-42.

Topside-Down and Inside-Out

I will put my law within them, and I will write it on their hearts;
and I will be their God, and they shall be my people.
No longer shall they teach one another, or say to each other,
"Know the Lord," for they shall all know me,
from the least of them to the greatest, says the Lord.
Jeremiah 31:33-34 (NRSV)

How can it be valid to rethink the tradition? Isn't our job simply to accept the faith as it has been given to us? Doesn't the tradition come from God? After all, theology is based on the Bible, and isn't the Bible God's word?

These are questions of authority. By *authority* I mean the standard for judging what or who to believe, the criteria for deciding what is true and worthy of our attention and trust. This is a very, very important issue. Religion asks us to take its teachings and doctrines seriously and to structure our values and our lives accordingly. That is, religion invites us to invest ourselves in its vision of reality. I use the word *invest* very deliberately, for Christianity seems to offer payoffs for that investment. Just as it would be foolish to invest your life's savings in a business venture you have not scrutinized, so too is it foolish to buy into Christianity, or any other faith, without being very clear about the terms of the deal, who is making the offer, and how trustworthy it is.

The dominant tradition regarding religious authority is that it derives from objectively observed divine revelation. This point of view holds that God has actively revealed "his" will and "his" plan through miraculous historical events and the scriptures, that the tradition has been guided by God to correctly interpret these sources—at least on the main points—and that it is simply up to humanity to accept what God has directly and plainly offered. This is a top-down view of authority: Truth resides with a transcendent God who intervened supernaturally at certain points in recorded history with a plan to save a hopelessly lost humanity. The church's main role is simply to report these events to later generations and interpret their significance. The church's authority is based on its claim to represent the God who has clearly demonstrated "his" power through these events. From this perspective it is often seen as sinful even to question the tradition, for to do so is to question God.

The dominance of the top-down orientation toward authority is rooted in developmental and psychological factors. We all start out learning from the world around us in a top-down manner. Our first concern when we are born is not to turn inward and find God but to come to terms with the overwhelming external reality into which we are literally thrust at birth. We spend a great deal of attention and energy learning from our parents and the rest of our environment. We look outside ourselves for answers and models. In religion also we must learn the tradition from external institutions and people of authority within those institutions. This is a very top-down process. It is generally only after we have acquired a significant level of familiarity with and competence in the outer world that we can turn to other modes of learning and growing. This is a transition that may not occur until later in life or it may not occur at all. The top-down model of authority is one that everyone can understand because it is the one that everyone starts with. Other orientations of authority may not make sense to those who have never seriously considered any but the top-down version.

Top-down authority has the extra appeal of providing a way to avoid much of the pain of doubt and uncertainty. As conscious, rational beings, we humans seem driven to understand the reality in which we exist. We want answers. We *need* answers. We are quite uncomfortable with doubt and the unknown. Top-down authority not only provides answers, but it also provides a conceptual framework that mitigates doubt. It tells the believer to believe, not because the teaching is necessarily believable, but because of the authority by which the teaching is given. It tells us that we have a duty to believe even if it makes no sense at all. By teaching the believer that it is wrong to question authority, religion based on top-down authority invites the believer to join in an unspoken conspiracy to ignore whatever causes for doubt there may be. This is religion at its worst, the "opiate of the masses", rather than an uncompromising search for truth.

Because the uncompromising search for truth can be difficult and painful, many are quick to join the conspiracy.

But there is another model of religious authority in the Judeo-Christian tradition that can be traced back at least to the prophetic tradition of ancient Israel. The prophetic tradition coexisted with the official religious institutions of the priests and Levites, who were the keepers of the Law, the tabernacle or temple, and the ritual life. These two aspects of Israel's religious tradition intertwined—some prophets were priests, and some priests were prophets—but the two roles were always different in essence: The priest was concerned with proper observance of the established tradition, especially ritual and the written Law. The prophet stood as a critic outside the official structures, challenging society to rethink its interpretation and practice of the same tradition.

Authority in the prophetic tradition flowed in a fundamentally different way. Rather than a top-down model, it was both a bottom-up model and, more importantly, an inside-out model. It was a bottom-up model in relation to the religious institutions and power structures of its day. Prophets generally had no official standing in the religious hierarchy; they had no institutional authority. They were individual human beings who claimed to speak God's truth—and that is where the inside-out part lies. As with the top-down model, the prophets and judges claimed to derive authority from God, but the mechanism was essentially different. In the prophetic model, God was not outwardly visible; God did not appear in pillars of smoke nor flame nor speak audibly nor carve words in stone. The prophets and judges experienced God inwardly—in dreams and visions, in inner voices, and in their own deepest convictions—but always inwardly. God's message through the prophets was always mediated by the individual prophet's own consciousness.

What we see in the prophetic tradition of Israel is a remarkable mechanism for renewing and redirecting the faith. Organized religion, like all other cultural institutions, has a tendency toward stagnation and inertia. Later generations lose touch with the fervor of those who went before. Visionaries and innovators are succeeded by conformists and bureaucrats. The more troubling or demanding aspects of the faith are reinterpreted, bit by bit, to be less so. The religious classes come to enjoy their positions of prestige and power within the society and align themselves with the institutions of political power. The focus of practice tends to slip from things ultimate and eternal to things immediate and tangible, from lofty ideals to comfortably calculated requirements, from deeply felt personal commitment to rote ritual.

We humans like to tame our religion. There seems to be an unspoken conspiracy to change it from an awesome and troubling encounter with the truest reality into a circumscribed, magical means of managing that reality. We don't want our faith to change us; we want it to make us feel comfortable and safe. The prophetic tradition served marvelously to counteract this tendency toward easiness.

Of course, this inside-out model of religious authority, as far as I have taken it, has its own potential drawbacks. How can we tell whose inspiration is genuine? After all, anyone can claim to have received a prophetic call. If we open our tradition to such a process, won't it lead to utter chaos?

But there is another piece to the model: the audience of the charismatic appeal. The other living members of the tradition must respond to the charismatic message from within themselves. The judges could only urge and lead, they could not compel. The prophets could only speak their message; they could force no one to listen. It is the other participants of the tradition who decide which prophetic messages ring true and are worthy of inclusion in the tradition. Israel almost certainly had many more prophets than we know about; it is only those whose messages were (eventually) accepted that have been remembered. In the inside-out model of religious authority, it is the inner conscience of the faith community that mediates God's authority. In this model the Spirit of God acts within people in two ways: God speaks from within some and listens from within all.

I submit to you that this inside-out model of charismatic authority has functioned every bit as much in the Christian tradition as it ever did in the faith of ancient Israel. We no longer refer to the people through whom this mechanism works as judges or prophets; instead, we label them saints and apostolic fathers and apologists and reformers and theologians and commentators and writers and mystics.

The two models of religious authority, top-down and inside-out, both play a role in human spiritual development. Each of us originally receives culture and tradition in a top-down manner. Each of us who would be a part of the tradition must first receive the tradition as it is transmitted to us from the past through the cultural institutions and writings that have preserved it. That is, we must first learn about it. Then, as we begin to understand the tradition, we can begin to interact with it. Individually and in groups, we struggle to interpret the received tradition in terms that make sense in our own lives and times. This is the inside-out process. Each generation makes its own modifications and additions and passes them on to the next. Each generation's inside-out theology changes what it had received as top-down theology, the result becomes the next generation's top-down theology, and so it goes. This is a sort of chicken-and-egg cycle that suggests the question: Which came first?

The more conservative, traditional point of view would hold that top-down authority came first, that the core revelations of the faith occurred in a top-down manner. According to this perspective, God acted directly in two ways to bring about Christianity. First, whether she does so today or not, in biblical times God sometimes acted in the world directly, supernaturally, and independent of human mediation. That is, God sometimes walked among people, appeared in columns of smoke and fire, wrote on walls, stopped the sun, knocked down fortresses, spoke audibly, etc. Second, God caused such events and many others things to be recorded into the Bible as "his" direct word to humanity. Thus, Christian authority is ultimately top-down in nature because it is ultimately based on God's direct, supernatural action in human history.

I disagree almost completely with this point of view. I must argue that inside-out authority came first, that the Judeo-Christian tradition came into being and has always been shaped by the inside-out mechanism. While I allow that a lesser, human-based form of top-down authority is at work in the way the tradition has been held together and passed down, I do not believe that God has ever revealed God's self in a supernatural, top-down manner. I believe that God acted no differently in the past than she does in the present, and I believe that the core mechanism by which the faith developed was no different in the past than in recent times.

In other words, I see God as being directly active in the inside-out mechanism but only indirectly active in the top-down mechanism. The top-down mechanism is really a process of cultural transmission. It is a mistake to connect the top-down mechanism to external, observable acts of God in the remote past. The stories of such acts are properly understood as myth. Revelation and inspiration seem to happen in the world we know today only via the inside-out mechanism and not by the top-down mechanism. The sorts of miracles described in the Bible don't happen today, but God does speak in our hearts. There is no good reason to believe it was ever otherwise.

I am saying that real revelation always happens from within, that revelation is always a spiritual experience, that revelation always ultimately originates from the Spirit of God moving and speaking within the soul. It may be triggered by external events and perceptions, but those external things are really no different in essence from any other external things. All external things are subject to the same rules of cause and effect, and breaking those rules is not how God makes God's self known. God is spirit, and God is experienced spiritually. God is experienced in our inner-most consciousness. It is where the creature's spirit connects to the creator's spirit that revelation happens.

I am not saying that religion can properly be a purely personal matter in which each individual can expect to experience all necessary revelation from within. On the contrary, I am quite sure that the real-world social dimension of religion is also very important. As I have already stated, the inside-out model of authority involves a two-sided process: God speaks from within each of us some of the time and listens from within all of us all of the time. God's love and truth bubble up from within individuals, are refined and tested by the community of faith, and may eventually find acceptance in the broader tradition.

This is how myths develop. Something happens that forms the seed of the myth, and, as the story is told and retold, it takes on deeper meaning shaped consciously and unconsciously by all the people who participate in passing it on. It is shaped, not by the direct, external control of any deity, but by the spirit that is the deepest essence of each of us. This process can expose meaning beyond what any of the individuals involved in shaping it were able to see and understand on their own. By the time the myth is well-formed, the historical truth about whatever inspired the myth is usually long obscured by the embellishments of imagination. The point and value of myth is never accurate history but the deeper layers of meaning the myth encodes. Discovering that meaning is a subjective process of interpretation; it involves aligning the elements and action of the myth with our experience of reality both outwardly and inwardly.

This process of interpretation applies not just to myth but to all aspects of religion including scripture and doctrine. It requires listening for what was referred to in the Hebrew Bible as a "still, small voice." (1 Kings 19:12 RSV) This is a metaphorical reference to deep intuition and spiritual resonance. When we think we have "heard" such a voice—when we feel inspired—the validity and worth of the inspiration must be discerned relative to the real world and in how others respond to it.

I equate the still, small voice—the experience of God in our inner-most consciousness—with what the tradition generally refers to as the Holy Spirit. I suggest that this action of the Holy Spirit in the human soul has no rational content. This is not to say that it does not have meaning, but rather that the meaning is not expressed to us in rational terms. The Holy Spirit does not communicate with us intellectually, on the level of ideas. The Holy Spirit interacts with us on a lower level of consciousness—more on the level of feelings and impulses. It is an ineffable experience, something beyond words and ideas. It moves us in our hearts and souls and leaves us to grope for the words and ideas to express the meaning of the experience. The Holy Spirit neither imparts nor directly validates doctrines but stirs us in a deeper place. We create doctrines on our own in response to this stimulus and out of the context provided by our culture and experience.

This concept is crucial. It is based on my own experience of the Holy Spirit. Ultimately, you are going to be able to accept what I have to say only if you find your own experience of the Holy Spirit (the spirit of God present in you) to be consistent with my contention that it speaks to us on a sub-rational or non-rational level. If this does not make much sense to you right now, I ask you to simply take in the ideas I offer so that you can judge them for yourself based on your own continuing experience and reflection.

I urge you to pay attention to how spirit works in *you*. Look within yourself and be mindful of how stirrings and inspirations arise. I think you will find that they start out devoid of thought and that, soon after you become aware of them, your mind kicks in to construct some sort of rational expression of the impulse.

In this regard I recommend a serious discipline of meditation. One of the things meditation accomplishes is to still the thought process enough to allow perception of the sub-rational roots of spiritual consciousness. This is a fairly subtle level of awareness that one must learn to perceive, but it can be perceived. Attaining this awareness requires more patience than effort. It is largely a matter of learning to be still and let the Spirit show you.

My contention that the activity of the Holy Spirit has no rational content does not invalidate reason. I am not saying that the inspiration of the Holy Spirit overrides reason or stands against reason but that it connects to us outside of reason. While it may be essentially sub-rational or extra-rational, it is not antirational. Our need to understand is a fundamental aspect of our humanity. Our faith should not have to stand in permanent conflict with the rational part of our minds. While faith does not rest on reason, neither should faith be opposed to reason. To be sure, there will be times when the two conflict, but this is always an opportunity for growth. Both faith and understanding are properly dynamic processes, not fixed states. Life is an adventure of growing in both dimensions and bringing them into harmony.

Making sense of our faith is our work—not the Holy Spirit's. Notice the idiom: *make* sense. It is not *receive* sense or *discover* sense or *find* sense. We *make* sense—*we* do it. Because the need to understand things runs so very deep in us, we cannot stop ourselves from making some sort of sense of these things. Our only choice seems to lie in the quality of the sense we make. While I don't think intellect can ever completely perceive or fully conceive of God, we can make substantial sense of our relationship to God if we are willing to leave some room for mystery and to recognize the honest limitations of rational thought.

All of this is important because it frees us from the tyranny of doctrine. It recognizes doctrines to be human constructs rather than divinely dictated, absolute, and immutable precepts. This is not to say that there is nothing of the divine in any doctrine, but rather that the divine part is not in the words, concepts, and formal logic of the doctrine. The divine part lies on a deeper, ineffable level that transcends and defies precise verbal expression and complete rational explanation. This frees us to question and rethink any and all doctrines.

God as the source and ground of being is the same reality always and forever. How we think and speak of that reality does not change the reality but may change us and how we are able to relate to it. Our task is to articulate and espouse doctrines that help us relate to the ultimate reality (God) as fully and positively as possible. We must not let ourselves be imprisoned by our doctrines; rather, we must recognize our responsibility to fashion our doctrines so as to free ourselves and others to be fully alive in relationship with God, one another, and all things.

This view of faith and religious doctrine anchors faith in an ineffable personal relationship with God in the here-and-now. That is, it anchors faith in the personal experience of spiritual relationship. This means that faith is not properly anchored elsewhere. Faith does not depend on the veracity of any particular historical events, fulfilled prophecies, miracles, or any particular interpretation of scripture. It also does not depend on institutional authority or personal charisma.

This view of religious doctrine also suggests that the same sort of ineffable spiritual experience may lie at the root of all religion. Is it possible that God has been just as active all throughout human history in India and China and Africa and America as God ever was in Israel? Is it possible that all the world's religions are just the different ways different cultures with different histories have tried to express the same inward reality? Contrary to what the Judeo-Christian tradition seems to imply, is it possible that God has not been playing favorites all along? It is my own experience that one does not have to look very deeply into other religions to begin to sense their common ground. I have, in fact, gained fresh and very helpful perspectives on Christianity from my experience with other traditions.

Many who call themselves Christian today seem to be engaged in a full-fledged and semi-deliberate flight from reason. I refer to Christians who hold doggedly to their particular literal interpretation of scripture and to theological systems that haven't changed much in hundreds of years. These people seem to understand the reality we all share to be a cosmic test of faithfulness—those who remain steadfast to what they have been taught will win salvation, and those who don't will go to Hell. The content of this faith does not seem to matter nearly as much as the authority by which they believe it to have been given to them. Reason is to be respected as long as it does not challenge the faith but is simply not to be heeded when it does. This sort of faith seems often to involve profound conversion experiences and/or conviction of the presence and guidance of the Holy Spirit. Such Christians can be very enthusiastic, articulate, well-rehearsed, and outspoken about what they believe. They can also be stubbornly irrational in the face of any evidence or argument that challenges their doctrinal framework.

Many of the doctrines such "Spirit-filled" or "born-again" Christians espouse to be literally true simply don't make sense if one is honest about it. It seems to me that this branch of the tradition behaves in this way because it connects the experiential side of its faith too rigidly to the doctrines by which it has come to understand its own experience. There seems to be a fear that if any part of the doctrine should be acknowledged as false, the whole thing would disintegrate leaving only confusion and despair. I believe this fear actually distorts their perception of spiritual guidance. Any prompting of the Spirit is filtered and nuanced to be compatible with the fundamentalist understanding of scripture and tradition.

I am suggesting in this chapter that there is, in fact, a gap between spiritual experience and doctrine—the two are not inseparable. Even if all the doctrines crumble, the experience of the Holy Spirit will remain. We need to be consciously aware that our faith resides ultimately in the love and grace of God that existed long before the first religious doctrine and will exist long after the last doctrine fades away. That still, small voice of the Holy Spirit remains real no matter how we understand it. To truly comprehend this is to find the freedom to doubt and to question and to rework the tradition.

Let me, then, return to the question posed as the focus of this chapter: Who is behind the offer represented by the Christian tradition and how much can they be trusted? God stands in the background of the offer, but the form and details of the offer come from the tradition itself, as the product and ongoing process of millennia of inside-out inspiration and topside-down transmission. The tradition is a less-than-perfect messenger. The tradition is many different groups of people over long periods of time trying to do the right thing according to their best understanding. It is ever a work in progress and never the final word. The tradition would seem to offer many things—truth, wisdom, prosperity, salvation—but we must realize that tradition speaks finally only very indirectly for God. What it can validly offer is not promises and guarantees but the opportunity to become part of its ongoing process. Investing in Christianity brings the opportunity to learn and grow and connect and, perhaps, to experience spirit ever more deeply—but what is validly offered is only opportunity.

The mystery we call God is there in it all, as God is in each of us, but God cannot be pinned down by any scripture or doctrine, and God does not make deals. The mystery at the center of all things, including us, enlivens being through love (agape) and calls us to know it and recognize it as that same love in ourselves and in all things. Tradition is simply the cultural memory of the many ways this has been perceived, understood, expressed, and pursued.

Religion is not properly a matter of just accepting someone else's story about God and then living out the rest of our lives according to the rules of that story in hopes of learning in the hereafter that the story is true. Religion is properly about using the wisdom, experience, and—yes—shortcomings of those who have gone before us to live our own story.

Ultimate authority must be understood to reside in the source—the working of God's spirit in our souls and our communities—and not in the outward product—the tradition. Because it is always a work in progress, there is nothing wrong with revising the tradition, as long as the revision is sincerely based on the best truth and greatest love we know. It is not only allowable but vital that we question and rethink the tradition. In fact, it is traditional to do so. Those who see the tradition as something to be accepted without question do not see the tradition very clearly at all. The several-thousand year history of the Judeo-Christian tradition is a great saga of people trying to relate to that which is beyond our ability to completely comprehend or express. It is a story in which each generation has used what it received from the previous generation to find its own relationship with God. It is an evolving story, and we are part of it.

This chapter was adapted from an earlier work by the author: *The Realm of Love: Toward a Believable and Worthy Christianity.* Self-published, 2002.

Mythic Literacy

Happy are those who find wisdom,
and those who get understanding,
for her income is better than silver,
and her revenue better than gold.
Proverbs 3:13-14 (NRSV)

In common usage we often apply the term myth to indicate something that is misleadingly false. To say, "That's just a myth," is to say that something is not worthy of our attention. Such an understanding of myth is unfortunate because myths can be very rich repositories of meaning and truth. The truth of a myth lies in its symbolism and in the dynamics of relationship among the characters of the myth. Myths are symbolic stories that express very important truths about human experience and relationship and the inner dimensions of reality. Myths are the native language of primitive and traditional religion. The real meanings and messages of religion are communicated every bit as much if not more through myth as through doctrine and theology.

In the Hellenistic world, religion was not expected to be especially rational. If you wanted to make sense of things, you turned to philosophy.[7] Religion was not so much about rationality and understanding as about relationship. What was most important in religion was ritual. Through ritual, human beings played their role in maintaining the proper order and flow of the cosmos. Through ritual, people tried to manipulate that order and flow for their own benefit and that of their community. The point was to connect with the greater reality emotionally and spiritually, not necessarily to understand it.

Our modern concern for scientific objectivity simply was not present in the culture of early Christianity. It is a concern based

---

[7] Karen Armstrong, A History of God: The 4000-Year Quest of Judaism, Christianity and Islam. (New York: Ballentine, 1994), 91-92.

on a way of thinking and understanding that has only come into its own in the last few hundred years. It took thousands of years for the underlying principles of mathematics and logic and philosophy to develop and mesh with discovery and technological innovation. Our culture is still struggling to come to terms with this new, scientific perspective. For most of human history, people did not think scientifically; they thought in stories and in terms of relationship. That is what myth is. Myth is a way of thinking about reality using stories about relationship.

We humans have always been creatures of meaning; we deeply need to make some sort of sense of our world. The conflict between religion and science is really a conflict between two different ways of doing that. Narrative and myth are very ancient ways of making sense of reality; science is a very, very new way.

The cultural process of myth making works according to the inside-out model of inspiration. Myths are a kind of cultural dreaming in which the group gives rise to a story of shared significance. Myths develop very much like rumors: Once they get started, they take on a life of their own. Little changes creep into the story as it is told and retold. Some of the changes are deliberate on the part of the story tellers, and some happen inadvertently as each successive teller speaks from his or her own understanding of the meaning and significance of the story. As connections are seen between two or more stories, they are combined into a larger story, and so on. The versions that seem most true and meaningful to the audience are the ones that are remembered and passed on.

The inside-out model of revelation sees God as inwardly active in this process both in the hearing and in the telling. However, the shallower levels of the human ego and psyche are also involved. Myths, then, can be a mix of deep spiritual truth and shallow human desire and prejudice. The longer the process continues, the more the deep parts have a chance to come through and the shallow parts to fall away, but the process can digress and has no definite end.

Our challenge is to learn to recognize and affirm the truth of religious narrative at whatever levels it exists. Traditionally the scriptures were believed to be both literally and symbolically true. As the emergence of our scientific worldview has called into question the literal truth of parts of scripture, we have tended to reject its symbolic truth as well. We need to find the middle road. We do not require a novel to be literally true to find meaning in it. We take it for granted that novels are fiction, but we read them looking for other levels of truth and meaning. A similar attitude is appropriate with the Bible or any other scripture. I am not saying that the entire Bible is fiction, for there is a lot of history there, but we must learn to see the other levels of truth and meaning apart from whatever fact or fiction is present at the surface. What really matters in the Bible are the deeper layers of meaning. These deeper layers deal with eternal truths that remain true whether we believe the stories that carry them to be fact or fiction.

I offer two examples. The first, from the Old Testament, is the story of Adam and Eve eating of the fruit of the tree of the knowledge of good and evil.

> Now the serpent was more crafty than any other wild animal that the LORD God had made. He said to the woman, "Did God say, 'You shall not eat from any tree in the garden'?" The woman said to the serpent, "We may eat of the fruit of the trees in the garden; but God said, 'You shall not eat of the fruit of the tree that is in the middle of the garden, nor shall you touch it, or you shall die.' " But the serpent said to the woman, "You will not die; for God knows that when you eat of it your eyes will be opened, and you will be like God, knowing good and evil." So when the woman saw that the tree was good for food, and that it was a delight to the eyes, and that the tree was to be desired to make one wise, she took of its fruit and ate; and she also gave some to her husband, who was with her, and he ate. Then the eyes of both were opened, and they knew that they were naked; and they sewed fig leaves together and made loincloths for themselves.
>
> They heard the sound of the LORD God walking in the garden at the time of the evening breeze, and the man and his wife hid themselves from the presence of the LORD God among the trees of the garden. But the LORD God called to the man, and said to him, "Where are you?" He said, "I heard the sound of you in the garden, and I was afraid, because I was naked; and I hid myself." He said, "Who told you that you were naked? Have you eaten from the tree of which I commanded you not to eat?" The man said, "The woman whom you

gave to be with me, she gave me fruit from the tree, and I ate." Then the LORD God said to the woman, "What is this that you have done?" The woman said, "The serpent tricked me, and I ate." The LORD God said to the serpent,
"Because you have done this,
cursed are you among all animals
and among all wild creatures;
upon your belly you shall go,
and dust you shall eat
all the days of your life.
I will put enmity between you and the woman,
and between your offspring and hers;
he will strike your head,
and you will strike his heel."
To the woman he said,
"I will greatly increase your pangs in childbearing;
in pain you shall bring forth children,
yet your desire shall be for your husband,
and he shall rule over you."
And to the man he said,
"Because you have listened to the voice of your wife,
and have eaten of the tree
about which I commanded you,
'You shall not eat of it,'
cursed is the ground because of you;
in toil you shall eat of it all the days of your life;
thorns and thistles it shall bring forth for you;
and you shall eat the plants of the field.
By the sweat of your face
you shall eat bread
until you return to the ground,
for out of it you were taken;
you are dust,
and to dust you shall return."
The man named his wife Eve, because she was the mother of all living. And the LORD God made garments of skins for the man and for his wife, and clothed them.

Then the LORD God said, "See, the man has become like one of us, knowing good and evil; and now, he might reach out his hand and take also from the tree of life, and eat, and live forever"— therefore the LORD God sent him forth from the garden of Eden, to till the ground from which he was taken. He drove out the man; and at the east of the garden of Eden he placed the cherubim, and a sword flaming and turning to guard the way to the tree of life. Genesis 3:1-24 (NRSV)

Isn't this a great story? On one level it is a primitive myth that explains why snakes have no legs, why childbirth is painful, and why survival is hard work. On a deeper level it holds profound psychological and metaphysical insight into the nature of humanity's separation from God. Because it is a symbolic story, its symbols are open to a variety of interpretations, more than one of which could be valid. I will offer two.

The story begins with the serpent. The story does not explicitly identify the snake with the devil or evil in any way; that is an interpretation that developed much later. Instead, it characterizes the snake as being the most subtle of God's creatures. The Hebrew word ('aruwm) translated here as subtle is translated elsewhere in the Bible as prudent and crafty. It can also mean sly, shrewd, and sensible. Thus, the snake is identified here with intelligence and reason.

Joseph Campbell has pointed out that the snake is also a symbol of life. Having no limbs, the snake is basically just a nervous system and digestive tract. It embodies the essential functions of life—consciousness and eating—and how the one depends on the other. Our consciousness rides in a physical body that must eat to live. Life eats life. Furthermore, the snake shedding its skin is a symbol of rebirth.[8]

The fruit of the tree of the knowledge of good and evil can be understood to symbolize human self-awareness, i.e. the ego. This story, then, is about the cyclical processes of life bringing human consciousness and intelligence to the point that we became aware of ourselves as separate from God and from one another. It is a

---

[8] Campbell, Joseph with Bill Moyers. *The Power of Myth.* (New York: Doubleday. 1988), 45.

story about evolution from the primal unity of being (the Garden of Eden) into the psychological separation of individual personhood.

Tradition has also equated this story of the fall with the process of creation itself by which unmanifest spirit gives rise to manifest, physical existence. Although the underlying unity remains, what we experience in manifest being is difference, separateness, and duality. There is no conflict in unmanifest unity because conflict requires two, but, in our world of multiplicity, there is always the potential for interests to clash. This is at the root of what we call sin.

There is, of course, much more that can be drawn from this story. My purpose is simply to indicate the deep and profound meaning that can be uncovered when myth is understood symbolically. It is truly amazing that people living thousands of years before the theory of evolution or the advent of psychology could develop a myth whose symbols carry insights of both. Does it not seem as though God herself must have spoken through this myth?

There is no need to believe this story in literal terms. It was okay that people believed it in that way when there was no evidence to the contrary, but nothing is lost if we cannot accept it literally today. In fact, those who insist on believing the story literally today are probably missing the point. If you are not willing to see the story symbolically, you just don't get it.

My second example is the story of Jesus' birth—or, should I say, stories—for there are two in the Bible? Neither Mark, surely the earliest of the four biblical gospels, nor John, probably the latest, pretend to know anything about Jesus prior to his ministry, nor do they seem to care. Only Matthew and Luke offer stories of Jesus' birth, and they are very different and incompatible stories.

Matthew begins with Joseph and Mary living in a house in Bethlehem. A star leads wise men from a far country to this house. On the way, the wise men stop in Jerusalem, where they ask Herod about prophecies regarding the king of the Jews whose birth they believe the star had announced. After the wise men depart, the family flees to Egypt to escape Herod's treachery, which culminates in the slaughter of all the baby boys remaining in Bethlehem. Only after Herod's death do they return to Palestine, but, being afraid to live under the rule of Herod's son in

Judea, they settle in Nazareth. In this story God communicates only through dreams. There are no visible angels in this story, nor shepherds, nor a stable, nor a manager. This story places the birth of Jesus before the death of Herod the Great, who died in 4 B.C.E.

Luke's is the more familiar story. Luke places the home of Joseph and Mary in Nazareth. They travel to Joseph's ancestral village of Bethlehem for a census. Because the inn in Bethlehem is full, they have to sleep in a stable, where Jesus is born and placed in a manager. In this story, angels appear to shepherds, who then visit the babe in the manger. After taking Jesus to be dedicated at the temple, the family returns home to Nazareth. There are no wise men in this story, no star, no slaughter of the innocents, and no flight to Egypt. This story places the birth of Jesus at the time of a census when Quirinius was Governor of Syria, which historians now place around 6-7 C.E. (Thus, the two stories place the birth of Jesus at least ten years apart.)

It is all but certain that neither of these stories is literally true. There is no historical evidence of the star or the slaughter of male children in Bethlehem. The historical records from that time are good enough that scholars would expect to find accounts of such things had they occurred. More importantly, though, the stories themselves contain some very big clues that they are fictitious.

In Matthew's story the biggest problem is the star. How is it that a star could lead the wise men to a specific house? All celestial bodies, even comets and planetary conjunctions, appear to move continuously with the rotation of the earth. They all rise in the East and set in the West every day. Objects in the sky never stand still unless they are in synchronous Earth orbit, but then they are too far away for someone without very sophisticated instruments to be able to tell which point on the surface of the earth is directly beneath them. So, either the wise men followed a very slow, low-flying UFO or someone made up that part of the story. The flight to Egypt is also a bit far-fetched; there were closer destinations where Joseph, Mary, and Jesus could have been safe from Herod.

In Luke's story the biggest problem, apart from apparitions of angelic choirs, is how the census was supposedly conducted. The purpose of the census was taxation, and tax collectors need to know who lives and works in their specific areas at the present time. It makes absolutely no sense to require people to return to their ancestral hometowns to register for paying tax. The civil and economic disruption would have been catastrophic. While the people were all traveling to register, none of their normal economic functions would be served. In the case of Joseph and Mary the trip was about seventy miles and would have taken at least three days one way, probably much longer considering Mary's condition. While most common people probably never moved far from the place of their birth, there were surely also many who moved long distances. Could the Romans really have expected such people to return for this purpose? What were the ill, the crippled, and the elderly to do? What type of recordkeeping and tax collection system could the Roman's possibly have used to make such an approach work? And how could they ever possibly have enforced such a requirement? The idea is utter nonsense. Other parts of the story are also suspicious. Why would Joseph have brought Mary along? He could have traveled much faster alone and could surely have registered her without having her present. Had she stayed home, the women of Nazareth could have helped her bear her child. And why did they need an inn? If Bethlehem were their ancestral home, wouldn't they have relatives there?

These stories were written seventy-five to ninety years after Jesus' birth, and the authors had absolutely no way of knowing what had actually happened. Remember, there were no birth certificates, no hospital records, no photographs, no newspapers, and no video cameras in those days. The only definite witnesses to Jesus birth, Mary and Joseph, were surely dead long before either book was written. Joseph seems already to have died before Jesus began his ministry. If we assume Mary to have been fourteen years old at the time of Jesus birth and to have lived to the age of sixty, she would have been dead more than twenty-five years by the time these stories were written down. The earliest Christian writings, the authentic letters of Paul and the gospel of Mark, make no reference to a virgin birth or anything special about Jesus' origins.

So, why did Matthew and Luke include these stories in their gospels? This question must be answered in at least four layers. First, these two gospels were written after the early Christians had thoroughly scoured the Jewish scriptures seeking evidence to support their belief that Jesus was the Messiah. The birth stories in Matthew and Luke were constructed to be consistent with the conclusions that emerged from this search. Matthew even went so far as to quote some of the specific prophecies that his birth story satisfies. For example, the fifth chapter of Micah predicts that a great leader will come from Bethlehem. Matthew quotes the pertinent verse, somewhat loosely, at 2:6. Apparently the idea that the Messiah would be born in Bethlehem was well enough known that somewhere along the line the Christian community came to assume that Jesus must have been born there. Matthew and Luke simply gave two different scenarios of how that might have happened. Other parts of these stories, such as the virgin birth and the slaughter of the innocents, appeared to fulfill other prophecies.

It should be noted that it was a real stretch to use many of these scriptural passages to prove that Jesus was the Messiah. When you read Matthew, the proof seems fairly reasonable. He says something about Jesus, follows it with a quotation of a corresponding prophecy, and everything seems to line up very nicely. If you dig a little, though, cracks appear. The quotations are sometimes rather loose and usually taken out of a context that does not otherwise fit Jesus or that was not especially prophetic in its original meaning. Yes, Micah 5:2 does mention a messiah figure coming from Bethlehem, but the rest of the prophecy really does not fit Jesus well at all. The same can be said for the mention of a virgin conceiving and bearing a son in Isaiah 7:14. Both prophecies are clearly addressed to the time in which they were given; both refer quite explicitly and prominently to conflict with Assyria and indicate that the events predicted will occur in the context of that conflict. The Assyrian empire was long gone in Jesus' day. Furthermore, both prophecies include other specific predictions that cannot be applied to Jesus.

Second, there seems to have been some concern about the legitimacy of Jesus' paternity. It is well documented that opponents of the early church spread rumors that he was a bastard. While their motives detract from their credibility, it is possible that something was known in Nazareth about Jesus' origins that made him vulnerable to the charge.[9] More importantly, the idea that Mary was pregnant before her

---

[9] Bruce Chilton's treatment of Jesus as a Mamzer in his book *Rabbi Jesus* provides a very interesting perspective on this topic.

marriage to Joseph had been consummated is one of the few details shared by both of the Biblical birth stories. Thus, one purpose of these stories may have been to smooth over a scandalous aspect of Jesus' origins.

On the third level, parts of Matthew's story echo stories from the Old Testament. It was, apparently, a common practice for Jews to make up stories about revered individuals that depicted them as having similar experiences or performing similar miracles as earlier revered figures.[10] The killing of the male children and the flight to and return from Egypt in Matthew's birth story are echoes of the Exodus story. These images symbolically liken Jesus to Moses, Judaism's most revered prophet. They suggest that Jesus carried the formative experience of the entire Jewish people within him.

On the fourth level, these stories contain symbolism that expresses the significance the authors found in Jesus and his birth. The magi from foreign lands suggest that Jesus is to be significant for all the world's people. The inclusion of astrology and the star suggest that Jesus' birth was of cosmic significance. Herod's treachery shows that Jesus' message was not to be welcomed by the entrenched powers of this world. It conveys Matthew's understanding that Jesus would stand in opposition to systems of domination. The manger conveys Jesus' humility. That the angels announced Jesus' birth only to shepherds, who were among the lowliest and least respected members of society, indicates Jesus' concern and special meaning for the poor and outcast.

These stories of Jesus birth, then, are symbolic declarations of who the authors believed Jesus to be. Through these stories, the authors of Matthew and Luke very effectively communicate how they and their communities felt about Jesus. While the stories may not communicate literal truth, they communicate tremendous symbolic and emotional truth. These non-literal truths have become central to the traditional view of Jesus, and the stories that convey them have become deeply imbedded in the larger Christian myth.

---

[10] John S. Spong, *Liberating the Gospels: Reading the Bible with Jewish Eyes.* (San Francisco: HarperSanFrancisco, 1997), 33-37.

In saying that these stories are mythic, I am in no way saying that they should not be celebrated. The real meaning of Christmas actually becomes clearer when we are able to distinguish the literal and symbolic layers of meaning in these stories. The feelings of expectation and awe and joy and great significance these stories elicit within us when we simply hear them as stories are as much a part of their true message as is the underlying symbolism.

If we insist on looking for objective truth in every story in the Bible, we will never be able to make sense of it. On the other hand, if we can learn to suspend our concern for objective, logical continuity and allow the text to speak to us subjectively, it will speak to us authentically. The Bible makes a lot of sense subjectively, but we have to learn to read it with our hearts and imaginations, which is how it was written. We need to learn to let the myths be myths.

People were once able to live in the world and in their myths at the same time without much awareness or concern for any distinction between the two. Part of the evolution of humanity over the past few thousand years has been the accelerating ability and increasing concern to sort out the objective and subjective sides of our experience. In the process, there have been attempts to live in just one side—either in the objectivity of science or in the subjectivity of myth. Neither has worked well. We must learn to live in both worlds at the same time, but with the awareness and concern to distinguish between them.

This chapter was adapted from an earlier work by the author: *The Realm of Love: Toward a Believable and Worthy Christianity.* Self-published, 2002.

An Introduction to Developmental Theory

When I was a child, I spoke like a child,
I thought like a child, I reasoned like a child;
when I became an adult, I put an end to childish ways.
1 Corinthians 13:11 (NRSV)

This chapter and the one that follows are the core of this book. This chapter does not speak directly to issues of theology and faith. Rather, it considers us and our patterns of thought and behavior both as individuals and groups. This topic is crucially important to understanding religion because religion arises from human individuals and societies. The shapes religions take are not random; they develop from human experience and are deeply influenced by how we are predisposed to think and understand. The way we think, understand, choose, and otherwise behave is deeply dependent on our brains and how we have learned to use them. An accurate understanding of religious development is impossible without at least a basic understanding of human psychosocial-spiritual development.

Our neurology is a product of evolution here in the material world. Its primary role and purpose from an evolutionary perspective is to help our species survive and thrive. It is specialized for this purpose. We can consciously control it to a limited extent, but our neurology and hormones influence our emotions, motivations, and understanding far more than we usually admit. In seeking to see God more clearly, we must be aware of what we bring to the search from our own creaturely nature. If our consciousness is the seeker, then our body with its neurology is the vehicle in which our consciousness rides on its spiritual journey, and the windows and instrumentation of that vehicle predispose us to see and understand things in certain ways.

We human beings have complex brains with multiple intelligences that arise from different parts of our brains and the way various parts of our brains interact. The two broad types of intelligence most important to the religious context are social intelligence and rational intelligence. Social intelligence consists of the instincts, emotions, and thinking abilities that enable us to live in communities. These include instincts of dominance and submission, loyalty, commitment, competition and cooperation, affection, fairness, compassion, revenge, and the abilities to interpret and respond to the behaviors of others. These instincts, emotions, and thought processes determine how our social groups cohere and function, including who leads and who follows. Rational intelligence, on the other hand, is the capacity to think abstractly and critically, as in basic problem solving, mathematics, science, philosophy, and self-reflection. Social intelligence resides primarily in the limbic system (paleomammalian brain) and especially in the amygdale. Rational intelligence resides primarily in the neocortex. At the very least, all animal species that reproduce sexually have some level of social intelligence. While many non-human species evidence some ability to reason, the human capacity for complex, abstract, critical reason seems to be unparalleled, at least among earthly beings.

We are first and foremost social beings whose survival depends on our connection to human society. We are not stronger or faster than other animals, so it is by functioning in groups and passing down knowledge and experience by way of our social culture that we are able to survive and dominate our world. We are all born with innate, instinctual intelligence to help us fit into the human social world on which we so much depend. Our capacity for rational intelligence is also inborn, but it is a much more recent evolutionary development and its full application does not come so naturally. While our social instincts are quite active from birth, we must learn to read and write and to use critical reason in a disciplined way. Thus, we are hard wired for social life at a deeper level than we are wired for rational consciousness. (To use a computer analogy, social intelligence is preloaded in our ROM while rational intelligence has to be programmed into our RAM.) Our default way of making sense of things is to model them in terms of human social relationships.

We resort to our rational intelligence only secondarily. It takes disciplined reason and careful scientific thinking to really see beyond our natural, socially-oriented, anthropomorphic way of structuring our understanding of reality.

Pre-scientific human cultures naturally anthropomorphized the world around them. Using their innate social intelligence, they attributed human-like motivations, emotions, and thought processes to other animals and to the unseen forces (nature, spirits, gods) that they believed affected their lives. This was a very subjective way of making sense of the objective world because it projected our human feelings and motivations onto everything else. During the modern period we have learned to use our rational intelligence to better distinguish the objective and subjective dimensions of our experience. It is important to extend this differentiation to our religious understanding.

If we think of God with our social intelligence, we tend to anthropomorphize God. The Bible predominantly speaks of God in this way, as though God were a bigger version of a human being: God is male and Lord and King and Father. God speaks, has feelings, walks in the garden, has a strong arm and a mighty hand, consciously controls everything that happens, and can be talked into changing "his" mind. This God is the ultimate social group leader.

If we think of God with our rational intelligence, we see God more abstractly. Though the Bible predominately speaks of God anthropomorphically, it also sometimes refers to God as something much more abstract, intangible, and all-pervading. Psalm 139, for example, paints God as being profoundly omniscient and omnipresent. The Book of Acts depicts Paul as understanding God to be the one *in* whom "we live and move and have our being" (Acts 17:28 NRSV). The First Epistle of John says that "God is love, and those who abide in love abide in God, and God abides in them" (1 John 4:16 NRSV). In the centuries since the last words of the New Testament were written, many Christian theologians and mystics have spoken of God in quite abstract terms. Anslem of Canterbury (c. 1033-1109), for example, defined God as "that than which nothing greater can be conceived" (*Proslogion*), and Paul Tillich (1886-1965) referred to God as "ultimate concern".

If we understand the types of intelligence behind these two ways of seeing God, we can see that each has its place. The anthropomorphic God of our social, subjective intelligence speaks importantly to our emotions and values but, being mythic, must today be understood not to be literally true. The abstract God of our rational, objective intelligence makes a lot more sense but can seem impersonal. One is a God of the heart; the other is a God of the head. BUT—they are both honest and meaningful attempts, using the intelligences available to us, to understand the same God. Both of these dimensions of our experience have arisen within us from the same ultimate source that has given rise to all things. In other words, God has given us both of these ways of thinking. We need both. Neither gives us the full picture and each helps clarify the other. Our emotion and our reason are both of God, and the spiritual journey should lead us to harmony between them.

It is crucial to understand that the balance of how we use these types of intelligence changes for us as individuals over the course of our life journey. We can think of our vehicle as having a series of gears, with the lowest gear being pure social intelligence and each subsequent gear adding more and more rational intelligence until reason provides as much thrust and then even more thrust than social intelligence. As babies we start out in first gear—all social intelligence. As our brains develop through childhood and into adolescence, we shift up through the gears to use more and more reason. If we are exposed to formal education, we can shift faster and farther. The important word here is *can*. As we move up toward the higher gears, the shifting becomes increasingly optional as education and disciplined thinking become increasingly a matter of opportunity, effort, and choice.

It is also crucial to realize that the quality of a society will vary according to how many of the spiritual vehicles (bodies and brains) that make up that society are running in which gears of consciousness. We can think of these different qualities of society as the traffic patterns we traverse on our spiritual journey. Societies where people run mostly on social intelligence will be driven by instincts of group cohesion and of dominance and submission. These will tend to be tribal and nation-state societies unified by a shared mythology and ruled by forceful leaders or aristocracies. As more members of a society shift up into more rational gears, there is a shift from myth to science with a tendency toward egalitarianism (democracy) and the rule of principle (law).

My analogies here are crude and oversimplified, but this is not, I think, a terrible way to introduce the topic of developmental theory. Over the past several millennia, many careful observers have noticed that people tend to change and grow psychologically according to noticeably consistent patterns. In more recent centuries, observers of history and culture have similarly noticed that societies also seem to develop through identifiable stages. The result is that these observers have provided us with many dozens of developmental theories. Jean Piaget, for example, has given us a well-accepted theory of cognitive development, and Erik Erikson has a widely used theory of psychological development. Jürgen Habermas and Jean Gebser are just two thinkers known for theories of sociocultural evolution.

Each stage theory has its own set of stages, and the number and names of those stages can vary quite a bit from one theory to the next depending on the focus of the theory. Nevertheless, because all of these stage theories are concerned with at least some part of the same core phenomenon—human psychosocial-spiritual development—one can recognize a great deal of congruity among them.

Ken Wilber has done an amazing job of collecting and correlating the most important developmental theories, past and present, in his book *Integral Psychology: Consciousness, Spirit, Psychology, Therapy*. There and in his other writings he has developed and continues to refine his own stage theory, which he calls Integral Theory and the AQAL (All Quadrants All Levels) map. His stated intention is to provide a conceptual framework that encompasses all developmental theories, evolution, spirit, and, really, everything else. I find his thinking VERY, VERY HELPFUL. I am not convinced that he is right on every point, but his analyses are deeply insightful and profoundly integrative. To this point in my own spiritual journey, it is Ken Wilber's thinking that has done the most to help me pull all the scattered bits together into a satisfying whole.

If you are not familiar with developmental stage theories, I highly recommend that you learn about them. It is simply something that cannot be ignored with any success. Your spiritual journey very much involves psychosocial development, and having some understanding of it will make your journey much easier. A good introduction to developmental stage theories in general can be found in Part II, "Windows on Human Development: A Fictional Conversation", from James Fowler's seminal book *Stages of Faith: The Psychology of Human Development and the Quest for Meaning*. He gives a very readable, interconnected overview of the stage theories of Jean Piaget, Erik Erikson, and Lawrence Kohlberg. For a gentle introduction to stages of spiritual growth, I recommend chapter seven, "Spirituality and Human Nature", from *Further Along the Road Less Traveled* by M. Scott Peck. Then there is Ken Wilber and Integral Theory, which wraps all developmental theories in a cosmological and broadly metaphysical framework. At the time I am writing this, a relatively short introduction in pdf format, "An Overview of Integral Theory: An All-Inclusive Framework for the 21st Century" by Sean Esbjörn-Hargens, is available at https://integralwithoutborders.org/sites/default/files/resources/In tro_Integral_Theory.pdf. If you want to read only one of Wilber's books, I recommend *The Essential Ken Wilber: An Introductory Reader*.

It seems to me that the biggest thing that almost all organized religion lacks in attempting to understand and come to terms with modernity and postmodernity is a robust understanding of the related topics of evolution and human psychosocial development.

Evolution is actually much better acknowledged and easier to talk about in religious circles than psychosocial development. Evolution is less personal; it has to do with how all of us humans together got here as a group. Psychosocial development, on the other hand, can become quite personal; it gets down to important aspects of how we may differ as individuals and why we associate into different groups. Evolution can more easily be rejected because it deals with the past; psychosocial development is happening now all around us and in us. This is, perhaps, a little too close to home. Real talk about psychosocial development necessarily stimulates self-reflection, which is not always a comfortable thing and can trigger personal defensiveness.

It is much easier to believe that salvation comes from simply believing and being loyal to certain predefined doctrines than to realize that we must all take responsibility for our own spiritual journey. The prominent religious perspective that faith is about believing and being loyal to received tradition is more a characteristic of a particular stage of psychosocial development than an accurate interpretation of the core meaning of any religious tradition. We humans like to tame our religions by filtering them down to a few beliefs, requirements, and rituals that we can accept and do without ourselves being changed much. Such beliefs and requirements are idols that must be smashed. The truth is that all real religion is about the inward growth of awareness and the outward change of behavior driven by such inward growth.

Until the church is willing to assertively enlarge its perspective beyond the worldview of traditional faith, it will continue to sputter and flounder and become increasingly irrelevant. Good religion has never been just about looking outward and relating externally to whatever God or gods might be believed to be lurking just beyond the edges of our perception. It has also always been about looking within and coming to know and understand oneself well enough to be able to see through the self to the larger spirit that rests deep in all things. Honest self-awareness and self-reflection are essential to the spiritual journey. Familiarity with stage theories of psychosocial-spiritual development is an extremely valuable tool for better understanding how the journey happens and to better see oneself in the context of that journey. This is a process of growth. You have to see yourself before you can see God in yourself.

The Crisis and the Way Out

Do not think that I have come to bring peace to the earth;
I have not come to bring peace, but a sword.
For I have come to set a man against his father,
and a daughter against her mother,
and a daughter-in-law against her mother-in-law;
and one's foes will be members of one's own household.
Matthew 10:34-36 (NRSV)

One of the gross oversimplifications I made in my introduction to developmental stage theories was to focus only on the balance between social and rational intelligence. If you have explored any of the resources I suggested there, you will realize that development involves far more complexity than just this balance. However, I chose to focus on this balance because it lies at the core of the crisis of religion and spirituality in our time. The crisis revolves around the question, **in which of these two forms of intelligence do we put the most trust for deciding what is true?** Everyone uses both types of intelligence, but which of the two do we trust when they are not in agreement?

Religion is in crisis today because humanity is in the middle of struggling through two big developmental transitions regarding this question. The names of the developmental stages involved vary in different stage theories, but for the purposes of my discussion I shall use these labels which I first encountered in the writings of Ken Wilber:

Prerational		**Rational**		**Transrational**
(Traditional)	$\rightarrow$	(Scientific)	$\rightarrow$	(Integrative)
Social Intelligence		*Rational Intelligence*		*Balance of Social &*
Dominates		*Dominates*		*Rational Intelligence*
Integral: Amber		Integral: Orange		Integral: Green+

I shall repeat myself just to be clear: The difference between these stages lies not in which of the two forms of intelligence, social or rational, is present—they are both present in all healthy, normal humans from childhood onward—but on which of these forms of intelligence one relies when they are in conflict. Do we trust the witch doctor or the medical doctor? Do we believe our creation myths literally, or do we believe the theory of evolution? Do we accept tradition as authoritative, or do we reserve the right to question and think for ourselves?

Before the sixteenth century the vast majority of Europeans put their trust in social intelligence and the traditions (which are social constructs) of their culture, which is to say that they operated at the prerational stage of consciousness. That began to change with the Protestant Reformation. Up to that point, religious authority resided in the institution of the church under the control of its leaders. As is usually the case where power, wealth, and privilege accumulate, the church became rife with corruption. People outside the Church's power structures deeply resented the abuses, yet on what basis could anyone challenge the church hierarchy? The Church was understood to be instituted by God, and its leaders were understood to be God's representatives on earth. The Protestants got around this by claiming what they regarded to be a higher authority in the Bible. Because they understood the Bible to be God's word, by going directly to the Bible they could, so to speak, cut out the middlemen.

Before Gutenberg, Bibles were expensive, rare, and available only in Latin or ancient Greek. Even many clergy had little access to or familiarity with scripture, and few lay people had direct access to it at all. The vast majority of Christians had to rely on the clergy for their knowledge and understanding of scripture. The invention of the printing press changed that. In 1522, only five years after publishing his ninety-nine theses, Martin Luther was able to publish his own translation of the New Testament in German. For the first time, ordinary Germans could read or hear the Bible read in their own language.

The effect of all this was to begin shifting the basis of how people judge truth from social intelligence to rational intelligence. Up to that point, one simply obeyed those in power because they were in power. But the Protestants found an objective reference point, the Bible, from which they could judge for themselves. This judging was an act of reason using the Bible as evidence. This was a huge shift, not just in the ideas about where authority resided but in how the human brain was used to determine what is religiously true. Of course, the authority of the Bible rested on the assumption that the Bible was God's inspired word, so conforming to the Bible was ultimately an act of obedience, which is a social behavior. Nevertheless, reason had come to take on a revolutionary and pivotal role in the faith life of ordinary Christians. Instead of simply having to trust what they were told, people could weigh the evidence and decide for themselves.

In the meantime astronomers were finding evidence in the heavens that the Church was in error in other ways. They weren't looking for a fight with the church, but the evidence could not be ignored. The Church insisted that Earth was the center of the universe and that everything in the heavens revolved around Earth. Astronomers found increasingly more evidence that such was simply not the case. This culminated in the condemnation of Galileo by the Inquisition in 1633. The Church won that particular battle by social and political coercion, but it was never able to put the genie of science back in the bottle.

In just a few hundred years, science and the rational intelligence that drives it have become entirely authoritative for most of us when it comes to understanding and interacting with the material universe. Space shuttles, cardiac catheterization, and smart phones don't work by magic or cajoling the entities involved to comply with our wishes through ritual and prayer and professions of faith or loyalty; they work because many, many, many people have carefully studied, analyzed, and shared detailed and precise information about every dimension of the structure, performance, and effects of all the materials, forces, energies, organisms, and processes involved. This is rational intelligence applied according to the discipline of the scientific method. Today critical reason—the careful, impartial weighing of evidence, which is the core process of science—dominates also in the social sciences and has even pushed into religion.

Those damned, misguided liberal Christians have dared go so far as to apply critical reason to studying Christianity itself, and they have come up with reprehensible conclusions. They think that quite a bit of what's in the Bible may not actually be true, like maybe Mary was not a virgin when Jesus was conceived or maybe Jesus was not born in a stable in Bethlehem of Judea or maybe Jesus never understood himself to be God's son in any unique way or maybe Jesus' resurrection did not involve his dead body coming back to life. The "progressive Christian" (oxymoron?) writing these very words has gone so far as to suggest that much of the content of the Bible is myth. And then, there are all those truly troubling social issues—divorce and premarital sex and homosexuality and abortion—where those same liberals have taken stances that clearly violate God's word. How can any of that be okay? How can anyone committing such offenses claim to be Christian?

This is the crisis that has assailed Christianity in recent centuries. It is a crisis of the clash of shifting cultural perspectives and worldviews. The basic movement is from prerational to rational modes of understanding the world and making choices. The shift is from reliance on social intelligence as dominant over rational intelligence to rational intelligence as dominant over social intelligence. In Integral Theory this is the shift from the amber level to the orange level. In Spiral Dynamics it is the shift from blue to orange. In M. Scott Peck's stages it is the shift from Formal-Institutional to Skeptic-Personal. As more and more people in the culture make this shift—and especially as those running the education, media, business, and government systems do so—the society tips more and more to being centered in rational perspectives, but the shift is not easy, it is not smooth, and it is not inevitable. It is a battle. Those exposed to liberal education and leading-edge culture and institutions can make the transition easily, but those embedded in more traditional segments of society find the shift confusing and threatening. Backlashes happen.

A Deeper Dive

At this point it may be helpful to look a little deeper at the differences between how the prerational and rational stages manifest in the real world. At the prerational stage, choices are driven by social factors like group identity, group norms, and deference (submission) to strong (dominant) leaders. Reason may be used to construct arguments to support the socially-driven choice, but reason is always secondary and is never allowed to oppose that choice. At the rational stage, these social factors often remain quite influential, but reason is respected to the point that any choice that is not in line with the facts and honest logic of the situation is not acceptable.

Take, for example, how the theory of evolution is regarded by conservative and liberal Christians. Conservative Christians generally occupy prerational worldviews. That is not to say that they are entirely irrational people, but they refuse to seriously consider any evidence or rational argument that challenges their core religious understanding. They place highest authority in the traditional perspectives of their group and its leaders, any evidence to the contrary be damned. They have gone so far as to create an alternate education system to prevent their children being exposed to anything that challenges their traditional perspective.

Liberal Christians, on the other hand, generally occupy rational or transrational worldviews, and they regard evidence to be authoritative. They understand enough about the scientific process, natural selection, and the fossil and other evidence to accept the theory. That does not mean they are all experts on the topic, but they trust that science moves toward ever better understanding of the objective world. They regard anything in traditional Christian understanding that conflicts with the theory of evolution to be mistaken and to require either reinterpretation or outright rejection. They have no problem reinterpreting the biblical accounts of creation as myth and poetry that carry valuable meaning but are not literally true.

The nature of truth is very different for these two stages. At the prerational stage, truth is a matter of loyalty to the group and its norms. Such truth is a quality not of an idea but of the person who holds the idea; it is the person, not the idea, that is true or false. This perspective on truth is expressed in statements of the sort, "They were true to the end." At the rational stage, on the other hand, truth is a property of ideas and is located in facts and the rules of common-sense logic. At this stage shame lies, not in giving up (betraying) an established norm, but in holding on to such a norm once facts and reason have shown it to be incorrect or outdated. At the prerational stage, those who point out unpopular truths are regarded as traitors; at the rational stage they are seen as heroes.

At the prerational stage, the attitude is very much one of "my group right or wrong." This can all too easily give rise to racism, nationalism, sexism, and all the other isms that involve prejudice against those whom we do not identify as being in our group. The others are judged negatively simply because they are other. Such simplistic prejudice does not fly at the rational stage where difference does not automatically carry a value judgment one way or the other. Instead, at the rational stage each person must be judged as an individual based on their own actions and attitudes.

A corollary of "my group right or wrong" is "might makes right." At the prerational stage, the concept of justice—by which I mean freedom from unfair coercion, exploitation, and aggression—is applied preferentially to members of one's own group. It may be applied to other groups when convenient, but is easily ignored when it might diminish the advantage of one's own group. We see this in the historical treatment of indigenous peoples around the world, including in the treatment of Native Americans by European invaders. Native peoples were slaughtered and relocated with the overwhelming approval of white America at the time. Slavery is another huge example. Today the more rational segments of American society express shame and regret about these aspects of our history. This shift of attitude reflects, at least in part, the shifting balance of American culture from the prerational to the rational stage.

However, we must also remember that higher stages of psychosocial development always rest on the lower stages, and that those lower stages are always present. We can always—and often do—slide back to a lower stage. In particular, fear or convenience make it easy to ignore our higher standards. When we feel attacked, we tend to circle our wagons together with those with whom we most identify and to accept the leadership of those we see as strong but whom we might not otherwise hold in high regard. We also far too often compromise our best selves for personal gain. It's just not that hard to look the other way while something bad happens if that something benefits us significantly, especially if the legal or economic systems say it's okay. After all, "Business is business, right?" If we get called out on it, we can always express regret after the fact.

As we move up the ladder of psychosocial development, commitment to values, carefully chosen principles, and self-discipline play an increasingly important role. At the lower stages we are ruled by our instincts and desires, which does not require a lot of effort even if the shortsightedness of such behavior can lead to a lot of pain. Responsible adulthood and the benefits of complex civilization come only by subordinating our instincts and desires to higher values and principles. This is one of the functions of good religion. Good religion leads its adherents through the prerational stages of development and into the rational stage.

Jesus' admonition that we love our enemies is absolutely not an expression of the prerational stage. It goes against instinct and the prerational preference for one's own group over all others. It requires levels of self-reflection and self-discipline (functions of the neocortex) that bring the individual to detach from the group-centric tendencies of the prerational stage and embrace the world-centric perspective of the rational stage. I must argue that early Christianity was, at its best, very much about moving people from the prerational to the rational stage and beyond. Central to this path of development was the practice of self-reflection that led to repentance and the commitment to deep personal change expressed through baptism.

The prerational stage does not demand that one know oneself, only that one know one's group and support its ethos. The rational stage moves the locus of choice from the group to the individual; it is the individual who must weigh the facts and exercise reason. The prerational decision-making process is simply a lot easier than at the rational stage because it does not require any self-examination. As we move into and beyond the rational stage, we do a lot of navel-gazing that we did not do at the prerational stage. This is because we come to recognize that our prerational decision mechanisms do not go away at higher stages but remain quite functional and ready to take control any time we allow it. We learn that we can easily slip back into our prerational ways if we do not keep an eye on ourselves. We are born prerational creatures, and it is a lot of work to grow into and function from our rational potential.

And Postmodernity?

All of this is complicated by the fact that, while many people are struggling between the prerational and rational stages, others are transitioning from the rational to the transrational stage. In my opinion, this is not as difficult a transition. It involves using reason to find an appropriate balance between reason and social intelligence and to recognize the limits of reason. Recognizing the limits of reason is a prime stepping-off point for experiencing contemplative awareness, which really does take one beyond reason.

I have already suggested that the shift from prerational to rational cognition corresponds closely to the transition from premodern to modern culture. The shift from rational to transrational corresponds, perhaps somewhat less closely, to the transition from modern to postmodern culture. At the risk of getting bogged down in discussing the differences between modernity and postmodernity, I shall try to wade in just enough to make my point.

Cultural periods do not have precise starting points; they build and wane like waves, and they overlap. The wave of modernity became significant in the sixteenth century with the peak of the Renaissance, the emergence of science, the Protestant Reformation, the discovery of the New World, and the rapid dissemination of information and ideas thanks to the invention of printing. Postmodernity began to emerge in late nineteenth and early twentieth century philosophy and art and has built momentum from disillusionment engendered by the wars of the twentieth century; from the common-sense-defying logic of the theories of Relativity and Quantum Mechanics; from post-colonial, human-rights, and social liberation movements; from the mingling of world cultures; and from the decentralizing effects of media and information technology starting in the late twentieth century.

Explanations of exactly what constitutes postmodernity vary a great deal. In my view, postmodernity is best understood as being about diversity of perspective and the decentralization and diversification of cultural identity. Premodernity was dominated by social intelligence, with a mythic worldview and centralized, hierarchical patterns of authority. Except for the often ostracized and persecuted Jewish minority, medieval Europe's culture, though diverse in language and local custom, was monolithically Christian and feudal. In modernity the mythic worldview began to be displaced by science. Also in modernity, movements of liberation and democracy made significant inroads against hierarchical power structures. However, in most prominent social, cultural, and political institutions and contexts, the dominant western cultural perspective—the one based on the thinking of a lot of old, dead, privileged, white men—remained dominant in modernity. This dominant perspective was regarded as superior to other perspectives even to the point of not acknowledging other perspectives. This was expressed in the colonial mindset that western technological civilization was superior and that it was a gift to share it with the benighted masses in other parts of the world, however much cruelty and exploitation that might have involved. Postmodernity is about leveling the playing field for cultural perspectives and worldviews. Whereas modernity carried forward premodernity's mindset that the dominant way of understanding things in a society is the best way; postmodernity denies any such privilege to any perspective.

This, again, relates to differences between social and rational intelligence. Social intelligence is very group conscious; it sees groups as being in competition with one another, and it sees otherness as a threat. This sort of intelligence is at play in xenophobia and knee-jerk anti-immigration sentiments. It seeks to preserve established tradition and order as the context in which all members of society know their place. Rational intelligence is more oriented to the individual and sees other groups as merely different, not inferior. The individual orientation of rational intelligence predisposes it to judge each member of a different group on their own merits rather than paint everyone in the group with the same brush. Rational intelligence thus finds no valid basis for society to relegate anyone to a particular class or role based on heritage, race, or gender; rather, it expects each individual to find or forge a place in society based on personal ability, ambition, and preference.

Based on this understanding, I see postmodernity as a second major phase of modernity, *not as an essentially different or opposing stage*. Postmodernity is simply bringing to fulfillment trends begun in modernity. These trends simply require time to mature. Social and cultural change is slow; it can take generations to work through. Growing from the default social orientation to the more rational mindset also takes effort. Modernity could rationally recognize the essential equality of all people, but overcoming patterns of prejudice and domination woven into the fabric and systems of society does not come easily, especially while major segments of the society remain in the premodern stage. It is one thing to recognize and declare that all people are created equal; it is another thing to actually end slavery and racial discrimination, give women the vote and equal pay, and treat LGBTQ people fairly. Modernity saw the leading edge of culture break through to embrace rational intelligence; postmodernity is mostly follow-through. In postmodernity we are seeing the implications of modernity's best achievements come to fruition. The social impacts of both modernity and post modernity are rooted in the rational recognition that culture, tradition, social roles, class, and economic and political systems are all human constructs and, underneath it all, people are essentially the same.

The end result of postmodernity is a fluid diversity and mutability of culture. This is not a balkanization, not a fracturing and hardening along existing cultural boundaries, which would be a premodern phenomenon. It is also not a homogenization that seeks to erase difference, which is where modernity tended to go. Instead, all the different perspectives and cultures slosh together in a chunky soup with each individual potentially identifying with a different mix. This is evident in the online world, which is today full of sites that appeal to a dizzying multitude of subcultures—gamers, makers, every imaginable variation of politics, religion, and sexuality—and more than a few unimaginable ones—and every kind of interest, hobby, and obsession. Individuals can identify with any mix that works for them, slipping back and forth between several different subcultures, and changing the mix as their lives progress.

Postmodernity relates to the transrational stage of development through its discovery of the limits of reason and science. The hope of modernity was that science and reason would bring us to full understanding and would solve all our problems. Science and reason have improved life in many ways, but they have also failed to solve many important problems—like poverty, conflict, and violence—and they have created new problems—like the possibility of destroying ourselves by war or environmental disaster.

Science has given us considerable power over the objective, material side of being, but it cannot give us mastery of the subjective, spiritual side. Science can help us understand what actually is and what is possible in the material world, but it cannot tell us where we ultimately come from, where we are ultimately going, what we should choose, or why we should choose it. Science is circumscribed within the material world and cannot give us all the answers we seek.

Central to postmodernity and the transrational stage is the realization that reality and our perception of reality are not the same. We do not perceive reality directly. Rather, our nervous systems use input from our senses to build representations of reality in our brains. What we perceive directly is not reality but this model of reality that we carry around in our heads.

For example, colors are a product of the brain. Different wave lengths of electromagnetic energy in the real world are interpreted by our brains as different colors. Colors do not exist outside the subjective experience of those who experience the colors. The brain does not just pass along the experience of red as it occurs in nature, rather certain wavelengths of light stimulate the experience of red in the brain, and only the person in whom that particular brain resides has that particular experience of red. My experience of red and your experience of red might be quite different, but we can never know because we can never have another person's experience of anything.

To be sure, our internal models are built in good part from direct inputs from reality and are usually congruent enough with reality that most of us are able to navigate reality well. However, they are also built of inputs from other people, which is our cultural milieu. Culture and personal psychology add to our internal models a lot of interpretation and value judgment that are not inherent in reality. So, we live and function, not directly in reality, but indirectly through these constructed models (worldviews) in our heads—and these models are different for each of us.

With this recognition of the constructed nature of human worldviews, the activities of deconstruction and reconstruction have risen to prominence in postmodernity. We can look critically at the cultural structures within which we live, analyze how they came to be, recognize their strengths and shortcomings, and rework them into something more true, good, and beautiful. This book is nothing if not an exercise in deconstruction and reconstruction of Christianity.

Reason happens within our mental models. When combined with careful, objective observation, reason can give us very useful insight into the structure and functioning of reality. This is what we call science, and we must realize that science is always a model, always an objectification of reality. Science cannot give us the subjective perspective. That is something we have to find within ourselves.

Of course, the subjective is always present. The journey from prerational through rational to transrational is about differentiating and reintegrating the objective and subjective. At the prerational stage, the objective and subjective are undifferentiated with subjective social instincts very much in control. In premodern Europe this was the world of Christendom in which subjective religious interpretation dominated all aspects of life. At the rational stage the objective and subjective are torn apart and control swings to the objective. In modernity this was the domination of science and business over religion and the arts. At the transrational stage, reason bumps into its own limitations, sees itself more clearly, and recognizes that subjectivity exists beyond its purview. In a healthy postmodernity, the subjective and objective are recognized as two sides of the same whole that must be taken in balance.

Ken Wilber has pointed out that, although prerational and transrational are quite different stages, they can appear much the same, especially to folks who have not reached the transrational stage. This is because, while the rational stage holds reason in highest regard as a mode of understanding and interacting with all levels of reality, the prerational and transrational stages both do not, which makes them look quite similar on the surface.

If one scratches those surfaces, however, the differences are most striking. Prerational folks fear and tend to reject reason because it questions the literal veracity of the traditional understandings those folks hold dear. Transrational people, on the other hand, have passed through the rational stage in which they have fully accepted reason and its implications for tradition but where they have also encountered the limitations of reason. Transrational folks fully trust and value reason as far as it goes but have come to recognize that objective understanding and subjective experience are not the same thing. In the context of the spiritual journey this means they realize that understanding God is not the same as knowing God. This distinction is not clear to prerational and rational folks, so the surface similarity between pre and trans can make for a lot of confusion. Folks in these three stages all do religion quite differently. Few churches have figured out any of this, so it is a mess.

The Faltering Church

The Christian church finds itself sinking in the postmodern cultural soup. The conservative churches remain grounded in and committed to the premodern worldview of traditional Christianity. Believing in the Bible as God's perfect, directly inspired word and rejecting the theory of evolution is no problem for such people. Conservative churches have prospered by riding the succession of antirational backlashes that have arisen from within the remaining premodern segments of society for the past century or so. There is evidence that they may be starting to decline as those segments shrink. While these churches continue to feed very significant conservative social and political movements, they are vestiges of the past and have very little of a truly spiritual nature to offer those who occupy modern and postmodern worldviews.

The more significant crisis is happening in the so-called mainline, liberal churches. Many leading thinkers on the topic of church decline and revitalization have tended to focus on the transition from modernity to postmodernity as the point of difficulty for the church. I think they have failed to understand what is really happening. The big problem for Christianity is rooted in the earlier shift, in the shift from premodern to modern. It is a mistake for the church to concentrate on postmodernity as though it has successfully come to terms with modernity. It has not.

Liberal churches opened themselves to Modernity and have paid a heavy price. Membership in many liberal denominations has plummeted. In my view, this is because they have tried to ride the wave of culture into Modernity and beyond without broadly, honestly, and explicitly coming to grips with the full nature and depths of the changes that doing so requires. As theologians and clergy took steps in that direction, they encountered deep resistance from within local congregations. Whereas some people were hungry for new perspectives on faith and eagerly welcomed trends of change, many others saw no need for it and were deeply threatened by it. Because working clergy could ill afford to alienate their religiously conservative congregants, a group that often included their most generous financial supporters, they tended to steer clear of deep change and the controversy that inevitably accompanies it.

But failure of nerve has not been the biggest problem. The real difficulty is that this sort of change is very hard to understand when you are going through it. There were no road maps, no how-to manuals, no master plans. The conflict between modern, scientific reason and the tradition-driven culture of the church was perhaps rather obvious, but what kinds of changes were really needed and how they could best be accomplished have been anything but clear. Those who were honest, insightful, and brave enough to set foot on the path of change had to take small steps, building the path as they went.

Large institutions simply do not handle radical change well. Changing culture very often results in the demise of old institutions and the emergence of new ones. This seems to be the fate of many, perhaps most, local churches in the mainline denominations. Because doctrine, liturgy, music, and talk in so many of these churches has remained largely traditional (premodern), most people who have grown into or been born into otherwise modern and postmodern worldviews have dropped out of church if they were actually ever involved. Liberal clergy found themselves shepherding congregations that became more conservative as they dwindled. As the laity grew more conservative, they became the pool from which subsequent generations of clergy were drawn. Because many of the theology schools have remained bastions of progressivism, the clergy have tended to remain more liberal than the laity, but the overall effect has been to push many mainline denominations in a conservative direction at the local level. Evidence of this can be seen in the acrimonious battles over gay ordination and gay marriage that have been so divisive for these once reliably liberal groups. More and more of these local congregations are simply dying out as the older generations pass on in the absence of sufficient younger people to keep the institutions afloat.

Of course, there are congregations in all these denominations where the liberal mindset has prevailed. Even in such congregations, however, much of the doctrine, liturgy, and hymnody has tended to remain traditional. This is to say that the words of the Sunday morning ritual still significantly reflect a premodern worldview. The sermon might be modernly ethical and progressive with only the occasional mention of God or Jesus, but the content of the rest of the service is often incongruently traditional.

Even those congregations that have consciously reworked the form and words of worship seem to avoid explicitly confronting the underlying doctrinal issues. It is most often in the area of social issues that these congregations and especially their clergy express their liberalism and channel their energy. This avoids direct doctrinal controversy and conflict within the congregation and between the congregation and the denomination. It also avoids the more fundamental problem that no clear, well-formed systematic theology has yet to emerge and be popularly accepted among progressive Christians. In other words, the most progressive churches are not really sure what their doctrinal and theological positions really are. It is as if they have set sail from the old home port headed for a new world that they can only hope is out there somewhere to be found—and it often seems that no one on the ship really wants to discuss it.

The Crux

So where am I trying to take all of this? It is this simple: The mythic conceptual structure of premodern Christianity provided a concise, systematic understanding for ordinary Christians of what Christian faith was all about. Specifically, that understanding was that **Jesus, through his faithful life, death, and resurrection, saves those who believe in him from eternal damnation and is the actor through whom goodness will ultimately prevail in all things**. This could be said in other ways, and theologians may have differed as to the details of how it worked, but ordinary Christians the world over could once recognize the core of their faith in this simple statement. Now modernity has exposed this to be a statement based on myth and not, therefore, literally true. Honest, educated people today simply cannot believe these words in the literal sense that Christians of the past believed them. So, what, then, is the literally true conceptual structure on which modern, rational Christianity can stand? Is there a similarly concise statement of faith that can unite within a Christian identity ordinary people who occupy scientifically-aware worldviews? I think there is.

Premodern Christian faith viewed the world from the perspective of its myth. The statement of premodern faith given above speaks from within the world of the myth as though that myth were literally true. Modern Christianity, if it is honest, recognizes that the myth is a myth. To speak literal truth, modern Christianity must speak from outside the myth, that is, from a perspective that accepts that the myth is not literally true. Yet, Christian identity cannot be separated from the myth. This means that the literal truth that modern Christianity can speak is not the myth alone but the myth acknowledged as myth together with its meaning. This could be referred to as *Transmythic Christianity*: what Christianity becomes when it moves beyond literal belief in its myths.

Myths are not just stories; they are stories that speak from the depths of our collective human consciousness about what it is to be human. Well-formed myths always tell us about ourselves, about the challenges of being human, about our journey through life and where it can lead, and about the larger reality of which we are a part.

The deep meaning of Christian biblical tradition for modernity and beyond is found in realizing that in the myth **Jesus, as the hero of the myth, represents every person**. The literal truth that follows from this is that **God is incarnate in all of creation and calls us to recognize and love the divine nature in ourselves, in other human beings, and in all things.**

It is obvious to me that this statement distills the meaning of the Christian myth and presents what the core of Christian faith ought to be in modernity and beyond, but I have been wrestling with this issue for quite some time. It may very well not strike you as obvious at all. That's fine. I invite you just to keep an open mind, to keep reading, to keep thinking, and to keep praying and meditating.

My point here is that the church flounders in its current crisis of decline among modern and postmodern people because it has not successfully transitioned from the old understanding of the faith to this new one or to something like it. The older summary of faith stated above could be and was believed literally by most

Christians for many centuries; it just does not make literal sense anymore. Nevertheless, the underlying needs and desires and concerns and hopes that drove that faith for all those people for all that time are still present in people today—even scientific, critically-minded, well-educated modern and postmodern people. The problem is not in the people; it is in what the church keeps trying to sell them.

Sola Scriptura

You shall have no other gods before me.
Exodus 20:3 (NRSV)

Sola scriptura means "only scripture" or "scripture alone". It was the quintessential battle cry of the Protestant Reformation and remains the core declaration of Protestant identity for many Protestants today. It means that the Bible, as God's inspired word, must be taken to be the ultimate authority in all matters of faith.

As previously stated, this perspective provided an opening at the time of the Reformation for ordinary Christians to exercise more independent reason in the context of faith than had been possible in earlier times. Instead of merely accepting what they were told by the church, individual Christians could read scripture for themselves and base their faith on this relatively more objective source. Scripture, being words written on paper, was a set of tangible, relatively fixed objects present in the physical world for everyone to see. The interpretation of these tangible objects was absolutely mired in subjectivity, and the objects themselves certainly had very subjective origins, but the objective nature of established scripture provided a way to start separating faith from the dictates of an all-too-human church hierarchy. As the Bible became more available in translation to an increasingly literate laity, the locus of interpretation began to shift from the institution to the individual.

What neither side in this battle really questioned was the authoritative nature of Scripture. The dispute was much more over who could properly interpret it than over the ultimate nature of its authority. Both sides held a top-down understanding of the nature of Biblical authority: the Bible was God's words to humanity as directly inspired by God into the minds of the authors. Hence, the Bible was regarded as a perfect and inerrant divine product.

Over the past several hundred years scholars have been punching holes in this understanding of biblical authority. Honest study of the Bible and its history and origins leads to the understanding that it is the product of fallible human beings—human beings trying to be faithful to their best understanding of God and God's will—but fallible human beings nonetheless. The Bible presents various and sometimes conflicting perspectives from different times and groups within the history of Judaism and early Christianity. If you think it is God's direct, perfect, and inerrant words that must be accepted literally and obeyed without question, then I suggest that you not continue beyond this chapter until you are able to recognize and accept the very complex and human nature of the Bible.

I am not going to try to convince you in great detail on this matter. Many others who are far more qualified than I have researched and written about it, so I see no value in trying to reproduce all the evidence and arguments here. I provide a list of resources at the end of this chapter to get you started investigating this topic more deeply for yourself. I will leave it to you to pursue the matter until you are satisfied one way or the other. My primary intention here is to provide a basic argument as to why strident belief in Biblical perfection is itself an error—a sin, actually—from a theological perspective.

In the past, the broadly accepted theological view was that the Bible, as God's word, came from God and therefore shared in and reflected God's perfection. There is a sense in which that is true, but there is a huge problem when that is understood to mean that the Bible is perfect in and of itself. It is the sin of idolatry—the transgression of the first and foremost commandment. It is the sin of granting ultimacy and priority to something that is not ultimate. God alone is ultimate. At its core, the sin of idolatry is believing the lie that any creature of God—which is to say, anything other than God: any object or being or idea—can have ultimate value in and of itself; it is believing the lie that anything can be equal to or greater than its source, which is God. Ultimate value and authority belong to and reside in God alone. Granting the Bible ultimate authority is the sin of regarding something that is not God with the respect and loyalty and importance that should be given only to God.

This is a sin of attention: when we focus so much on any of the trees (created beings and things) in the forest of God that we forget that they are all subordinate parts of that much bigger reality, then we have let something else usurp God's place in our consciousness. Fundamentalists and conservative Christians have done this with the Bible. They have elevated it to such a high status in their own minds and hearts that it has pushed out all the other ways God speaks to us and is present to us. By seeing God only through the Bible, what they see is only the Bible; God has been replaced by a thing.

This is a pivotal issue for what I am trying to say. I am arguing that Christianity can and should survive in contemporary, scientifically-aware culture only if it can shift its understanding of theological authority from the top-down model to the inside-out model. That is, Christianity must come to see that its outward, objective forms and structures—i.e., its traditions, doctrines, and institutions—are valid only to the extent that they derive from and remain faithful to the inward, subjective reality of divinity in and beyond all things. True faith must ultimately rest in the experience of the ineffable presence of the living God in the human soul. This means that ultimate authority cannot be accorded to any object, not even the Bible. Only God is perfect, and only God is ultimate.

Of course, we humans with our limited consciousness are incapable of holding an infinite God in our attention very well at all, let alone in the midst of the busyness and distractions that fill most of our time here on earth. I would argue that therein lies original sin, but that topic must wait. What must also wait is a more thorough explanation of what exactly I am using the word *God* to mean.

As I said, there is a sense in which the Bible is perfect. It is the sense in which everything that comes from God and that God sustains—which is everything—is perfect in every moment, but this is a derived and dependent perfection. It is the perfection of every imperfect part in a perfect whole. It is a big-picture perfection that recognizes and encompasses all the flaws, failures, conflicts, and sins of every constituent part. It is a perfection grounded in the love that connects all things within God—the love that forgives what we normally count as imperfections.

That is not what biblical literalists mean by *perfect*; they mean the Bible is without flaw, error of fact, or internal conflict of meaning. Any honest student of the Bible cannot believe such things.

Perfect means complete. God alone is complete. Everything else is perfect only in the sense that it shares in God's perfection. *Share* is the important concept here. No creature is complete in and of itself; its completeness, its perfection, lies in its connection to and its place within the larger reality that we call God. It is a serious theological mistake to ascribe full perfection to the Bible.

Could it be possible for the Bible to be imperfect in the sense of being limited and incomplete without also containing errors and inconsistencies? Yes, theoretically, but honest examination of the Bible simply reveals that not to be the case—and that's fine.

The deeper issue here is the lack of trust, courage, and imagination on the part of the Bibolators—those who have allowed their reverence for the Bible to usurp the place of God. They have a nice comfortable systematic understanding of what life and Christianity are all about. It is an understanding that makes sense to their social intelligence, and they repress any part of their rational intelligence that might allow that understanding to be challenged. This is a refusal to grow that is deeply rooted in fear and ignorance. They are like children who refuse to grow up and accept that maybe Santa Claus is not literally real. They think that faith is about holding fast to their current, often childish, understanding no matter what. They think that the "culture wars" are a test of their faith and that God will reward them for not giving in, for not allowing themselves to truly consider any other perspective. But God is found in truth, not in obstinacy. Real faith is trusting that God really can be found in the truth, whatever it is. That can be scary, but real faith is not for cowards.

So, if you think being a Christian obligates you to believe that the Bible is inerrant, flawless, and entirely without contradiction, give it up! You are free to let the Bible be what it is. It is a very great and important book, and that greatness does not depend on being inerrant, flawless, or entirely without contradiction. Let yourself learn from it rather than feeling obligated to impose any sort of predetermined meaning on it.

Resources for Personal Study

When you let the Bible be what it actually is, it becomes absolutely fascinating and also liberating. It is a window into the experiences and worldviews of people who lived 1900 to 3000 or more years ago. It presents itself to us as a foundation for faith, hope, and wisdom and also as a complex set of puzzles that cannot be ignored if we desire to truly understand it. The Bible was written, edited, and redacted largely by people working from the deepest inspiration they could find. It is, thus, a product of myth-building through which spirit can speak to us in very deep ways if we simply let it be what it is: perfectly imperfect.

The books listed here are concerned especially with the understanding dimension, but certainly do not ignore the faith, hope, and wisdom. The authors of these works do not agree with each other on every point, nor can I say that I agree entirely with any of them. Part of the learning here is to realize that we humans always filter our understanding through our own perspectives. The goal in critical study is to let the facts correct our perspectives, but facts regarding the Bible tend to be sparse and soft, so personal judgment is often necessary. I suggest that the goal should be to not let this need for personal judgment become the occasion of personal dishonestly. That means you must have one eye studying yourself while the other eye studies the Bible.

I recommend the first two books in the list as good places to start. The Ehrman book is more academic than Borg's, so pick accordingly. In my opinion the most important book in the list is Bishop Spong's; it holds some crucial insights as to why our New Testament gospels are structured as they are.

Borg, Marcus J. *Reading the Bible Again for the First Time: Taking the Bible Seriously but Not Literally*. San Francisco: HarperSanFrancisco, 2001.
A guide for reading the Bible with basic understanding of its origins, historical context, and literary nature.
Ehrman, Bart D. *A Brief Introduction to the New Testament*. New York: Oxford University Press, 2004.
_____. *Misquoting Jesus: The Story Behind Who Changed the Bible and Why*. San Francisco: HarperSanFrancisco, 2005.
_____. *The Orthodox Corruption of Scripture: The Effect of Early Christological Controversies on the Text of the New Testament*. New York: Oxford University Press, 1993.
In the introduction to *Misquoting Jesus*, Ehrman tells how his one-time conservative evangelical "commitment to the Bible as the inerrant word of God" (8) eroded as he studied it in depth. I commend these three books and any of his other books about scripture as excellent resources for seeing the human fingerprints

that are all over the New Testament. The first book above is an
entry-level college textbook.

Friedman, Richard E. *Who Wrote the Bible?* San Francisco:
HarperSanFrancisco, 1989.
An overview of the current scholarly understandings of the origins
of the first five books of the Old Testament, also called the
Pentateuch or Torah.

Funk, Robert W., Roy W. Hoover, and The Jesus Seminar. *The Five
Gospels: What Did Jesus Really Say?* San Francisco:
HarperSanFrancisco, 1997.
This book is the result of voting by the Jesus Seminar as to the likely
authenticity of the words attributed to Jesus in the Bible and the
Gospel of Thomas. It analyzes virtually every such passage. This is a
very important resource for understanding the gospels.

Mack, Burton L. *Who Wrote the New Testament? The Making of
the Christian Myth.* San Francisco: HarperSanFrancisco, 1995.
A scholarly analysis of the development of early Christianity as
reflected in the New Testament.

Metzger, Bruce M. and Michael D. Coogan. *The Oxford Companion
to the Bible.* New York: Oxford University Press, 1993.
A basic reference. Something newer might be better.

Ramsey, William M. *The Westminster Guide to the Books of the
Bible.* Louisville: Westminster John Knox Press, 1994.
A basic reference. Something newer might be better.

Spong, John S. *Liberating the Gospels: Reading the Bible with
Jewish Eyes.* San Francisco: HarperSanFrancisco, 1997.
Uses an understanding of Jewish tradition and practice in Jesus time
to make sense of the structure and content of the four New
Testament gospels.

The Objective Jesus

Jesus came to Galilee, proclaiming the good news of God,
and saying, "The time is fulfilled,
and the kingdom of God has come near;
repent, and believe in the good news."
Mark 1:14-15 (NRSV)

Who was Jesus of Nazareth really? What did he really do? What did he really say?

The only significant things I can say with any confidence about Jesus of Nazareth are that he was a Galilean Jewish peasant whose teachings attracted followers, that he was crucified in Jerusalem by the Romans, and that he was survived by followers whose various movements eventually gave rise to Christianity. We probably know other bits of accurate information—like the gist of some of his teachings and the names of his family members and closest followers—but there is almost nothing we think we know about Jesus that cannot be *legitimately* doubted.

We have no written sources that recorded the things Jesus actually said and did at the time he actually said and did them. Our best evidence for trying to discern who Jesus really was is the New Testament and especially the four canonical gospels. The recently discovered Gospel of Thomas is also helpful. The various parts of the New Testament were written twenty to seventy or more years after Jesus died. None of them was written to be objective history in the sense we use the term today. The author of the Gospel of Luke claims to have written "an orderly account" so that the person to whom he addresses the gospel, the "most excellent Theophilus", who may or may not have been a real person, "may know the truth concerning the things about which you have been instructed" (Luke 1:3-4 NRSV), but even Luke fails to acknowledge his sources and to evaluate their veracity.

The earliest gospel, Mark, appears to have been completed sometime shortly before or after Jerusalem was destroyed by the Romans in 70 C.E., more than 35 years after Jesus was crucified. It appears to have been written, not as a historical account, but to provide liturgical readings and to instruct new converts in preparation for baptism. The Gospels of Luke and Matthew clearly adopted their chronologies of Jesus life from Mark. These first three gospels—Mark, Matthew, and Luke—are together referred to as the Synoptic Gospels because they see Jesus life from pretty much the same chronological perspective. The Gospel of Matthew appears to have been structured to provide an annual cycle of liturgical readings to compliment the traditional cycle of Torah readings in the synagogues.[11]

The Gospel of John presents a very different chronology and a Jesus who speaks very differently from the Jesus of the Synoptics. The Gospel of John is more a theological reflection on the risen Christ (post-Easter Jesus) than a historical report about the earthly (pre-Easter) Jesus.

All of the gospels seem to be based on orally transmitted memory and some earlier written sources that have since been lost as separate works. All of the gospels also show evidence of additions, interpretations, corruptions, and a great deal of outright invention by the authors themselves or from the individuals and communities who passed their memories and understandings of Jesus to the authors. Thus, the New Testament carries layers of tradition, some quite old and more historically authentic and some later and substantially shaped by the biases of their authors and various proto-Christian communities. While some bits of the gospels may seem clearly to fall into one layer or another, it is impossible to know precisely what truly derived from the historical Jesus.

While Christianity has tended to understand the biblical account of Jesus in keeping with its theology, Jesus was not a Christian and did not intend or understand his actions and teachings from the perspective of Christian theology. In particular it is pretty clear that he did not understand himself to be the eternal, divine Son of God descended from heaven to die in order to secure salvation for believers. The Gospel of John, the last biblical gospel written, takes things in that direction, but the New

---

[11] John S. Spong. *Liberating the Gospels: Reading the Bible with Jewish Eyes.* San Francisco: HarperSanFrancisco, 1997.

Testament contains no credible statements from Jesus that he ever thought such a thing.

The search for the historical Jesus is a scholarly effort that has been going on for hundreds of years. It is an attempt by various independent and interdependent scholars and groups of scholars in Europe and America to make sense of the layers of tradition in the gospels and any related historical, archeological, and anthropological evidence. Their hope has been to arrive at a clearer understanding of what Jesus of Nazareth actually said and did and from that, perhaps, what he might have actually thought and believed.

Familiarity with the work of recent Jesus scholars has been very important to my own religious and spiritual development. It has helped me make much better sense of what I find in the gospels. It has also convinced me that the real, historical Jesus and the actual events of his life and death can never be known with confidence in much detail. There simply is not enough solid source material to be definitive. What source material there is requires enough interpretation that there is always room for the biases of the interpreters to come into play. In other words, seekers after the historical Jesus tend to assemble the bits of evidence so as to find the Jesus they expect or want to find.

Critically honest scholars pretty much all agree that the New Testament Gospels are literary constructions that draw to some extent from historical memory. What they have not been able to agree on is the extent. At one extreme are those who see most of the material in the gospels as being derived from historical memory even if that memory may have been distorted in the transmission or rearranged, bent a little, or embellished to suit the purposes of the gospel writers. At the other extreme are those who think that only the most basic material such as some of Jesus' sayings and the most pivotal events, such as his crucifixion, are historically accurate.

As with my treatment of the subject of scripture, I am not going to go very far into the scholarly analysis that has been done regarding Jesus. You will find a list at the end of this chapter of resources that I have found especially helpful on the subject. What I will do is give you a brief picture of how I, at the moment I am writing this, understand who Jesus really was and what he was about. This is my best judgment based on the evidence and opinions I have been exposed to so far and, objective though I try to be, it must inevitably reflect my own biases. In keeping with my belief that the evidence is sparse and often distorted by the process of transmission, my sketch will be brief and vague. I think the general picture is probably fairly accurate, but I would not bet on any of the details.

I find Aslan's analysis quite compelling that Jesus was a (little-z) zealot—not a member of the later Zealot political party, but one who acted out of zeal for Israel and Israel's God. Herzog's understanding of Jesus as an interpreter and teacher of the Torah according to the "little tradition" of Galilean peasant villages also makes a lot of sense.

To paint a picture of Jesus, I shall first paint the background of the picture—the social, cultural, religious, political, and economic situation in which he lived. Jesus was a Jew living in Roman-occupied Palestine. The Roman occupation was brutal. The Romans slaughtered and crucified many thousands of Jews in Galilee and Judea to maintain their control of the area. Thirty-five to forty years after Jesus' own crucifixion they would actually go so far as to destroy the temple, level Jerusalem, and slaughter everyone there.[12] The Romans also controlled who was appointed High Priest of the Temple in Jerusalem and used the Jewish elites of Jerusalem to help control the masses. Although the Jewish elites may have despised the Romans, they were willing to hold their noses and work with the Romans to maintain what they could of traditional Jewish institutional life and/or in exchange for power and privilege.

The Roman and Jewish upper classes presided over a system that squeezed wealth out of the ordinary people. Peasants and artisans were taxed into debt at high interest rates and then forced to forfeit their land or businesses when they could not repay their loans. This left most of the peasants working as tenant farmers on land that once belonged to them or working as landless day-laborers, which is what Jesus was. For the vast majority of peasants in first-century Palestine, life was a harsh, stressful, day-to-day struggle—and more than a few lost that struggle.

---

[12] In fact, the Romans destroyed Jerusalem and killed most of its occupants twice: in 70 and 135 C.E.

The Jews of Jesus day believed that their God had the power to free them from Roman occupation. Their tradition included prophecies that God would someday restore Judea and greater Israel to independence as a kingdom of justice ruled according to God's law as given in the Torah. More than a few of these prophecies included *messianic* figures who were expected to play important roles in bringing about the promised change. The word *messiah* means "anointed one". In Israel's history, kings, prophets, and priests were often anointed with oil to signify their appointment or acceptance by God. The prophecies that came to be regarded as predicting a messiah varied enough that a wide range of opinions existed as what sort of leader the messiah might be—military, political, priestly, prophetic—or even how many messiahs should be expected. These differences aside, most Palestinian Jews of Jesus' day, desperate as they were, seem to have put more than a little hope in these prophecies.

First-century Palestinian Jews also believed the fulfillment of these prophecies to depend on their faithfulness to the covenant that they understood to exist between them and their God. So, in the Jewish mind, religious thought and observance were deeply enmeshed with their political and economic situation.

The Jewish peasants of Galilee revered the Temple but despised the priests and their underlings who collaborated, however grudgingly, with the Romans. In addition to the taxes and tributes required by the Romans and their local surrogate rulers, the Temple levied one or more tithes on Palestinian Jews. The Jerusalem priesthood could not force the payment of these tithes, but those who failed to pay them were labeled as sinners and regarded as being excluded from the blessings of Israel's covenants with God—at least in the eyes of the Jewish elites. Many peasants simply could not afford to pay their tithes, which was one more source of humiliation and despair.

Within this context it is not surprising to find Jesus, a poor Jew from the hinterlands of Galilee, in conflict with the Jewish elites centered in Jerusalem. It makes sense to me that Jesus believed himself to be a messiah called by God to lead God's people back into proper compliance with the covenant and thereby to set in motion the prophecies of Israel's liberation and renewal. As well documented by Aslan and some of the other Jesus scholars in my resource list, Jesus would be far from the first or the last to regard himself in such a way. There were many would-be messiahs in Palestine in the centuries before and after Jesus.

Jesus seems to have understood the covenant to be about purity and proper ritual and even more about justice and being a community in which everyone—but especially the poor, the sick, the weak, and the outcasts—were treated with compassion. I think he tried to create such a community among his followers. His parables about the mustard seed and the leaven suggest that he believed that once he and his followers got it right on a small scale, it would grow and spread.

Jesus taught an interpretation of Torah that supported this perspective. For Jesus and many other devout Jews of his day, the intention of the Law and the Covenant of Moses was summed up in the Great Commandment: that we love God with all our heart, soul, and mind and our neighbor as our self. He seems to have held the conviction that loving one's neighbor in this way is possible only through forgiveness.

Jesus seems not to have been concerned with fighting the Romans and paid little attention to them, perhaps because he believed God would supernaturally handle that problem in due time. His concern was to bring about the necessary relationship among the Jewish people and between the Jewish people and their God so as to set the messianic prophecies in motion.

It seems that in Jesus' mind, part of that necessary relationship included proper operation of the Temple. I believe his action to drive the sellers and money-changers from the Temple was not just a bit of symbolic street theater to teach a religious lesson, but that it was an organized, violent attempt to change how the temple grounds were used. It was that action that brought him to the attention of the Roman authorities and led to his crucifixion. Because the Jewish Temple was a major trouble spot for the Romans, they had zero tolerance for anyone causing problems there.

One of the most telling verses of any of the gospels is the last words of Jesus from the cross in the Gospel of Mark, the earliest gospel: "My God, my God, why have you forsaken me?" (Mark 15:34 NRSV). This is a cry of utter, utter despair. Clearly things did not work out as Jesus had expected. Apparently Jesus thought he could get away with his action in the Temple courtyard, which amounted to poking his finger in the eyes of the High Priest and the Romans. Since he seems not to have organized any sort of military force, Jesus must have believed either that his actions would spark a widespread popular rebellion or that driving the commercial activity from the Temple would trigger divine intervention. The last verse of Zechariah states that "there shall no longer be traders in the house of the Lord of hosts on that day." (Zechariah 14:2 NRSV). Perhaps Jesus thought that driving the merchants and money-changers from the Temple courtyard was the action that would initiate the supernatural advent of the Day of the Lord that Zechariah and other prophets had predicted. Whatever he thought, his dying words as reported in the earliest gospel indicate that he was very mistaken.

Once his action in the Temple failed, Jesus must have known that his days were numbered. It is interesting that the gospels report that he alone was crucified and that all his followers escaped. That is odd because when the Romans crushed such movements they tended to kill many people. That Jesus alone died suggests to me that Jesus may have arranged to turn himself over to the Jewish authorities in exchange for sparing his followers. So, perhaps Judas was not the betrayer that orthodox tradition has made him out to be. Perhaps he was doing Jesus' bidding when he arranged Jesus' arrest. There are strands of early Christian tradition that suggest as much.[13]

In this regard there is also an interesting passage in the Gospel of John when Jesus prays for his disciples after the last supper. An odd thing about this prayer is that Jesus speaks has though he has already departed mortal life, as though the crucifixion is already behind him, which is one of the reasons many scholars regard the fourth gospel to be more about the post-Easter Jesus of faith than the pre-Easter Jesus of history. In one short part of this prayer Jesus says, "While I was with them, I protected them in your name that you have given me. I guarded them, and not one of them was lost except the one destined to be lost, so that the scripture might be fulfilled." (John 17:12 NRSV). This could be an echo of an orally transmitted memory of Jesus being concerned to protect his

---

[13] Cockburn, Andrew. "The Gospel of Judas", *National Geographic Magazine*, May 2006. Online:
http://ngm.nationalgeographic.com/2006/05/judas-gospel/cockburn-text.html

followers, which, in turn, may have been the seed of the idea that Jesus died to save those who follow him.

Some Jesus scholars suggest that Jesus did not understand himself to be a messiah and that he did not preach an apocalyptic message. Rather, they suggest, his followers came to understand him to be the Messiah only after he was dead and only then added the apocalyptic material to the tradition about Jesus. According to their perspective, Jesus was killed, not because of any overt seditious actions, but because he stirred up anti-establishment sentiment by peacefully advocating for justice within a corrupt and unjust system. This view has the Jewish elites finding Jesus guilty of a trumped up charge of blasphemy and denouncing him to the Romans. While I do think the High Priest and his allies wanted to see Jesus dead and that they undoubtedly played a major role in his demise, the fact remains that the punishment for blasphemy was death by stoning whereas crucifixion was a Roman punishment for sedition.

When the Romans crucified someone, they posted a sign (titulus) at the top of the cross indicating the name of the crucified person and their crime. Jesus' titulus, if we can believe the Gospel of Mark, read "King of the Jews". I think that is how Jesus thought of himself. Nowhere in the New Testament does Jesus deny the charge. Although the Jesus of the Gospel of John claims that "My kingdom is not from this world" (John 18:36 NRSV), it is highly doubtful that Jesus ever spoke those words. The evidence strongly suggests that Jesus saw himself as the rightful King of the Jews consistent with the common understanding of Messiah among the Jews of his day.

The suggestion that Jesus did not preach an apocalyptic message is highly doubtful. The word *apocalyptic* refers to revealed knowledge of the cataclysmic end of the existing world order. All of the canonical gospels agree that Jesus preached of the imminent coming of God's kingdom. In the context of first-century Judaism, such a message was inherently apocalyptic. The Lord's Prayer, Jesus' predictions of reversals—i.e., the first being last and the last being first—and many of the Beatitudes and parables are easily interpreted to have apocalyptic meaning.

As I have already confessed, my picture of the historical Jesus is based on a lot extrapolation. I fully acknowledge that I could be quite far off the mark of what really happened, and I am aware of other scenarios that are just as plausible. While I very much enjoy trying to unravel the mystery of the historical Jesus, I must emphasize that it is a mystery that we may never fully unravel.

The Jesus presented in the New Testament, though echoing some of the words of a real person, is truly myth. The uniquely divine Jesus of Christianity is a human invention, just like all the other divine personalities that populate myths the world over.

It is really only natural that the objective truth about Jesus of Nazareth should have been overshadowed by the subjectively constructed Jesus of faith, the Jesus of the Christian myth. Before Modernity this distinction between objective and subjective, between fact and faith, received little attention, but the essence of Modernity is the differentiation of these two aspects of human cognition and experience. Science claimed the objective domain and left the subjective to religion and the humanities. Religion is destined for obsolescence if it ignores this differentiation. Not ignoring it means being honest about what is objective fact and what is subjective myth—and this goes for how we understand Jesus as much as anything.

Much of what is attributed directly to Jesus would be more honestly attributed to the constructed tradition about Jesus. Some of it surely goes back to Jesus, but exactly what and how much is unclear. Other teachings may have entered the tradition with followers of John the Baptist or from James, the brother of Jesus, or Peter or Paul or other apostles or the authors of the gospels or unknown leaders in local groups of the early Christian movement or even just from popular imagination. This is precisely how the inside-out mechanisms of authority and inspiration operate.

Jesus was not supernatural and not the divine authority the tradition made him out to be. He was a human being trying to make sense of and be faithful to his own religious tradition. The teachings attributed to Jesus in the New Testament carry much insight and wisdom and hope that can be of great benefit to people today, but insisting that they are all rooted in the authority of a real, historical, uniquely divine Jesus only muddies the waters. The tradition that speaks through scripture and the Church was shaped by many people.

The historical Jesus did not believe himself to be a divine being descended from heaven. He knew himself to have earthly parents, and he did not believe himself to have been begotten by

God in a virgin. Jesus was a notable religious teacher and social leader, but not necessarily exceptional in comparison to other similar figures of the period. There is no objective reason to believe that the real Jesus was anything more than a quite human apocalyptic preacher who possibly believed that God had chosen him to be the Messiah. His story as presented by his followers, the lifestyle of those followers, and various streams of history and culture simply came together in such a way as to capture the interest, hope, and imagination of expanding numbers of people in the centuries of early Christianity. That interest, hope, and imagination and those streams of history and culture shaped a mythical Jesus of faith substantially different from the historical person who was the seed of the myth. The myth is not unrelated to the historical Jesus, but it is more an expression of the deeper meanings that others associated with him.

A major pitfall lies in the temptation to replace one subjectively constructed (mythical) Jesus with another and call him the objectively real Jesus. One such constructed Jesus is the fully realized spiritual master. Jesus may have been adept at spiritual practices such as prayer and meditation, perhaps of the Merkabah tradition of Jewish mysticism, but Jesus probably did not break through into some previously unattained level of (Christ) consciousness. That is a modern interpretation that seeks to retain for Jesus a special level of power and authority.

Other examples of a constructed Jesus are the postmodern reformer and the Marxist-leaning revolutionary. Theologians and religious teachers often filter the gospels to come up with a theology and a corresponding Jesus of their liking. This is fine and proper until they suggest, directly or by implication, that their Jesus is an accurate reflection of the real Jesus. Sometimes this is an attempt to preserve a supernatural Jesus. More often it is an attempt to identify their own understandings and values with Jesus as an authoritative figure. After all, Christianity has for two-thousand years regarded Jesus to be God in a unique way and granted him divine authority. It is only natural to try to ride those coattails of authority as we try to reshape the tradition for a new age. I have played this game myself, but it is dishonest. Authority does not reside in the historical Jesus; it resides in the living spirit that is present in everyone. The Jesus of faith, which is the Jesus of the Christian myth, can validly be seen as an expression of that living spirit because the myth has been shaped in the inside-out manner by the spirit within many people throughout the development of the tradition. It is simply crucial to recognize that the Jesus of faith is not ultimate truth but metaphor and symbol that points to ultimate truth.

Detailed historical truth about Jesus is lost to us in the dust of time. Seeking that truth has been and may very well continue to be a very helpful exercise, but we must be realistic about how far it can really take us. It will never become a magical time machine that can take us back to see for ourselves what really happened in Galilea and Judea two-thousand years ago. What the tradition gives us is not historical truth but spiritual truth encoded in the myth of Jesus.

What then, you might ask, does all of this mean for the traditional Christian understanding of Jesus as the second person of the Trinity? This is a very, very important question that I shall address at various points in what follows. First I shall turn my attention to the miracles of Jesus and some strong evidence that the writer of the first gospel, the gospel that lays out what has come to be called the "synoptic" view of the events in Jesus ministry (i.e., the view shared by Mark, Matthew, and Luke) did not intend that we take what he wrote entirely literally.

Resources for Personal Study

This list of resources present a range of opinions about the historical Jesus from scholars whom I think are at least trying to be open and honestly objective about the evidence. The Borg and Crossan books are a good place to start. Mack's book goes the deepest of those listed but is also the most scholarly. I also refer you back to the list of resources at the end of the chapter on scripture, since it is pretty much impossible to separate the study of Jesus from the study of the New Testament.

Aslan, Reza. *Zealot: The Life and Times of Jesus of Nazareth*. New York: Random House, 2013.

Borg, Marcus J. *Meeting Jesus Again for the First Time*. New York: HarperSanFrancisco, 1995.

Chilton, Bruce. *Rabbi Jesus: An Intimate Biography*. New York: Doubleday, 2000.

Crossan, John Dominic. *Who Is Jesus*. New York: HarperPaperbacks, 1996.

Funk, Robert W. *A Credible Jesus: Fragments of a Vision*. Santa Rosa: Polebridge, 2002.

Herzog, William R., II. *Prophet and Teacher: An Introduction to the Historical Jesus*. Louisville: Westminster John Knox, 2005.

Hoover, Roy W., ed. *Profiles of Jesus*. Santa Rosa: Polebridge, 2002.

Mack, Burton L. *A Myth of Innocence: Mark and Christian Origins*. Philadelphia: Fortress, 1988.

Robinson, James M. *The Gospel of Jesus: In Search of the Original Good News*. New York: HarperSanFrancisco, 2005.

Mark's Puzzle

Then he said to them, "Do you not yet understand?"
Mark 8:21 (NRSV)

I shall begin this chapter with a little recap: I believe that the traditional Christian understanding of Jesus is a myth and that, if Christianity is to play a positive role in the future of humanity, it must acknowledge its myths to be myths and shift its emphasis away from literal belief to faith rooted in the meanings of the myth and the non-literal dimensions of truth long present in the tradition. Such thinking may be welcomed by Christians and would-be Christians trying to reconcile faith with a scientific-rational worldview, but I know it can be frightening for Christians who are deeply rooted in a traditional perspective. I was taught from that traditional perspective to understand the gospels as historically reliable accounts that supported the evangelical version of Christian orthodoxy. It took me a long time and a lot of study and thinking and reflection to see them differently, to see them, I think, much more for what they really are. They are not historical accounts; they are documents of faith. They seem to be loosely based on historical realities, but they do not describe those realities in objectively reliable detail. As a group they undoubtedly include some authentic memories of what Jesus said and did, but those memories have been corrupted, obscured, and diluted by processes of transmission, interpretation, theological projection, and imagination. It is impossible to know the exact truth behind the gospel material.

What I have just said about the New Testament is pretty well accepted among liberal Christians. The jump from there to my statements about myth will make some of those same liberals squirm a little, and it will make all traditional Christians squirm a lot. The jump is fairly straightforward logically—more of a simple step than a leap really—but the implications would seem to be immense. The idea that the Jesus of faith is a myth rather than a historical reality is such a radical departure from traditional Christianity that one might fairly ask if a Christianity that accepts the premise is really any longer Christianity at all. Haven't true Christians always accepted the New Testament gospels as literally true? Furthermore, if the gospels are so historically inaccurate, then their authors must have been deliberate liars, or they were delusional regarding the quality of their own inspiration, or they credulously accepted a lot of popularly invented rumor and fantasy. But does it really even matter why they got it 'wrong'? If it is not literally true, shouldn't we just toss the whole thing and be done with it?

I have already told you that I don't think that is a good idea. Human culture is passing through a difficult transition from an old set of worldviews rooted in our social intelligence to a new set of worldviews more centered in our rational intelligence—from worldviews centered in tradition and myth and dominance-submission relationships to worldviews centered in reason and science and egalitarian relationships. If Christianity cannot accommodate itself to the new worldviews, it will eventually be left behind, but that would be unfortunate. We humans need religion. Religion is a universal human phenomenon that arises from our deepest nature. We don't need to be rid of it; we need it to grow with us. I think that is possible for Christianity, and that there is much of great value in the Christian tradition.

Before I turn my attention to how Christianity might make the necessary transition, I am going to suggest something that I have never found fully expressed by anyone else. What I have to say in the rest of this book really does not depend on whether my hypothesis in this chapter is accurate, but, if it is, the rest of what I have to say may be a lot easier for the Christian community to accept.

Was Jesus a Miracle Worker?

My suggestion arose somewhat unexpectedly from my interest to make sense of the miracles of Jesus. Other than the resurrection, no miracles of Jesus are mentioned in our earliest Christian scriptures, which are the authentic letters of Paul. Either Paul did not know Jesus to have been a miracle worker or he did not think it was important. The lost gospel Q—a hypothetical early source of the sayings of Jesus common to the gospels of Matthew and Luke but not Mark or John—seems to have credited Jesus with healings but provides little detail. The next earliest Christian scripture after Paul's letters is the Gospel of Mark. The Jesus of Mark performs many miracles. Some scholars have suggested that the author of Mark actually invented most or all of these miracles. Perhaps he did so to make Jesus a better fit for Old Testament prophecy. Perhaps he did so to make Jesus more appealing to the masses of the Roman world, who would have expected a religious hero or divine being to perform wonders. Perhaps he did so to metaphorically represent the meaning and power that he and his community found in Jesus. Perhaps he did so for all these reasons. In any case, I agree with those who think Mark or his sources invented many of the miracles he attributed to Jesus.

The authors of the gospels of Luke and Matthew used Mark as a major source. (Following common practice, I shall refer to the authors of the gospels by the names traditionally associated with those gospels. The identity of none of those authors is known with any certainty.) Luke incorporated about half of Mark in his gospel, and Matthew incorporated ninety-percent in his.[14] By bringing Mark's miracles into their own works, Luke and Matthew established the miracles firmly at the center of Christian scripture.

The miracles of Jesus can be divided into three categories: healings, exorcisms, and wonders. Healings are the cure of physical ailments and diseases. Professional medical care in the Roman Empire was crude and not widely available, so many sick and disabled people, and especially the poor, would turn to faith healers. Such healers were not uncommon in Jesus' day. They must have been similar to faith healers today. Jesus may have been successful as such a faith healer but probably no more successful than other faith healers of the time. His success would have depended mostly on the natural healing capacities of the human body and the placebo effect enhanced by his personal charisma. In other words, having a renowned person like Jesus focus his attention on them and their wellbeing would have

---

[14] Funk, Robert W., Roy W. Hoover, and The Jesus Seminar. *The Five Gospels: What Did Jesus Really Say?* (San Francisco: HarperSanFrancisco, 1997), 10-11.

boosted the healing processes in many of the sick people he treated. This effect would tend to be strongest in cases of psychosomatic illness, but would have been significant with many other types of ailment as well. In some instances Jesus is even reported to have specifically said that it was the person's own faith that healed them. He probably could not help everyone who came to him, but those who believed he had helped them would have testified to his power.

I doubt that many of the accounts of healing miracles attributed to Jesus in the gospels are historically accurate in their specifics simply because the amount of time that passed before the accounts were written down was just too great for details to be remembered. Also, many of the healing miracles seem to have metaphorical meanings that fit the immediate context where they have been placed in the gospels, which suggests that the authors fashioned them to fit that context. However, I think the attribution of healings to Jesus may have been based on authentic memory that he acted as a healer. The mention of healings in the Q material is consistent with this view.

Exorcism is the casting out of demons. In Jesus' day what we call mental illness was generally thought to be caused by demonic possession. Like faith healers, exorcists were not uncommon. The evidence suggests that Jesus was also an exorcist. His method seems to have been to speak forcefully to the demons and command them to depart. This may well have been a very effective psychotherapeutic technique in Jesus' culture. Again, while I doubt that any of the exorcisms described in the gospels are accurate memories of specific historical events, I absolutely believe they are based on authentic memory that he performed exorcisms. Strong evidence of this is found in Mark 16:9 where Mary Magdalene is identified as someone "from whom he had cast out seven demons." The author does not try to describe those exorcisms, the specifics of which he would not have known. Rather, he uses them as identifying information to help his readers know who Mary was and her relationship to Jesus. This strongly suggests that this information about Mary was an authentic memory within the early Jesus movement.

Wonders are all the miracles other than healings and exorcisms, miracles like feeding crowds, walking on water, changing water to wine, calming storms, and raising dead people.

These, I think, were invented out of whole cloth by the authors of the gospels or by the early Christian communities from which the authors drew material. I think the author of the Gospel of Mark played an especially pivotal role in this activity.

Before turning my attention to the Gospel of Mark and the important clues it holds, I owe it to my readers to be clear once again as to my perspective on supernatural miracles both scientifically and theologically. By *supernatural miracles* I mean events that defy the laws of the physical sciences. I simply do not believe that Jesus had supernatural powers. I see no credible reports of supernatural miracles today, and there is no scientifically credible reason to believe that they happened in the past. I have already explained Jesus' success as a healer and exorcist without playing the supernatural card. Might he have had psychic healing ability? I am open to the possibility that such abilities exist, but I remain to be convinced, so I am not willing to place any faith in the idea that Jesus had such abilities. The ability to heal and cast out demons was attributed not just to Jesus but to many of his disciples and followers and to many other Jewish and pagan figures of the period. I think these reports have more to do with the culture of the day than with special powers. As for wonders, I have already made it clear that I think they are products of the early Christian imagination. Such wonders do not happen today except by sleight of hand and trickery. Some scholars have suggested that Jesus was a magician of that sort. That is a silly attempt to preserve the notion that the gospels are historically reliable reports of what people actually saw or thought they saw. Just as silly is the notion that miracles really did happen in the past but, for whatever reason, no longer happen. The laws of the universe have not changed. Jesus lived in the same space-time continuum we inhabit today, and the fundamental laws and processes of physics and chemistry and biology functioned in the same way two-thousand years ago as they function today. What is different is that we understand the world very differently today from how it was understood in the first-century.

More important than this scientific reasoning, however, are the theological reasons for not believing in supernatural miracles. I will give this topic more attention later, but here is a condensed version: A god who could dispense supernatural power to alleviate our suffering and to make us more aware of that god's existence and of that god's will for us—a god who could do that but chooses not to do that except at a few rare moments in an obscure part of the world—is a monster. This is the old problem of theodicy, and the standard rationalizations about God choosing to respect our free will are garbage. The only way out of this problem is to stop believing in a capricious god of supernatural power. Such a move has major implications for how we should properly understand God, and I shall leave that discussion for later.

My goal in this chapter is to suggest that, not only should we not believe the miracles literally, but that the writer of the first Christian gospel did not believe them literally either. That is, I propose to show that the author of the Gospel of Mark attempted to be transparent about the symbolic nature of the miracles he composed.

Let me begin by giving a little background about the Gospel of Mark. Scholars today seem largely to agree that it was written around the time of the fall of Jerusalem in 70 C.E. We really don't know where or by whom the first gospel was written. It was written in crude Greek, probably by someone who was not a native speaker of the language.

The Gospel of Mark has been regarded from the early years of New Testament study as unsophisticated. For a long time it was assumed that the Gospel of Matthew was written first and that Mark was merely a poor-quality condensation of Matthew. Today the overwhelming consensus is that Mark was written first and provided the narrative structure of Jesus' ministry for both Luke and Matthew. Some scholars have credited Mark with inventing gospel as a literary form. I am not the first to propose that, crude though its Greek may be, the Gospel of Mark is a sophisticated literary work with a carefully designed structure.

The Feeding Miracles

I invite your attention to the passages in Mark having to do with the miraculous feeding of large crowds on two separate occasions. Here are the excerpts:

The apostles gathered around Jesus, and told him all that they had done and taught. He said to them, "Come away to a deserted place all by yourselves and rest a while." For many were coming and going, and they had no leisure even to eat. And they went away in the boat to a deserted place by themselves. Now many saw them going and recognized them, and they hurried there on foot from all the towns and arrived ahead of them. As he went ashore, he saw a great crowd; and he had compassion for them, because they were like sheep without a shepherd; and he began to teach them many things. When it grew late, his disciples came to him and said, "This is a deserted place, and the hour is now very late; send them away so that they may go into the surrounding country and villages and buy something for themselves to eat." But he answered them, "You give them something to eat." They said to him, "Are we to go and buy two hundred denarii worth of bread, and give it to them to eat?" And he said to them, "How many loaves have you? Go and see." When they had found out, they said, "Five, and two fish." Then he ordered them to get all the people to sit down in groups on the green grass. So they sat down in groups of hundreds and of fifties. Taking the five loaves and the two fish, he looked up to heaven, and blessed and broke the loaves, and gave them to his disciples to set before the people; and he divided the two fish among them all. And all ate and were filled; and they took up twelve baskets full of broken pieces and of the fish. Those who had eaten the loaves numbered five thousand men.   Mark 6:30-44 (NRSV)

In those days when there was again a great crowd without anything to eat, he called his disciples and said to them, "I have compassion for the crowd, because they have been with me now for three days and have nothing to eat. If I send them away hungry to their homes, they will faint on the way—and some of them have come from a great distance." His disciples replied, "How can one feed these people with bread here in the desert?" He asked them, "How many loaves do you have?" They said, "Seven." Then he ordered the crowd to sit down on the ground; and he took the seven loaves, and after giving thanks he broke them and gave them to his disciples to distribute; and they distributed them to the crowd. They had also a few small fish; and after blessing them, he ordered that these too should be distributed. They ate and were filled; and they took up the broken pieces left over, seven baskets full. Now there were about *four thousand people. And he sent them away. And immediately he got into the boat with his disciples and went to the district of Dalmanutha.* Mark 8:1-10 (NRSV)

Now the disciples had forgotten to bring any bread; and they had only one loaf with them in the boat. And he cautioned them, saying, "Watch out—beware of the yeast of the Pharisees and the yeast of Herod." They said to one another, "It is because we have no bread." And becoming aware of it, Jesus said to them, "Why are you talking about having no bread? Do you still not perceive or understand? Are your hearts hardened? Do you have eyes, and fail to see? Do you have ears, and fail to hear? And do you not remember? When I broke the five loaves for the five thousand, how many baskets full of broken pieces did you collect?" They said to him, "Twelve." "And the seven for the four thousand, how many baskets full of broken pieces did you collect?" And they said to him, "Seven." Then he said to them, "Do you not yet understand?" Mark 8:14-21 (NRSV)

This last passage clearly confronts us with a puzzle. It is a puzzle that did not originate with Jesus. It is the author of the gospel who has composed this scene and placed these words on Jesus' lips, thus posing the puzzle to his audience—including us— but especially to the audience of his day. He seems to think they should understand the significance of the numbers five, twelve, seven and seven.

The standard interpretation of this passage is that it is intended to demonstrate the disciples' lack of faith and understanding. It is true that there is a recurring theme in Mark that even Jesus' closest followers did not fully understand who he was and what he was about. This may, in fact, reflect that the early Jesus movement came to understand Jesus very differently after his death—a death that neither they nor he expected—than they had understood him when he has alive. But this passage goes beyond simply highlighting the disciples lack of understanding. This is a very specific and carefully crafted puzzle, and Mark is very direct about it: "Do you still not perceive or understand? Are your hearts hardened? Do you have eyes, and fail to see? Do you have ears, and fail to hear? And do you not remember? ... Do you not yet understand?" The puzzle begins with a rather direct clue that it is not really about bread: "Why are you talking about having no bread?" It all culminates with specific questions about the numbers of loaves and baskets. Mark is saying in so many words, this is important; figure it out!

So, what are we supposed to do with this nearly two-thousand years later?

Let me first address the issue of why there are two feeding miracles. Scholars have identified two chains of miracle stories in Mark (4:35-6:44 and 6:45-8:10), each consisting of five miracles, each beginning with a sea crossing, and each ending with a feeding story.[15] Other scholars have suggested that many parts of the gospels of Mark and Matthew were written to correspond to stories in the Torah and that they were intended to be read in parallel with those stories according to the annual cycle of Torah readings or to be read during thematically appropriate Jewish festivals.[16] It is clear to me that the two chains of miracle stories in Mark are intended to parallel the story of the Exodus from the crossing of the Red Sea to the feeding of the Israelites with manna in the wilderness. This sequence of stories appears twice in the Torah, first in the book of Exodus and a second time in the book of Numbers. Mark has deliberately paralleled these two sets of stories. Mark's point with these stories and with much of the rest of his gospel is to portray Jesus as a new Moses.

But what about the numbers in Mark's puzzle? Mark might have expected his original audience to recognize the meaning of five, twelve, seven and seven, but what hope do we have? Well, as it turns out—and this may be simple dumb luck—Luke relates an event in the early church that I believe holds the key to this puzzle.

Now during those days, when the disciples were increasing in number, the Hellenists complained against the Hebrews because their widows were being neglected in the daily distribution of food. And the twelve called together the whole community of the disciples

---

[15] Paul Achtemeier is credited with first recognizing this pattern by Burton Mack in *A Miracle of Innocence.*

[16] See John Spong's explanation based on the work of Michael Goulder in *Liberating the Gospels.*

and said, "It is not right that we should neglect the word of God in order to wait on tables. Therefore, friends, select from among yourselves seven men of good standing, full of the Spirit and of wisdom, whom we may appoint to this task, while we, for our part, will devote ourselves to prayer and to serving the word." What they said pleased the whole community, and they chose Stephen, a man full of faith and the Holy Spirit, together with Philip, Prochorus, Nicanor, Timon, Parmenas, and Nicolaus, a proselyte of Antioch. They had these men stand before the apostles, who prayed and laid their hands on them.

Acts 6:1-6 (NRSV)

What we have here is the first obviously divisive moment in the early Jesus movement. Jesus and his first followers were Aramaic-speaking Jews from rural Galilee, referred to here as the Hebrews. Within a few months or years after the crucifixion, the movement became centered in Jerusalem to have access to the Temple and to spread the word about Jesus among the Jews who came there from all over the Roman world. Many of these Diaspora Jews, such as Saul of Tarsus, were urbanized and Hellenized, meaning they spoke Greek and participated in Greek culture as much as their Jewish precepts would allow. Besides the language difference, other cultural differences between the two groups would have been significant. As these Hellenized, urban Jews began to be drawn into the Jesus movement, tensions arose between them and the original native-Palestinian members of the movement. Apparently the Hellenists felt they were being short-changed in the distribution of food. The solution was to appoint a separate set of leaders for the Hellenists. All seven of those appointed have Greek names.

So, there we have the Twelve for the Hebrews and the Seven for the Hellenists. That these are what Mark was actually alluding to is supported by his geographical references. Before the feeding of the five thousand, Jesus is in Galilee in his hometown and the nearby villages, which is a Hebrew cultural environment. Before the feeding of the four thousand, he travels to Gennesaret, Tyre, and to the Decapolis (a region named for its 10 Greek cities) by way of Sidon. (Mark's familiarity with Palestinian geography has been questioned because Sidon is north of Tyre and the Decapolis is south, so this would be very circuitous route.) All of these were

Hellenized cities, which works to place the second feeding miracle in a Hellenistic cultural context.

That leaves us to figure out five and another seven. That's child's play for anyone at all familiar with the history of the Bible. The Torah (the five books of Moses) were and are still known as the Pentateuch, from *penta*, Greek for five. The early Greek translation of the Old Testament, which seems to have been done in the third and second centuries B.C.E. in Alexandria Egypt, was known as the Septuagint, which means the Seventy. That is not exactly seven, but the miracle would not be nearly so impressive if Jesus had seventy loaves to work with. Seven, *septa* in Greek, is quite adequate to point to the Septuagint.

Put all of this together and these feeding miracles become entirely consistent metaphorical representations of how Jesus' interpretation of scripture fed people starving for a fresh take on God's word (the five and seven loaves) in two separate Jewish cultural contexts and how his authority for interpreting scripture passed after him to the leaders of those communities (the twelve and seven baskets). Less sophisticated readers and hearers of the gospel—the peasant masses who wanted a magic Jesus—could believe the miracles literally, but these passages are more than a nod and a wink from the author of the Gospel that their real meaning lies elsewhere.

I have encountered only two interpretations of the feeding miracles: 1) They really happened literally as described, or 2) the generosity of those who gave the first loaves and fishes inspired others to share food they had been concealing. I was never satisfied with either interpretation. It now makes complete sense to me that the feeding miracles are entirely symbolic representations showing that Jesus' interpretation of Jewish scripture nourished the movement that survived him.

We might also wonder about the other numbers in the feeding stories. Perhaps five-thousand and four-thousand were accurate historical counts of the two early Christian communities at some point in their history. Perhaps groups of hundreds and fifties are accurate descriptions of how those communities were divided up for administrative and pastoral purposes or how they were distributed geographically. And what about the two fish? Mark does not make that number a part of his puzzle, but maybe it too had some significance that escapes my understanding.

What is critically important is that the author of the gospel clearly wanted us to figure out the symbolic nature of these two miracle stories. I think he did not want us to stop there.

Gospel As Parable?

I invite your attention to a passage that appears after the second feeding and immediately before the puzzle.

> *The Pharisees came and began to argue with him, asking him for a sign from heaven, to test him. And he sighed deeply in his spirit and said, "Why does this generation ask for a sign? Truly I tell you, no sign will be given to this generation." And he left them, and getting into the boat again, he went across to the other side.* Mark 8:11-13 (NRSV)

What does it mean that the statement, "Truly I tell you, no sign will be given to this generation," is placed in just this spot? Many scholars feel that this passage refers to the generation of Mark's own time rather than of Jesus' time. However, if the words hark back at all to something Jesus actually said, then perhaps the historical Jesus actually refused or even denied having the ability to perform wonders. Luke's version of this same saying brings something else into view:

> *"This generation is an evil generation; it asks for a sign, but no sign will be given to it except the sign of Jonah. For just as Jonah became a sign to the people of Nineveh, so the Son of Man will be to this generation."* Luke 11:29-30 (NRSV)

Christians have understood "the sign of Jonah" to reference the resurrection, which occurred after Jesus had been in the tomb three days just as Jonah had been in the belly of the fish three days. However, there was no indication in the book of Jonah that he told the people of Nineveh anything about the fish. What saved the people of Nineveh, much to Jonah's displeasure, was that they believed his apocalyptic preaching. Perhaps Jesus was saying that the only sign he would give was his own preaching.

Whether or not Jesus ever actually said such a thing, Mark's placement of the passage is very interesting. It comes after the two feedings and Jesus walking on the water and immediately before he poses his puzzle about what the feeding miracles really mean. Even if Jesus never refused to give a sign, Mark seems to be saying that the real wonder performed by Jesus was the interpretation of Torah given in his preaching.

I next draw your attention to the wonder of Jesus walking on the water.

> Immediately he made his disciples get into the boat and go on ahead to the other side, to Bethsaida, while he dismissed the crowd. After saying farewell to them, he went up on the mountain to pray.
> When evening came, the boat was out on the sea, and he was alone on the land. When he saw that they were straining at the oars against an adverse wind, he came towards them early in the morning, walking on the sea. He intended to pass them by. But when they saw him walking on the sea, they thought it was a ghost and cried out; for they all saw him and were terrified. But immediately he spoke to them and said, "Take heart, it is I; do not be afraid." Then he got into the boat with them and the wind ceased. And they were utterly astounded, for they did not understand about the loaves, but their hearts were hardened.   Mark 6:45-52 (NRSV)

The last sentence clearly indicates that this miracle must be understood in a way similar to the feeding miracles, and it is located between them in the text. If it is as symbolic as they are, the symbolism is a little less obvious. As I have already mentioned, it is clearly intended to parallel the crossing of the Red Sea, just as the feeding miracles parallel the feeding of the Israelites in the wilderness, but that does not explain its internal meaning for the early church.

I regret that I do not recall who to credit with this idea, but at some time in the past I came across the idea that boats in miracle stories represent the early church after the crucifixion. That is also suggested here by the disciples thinking Jesus was a ghost. Perhaps this story is telling us metaphorically how Jesus' disciples came to experience and believe in the resurrection. Translation may also be an impediment to our understanding. Where the passage reads, "it is I," the literal translation is "I am." These words serve to identify Jesus with God (Exodus 3:14). They also reinforce a resurrection context: I am not dead; I am (alive)! If this is accurate, then the meaning of the passage would be that Jesus' followers as a group had a very difficult time after the crucifixion until they came to know and accept his "resurrected" presence.

The biggest problem with this interpretation is the sentence, "He intended to pass them by." Perhaps that is a later addition. The passage actually makes better sense if that sentence is omitted. The preceding sentence suggests that he was coming to help his disciples because he could see that they were struggling against the wind. In any case, it is odd that he would ignore them and just pass them by, struggling or not. Perhaps that sentence had a significance to Mark's community that I do not see.

I invite your attention to another interesting miracle:

> They came to the other side of the sea, to the country of the Gerasenes. And when he had stepped out of the boat, immediately a man out of the tombs with an unclean spirit met him. He lived among the tombs; and no one could restrain him any more, even with a chain; for he had often been restrained with shackles and chains, but the chains he wrenched apart, and the shackles he broke in pieces; and no one had the strength to subdue him. Night and day among the tombs and on the mountains he was always howling and bruising himself with stones. When he saw Jesus from a distance, he ran and bowed down before him; and he shouted at the top of his voice, "What have you to do with me, Jesus, Son of the Most High God? I adjure you by God, do not torment me." For he had said to him, "Come out of the man, you unclean spirit!" Then Jesus asked him, "What is your name?" He replied, "My name is Legion; for we are many." He begged him earnestly not to send them out of the country. Now there on the hillside a great herd of swine was feeding; and the unclean spirits begged him, "Send us into the swine; let us enter them." So he gave them permission. And the unclean spirits came out and entered the swine; and the herd, numbering about two thousand, rushed down the steep bank into the sea, and were drowned in the sea. Mark 5:1-13 (NRSV)

I include this passage to demonstrate that a miracle having no reference to the loaves can also be symbolic. Here *Legion* is a blatant allusion to the Roman army. The swine, that Jews considered to be unclean and wanted nothing to do with but that pagans loved to eat, are a symbol of Hellenistic, foreign culture. The passage as a whole is a very thinly veiled declaration that Jesus, at least in the minds of some in the early Christian movements, intended to see the Romans driven from Israel.

Finally, let's consider a very odd comment attributed to Jesus in Mark's gospel. It comes after Jesus has preached the parable of the sower to a large crowd.

> When he was alone, those who were around him along with the twelve asked him about the parables. And he said to them, "To you has been given the secret of the kingdom of God, but for those outside, everything comes in parables; in order that
> 'they may indeed look, but not perceive,
> and may indeed listen, but not understand;
> so that they may not turn again and be forgiven.'"
> And he said to them, "Do you not understand this parable? Then how will you understand all the parables?"   Mark 4:10-13 (NRSV)

The indented material here comes from Isaiah 6:9-10. It suggests among other things that Jesus was conscious of fulfilling Isaiah's prophecies. However, it is extremely odd that Jesus would say such a thing. He was about spreading the good news of God's Kingdom, not hiding it. He spoke in parables, not to hide his message but to make it accessible to the peasants of Galilee. He used images of things they understood, like sowing crops, to teach them about spiritual things. There is, in fact, wide scholarly agreement that Jesus did not say these words but that they are the invention of Mark or Mark's community.

The question is, why were these words important to Mark and his community? This is the first place in the gospel where we are confronted with the question, "Do you not understand?" The puzzle about the loaves is the last. Mark is known to bracket or bookend sections of his gospel with parallel material. Is he doing that here? Might he also be telling us that, just as Jesus spoke in parables, he, Mark, is writing in parables? If that is the case, what is the deeper message, and who is it that Mark and his community do not want to understand it? The Roman authorities or certain Jewish leaders perhaps?

I could go on. The Gospel of Mark is loaded with symbolic meaning, both in its individual passages and in how those passages are organized in relation to one another. As many scholars have done good work on this subject, I shall let these few examples suffice.[17]

As previously stated, the author of Mark is generally credited with inventing the literary form of gospel. That form is commonly understood as being religious biography, but none of the gospels is true biography as we understand the term. The gospels place the concerns of faith and theology far above historical accuracy, if that was ever even a concern. They draw some of their content, such as major events and some of the words of Jesus, from historical memory, but their narrative structures and details are almost entirely the inventions of the authors and their sources, both written and oral. Their concern was not to ferret out the truth about the Jesus of the past but to bring their audiences into faith and relationship with the Jesus they believed to be alive in the eternal present.

I believe that the gospel writers were consciously aware that they were writing foundational documents (scripture) for their religious movement. All four of the canonical gospels show strong evidence of invention on the part of their authors. As examples I suggest the birth narratives in Matthew and Luke, the post-resurrection appearances in all four gospels, and almost everything Jesus says in John. I believe that Mark and Matthew consciously wrote their gospels to serve as scripture to be read during weekly worship in their religious communities and that their narrative structures were consciously based on the Jewish liturgical calendar and Torah readings.[18] I think that Mark also

---

[17] If you want to delve deeper into the Gospel of Mark, good places to start are *Maverick Mark: The Untamed Gospel* by Bonnie B. Thruston (Collegeville, MN: Liturgical Press. 2013) and *What Are They Saying About Mark?* by Daniel J. Harrington, SJ (New York/Mahwah, NJ: Paulist Press. 2005). The heavyweight on the topic would be Burton L. Mack's *A Myth of Innocence: Mark and Christian Origins* referenced at the end of the chapter on the historical Jesus.

[18] Michael Goulder has an interesting, well-supported, and very important theory that the synoptic gospels in general and the Gospel of Matthew in particular are structured to provide an annual cycle of

structured his gospel for use in instructing and preparing new converts for baptism.

In other words, I am saying that the authors of the New Testament gospels more or less consciously engaged in the compiling and writing of myth and that at least one of those authors, the first, wanted us to know that he was doing so. That means that there were at least a few very important people of very genuine faith in the early Christian movement who did not literally believe many stories that Christians ever since have felt dutybound to believe altogether literally.

Christians, it is time to wake up and let yourselves off the hook! It is okay to question the literal veracity of all the stories in the Bible and to seek out other levels of meaning in them.

Christian readings to parallel the cycle of Torah readings in the synagogues. See: Rollston, Christopher A., ed. *The Gospels According to Michael Goulder: A North American Response.* Harrisburg: Trinity Press International, 2002. See also John Shelby Spong's *Liberating the Gospels: Reading the Bible with Jewish Eyes*, which is listed as a resource at the end of the chapter on scripture.

The Nameless God

But Moses said to God,
"If I come to the Israelites and say to them,
'The God of your ancestors has sent me to you,' and they ask me,
'What is his name?' what shall I say to them?"
God said to Moses, "I am who I am."
He said further, "Thus you shall say to the Israelites,
'I am has sent me to you.'"
Exodus 3:13-14 (NRSV)

God.

This is a name that is not really a name. It is a noun we have made into a name by capitalizing the first letter. Just as Tarzan gave his boy the name Boy and some people give their dogs the name Dog or their cats the name Cat, we have given our god the name God.

It was not always so. All of the ancient gods had names. Even the god of the ancient Hebrews, from whom the Christian God is derived, had a name, and that name was at one time spoken. The earliest writings of the Old Testament (Joshua, Judges, Ruth, Samuel, Kings, and Chronicles) paint ancient Palestine as a mix of tribal and monarchic societies, each with their own gods. At that stage the Hebrews did not believe that theirs was the only god but only that their god was *their* only god. For them the gods of other peoples were just as real, and for them the choice of which god to follow was a real choice. It was only around the time of the Babylonian exile, a mere six-hundred years before Jesus, that the idea of monotheism—that theirs was the only *real* god—emerged for the Jews.

The third commandment of the Law of Moses forbade the misuse of the name of the god of Israel, especially by invoking the name in false oaths or in curses against one's personal enemies. Because it was unclear exactly where the line was drawn between the proper use of the god's name and using the name "in vain", Hebrew tradition chose to err on the side of caution by not speaking the sacred name at all. Thus, by the time this god became the God of Christianity, it was, for all practical purposes, a nameless god.

By the time of Jesus, increasing numbers of pagans doubted that their gods were real. Their loyalty to Paganism often had more to do with respect for tradition and maintaining social unity and order than with strong belief in the literal truth of their myths. Because Jews in the Diaspora had translated their scriptures into Greek, people in the Hellenistic world could learn about the nameless god without learning the language of the culture from which that god had come. With the destruction of the Temple in 70 C.E., the practice of Second Temple Judaism ended. That meant that the nameless god was cut loose from any particular holy place and from most of the culturally specific worship practices that had previously been associated with it. All of this made it easier for Christian theology to understand God in increasingly abstract terms. This nascent namelessness and abstractness reduced the resistance the new religion faced as it spread across cultures. It was easier to accept this new kind of nameless god than to accept a god with a foreign name and culturally unfamiliar worship traditions.

Christianity's appropriation of Judaism's single god provided gentile culture with a fresh god that could be understood more abstractly than the old pagan deities and, therefore, better adapted to the esoteric Greek philosophy of the period. This supported dual strands of religious conceptualization: the simple supernatural theism of the masses and a more abstract philosophical understanding that appealed to the intellectual classes. But these two stands—one that takes the myths of the tradition quite literally and one that is more concerned with deeper meaning—have pretty much always been around, and they have pretty much always gotten along. It is only in Modernity that the strands have been torn apart.

As I have stated before, the concept of gods is rooted in our social intelligence. Because our relationships with other members of our species have for countless millennia been the greatest single influence on our survival and evolutionary success, we humans have evolved to think primarily in terms of human motivations and relationships. Our ancient ancestors were predisposed to view everything through this lens. It is said that if the only tool in your toolbox is a hammer, everything starts to look like a nail. Just so, if your brain is wired primarily to help you successfully manage human relationships, everything starts to look like a human relationship. Our ancestors attributed human-like motivations and thought processes to the other creatures in their lives. In situations where no living beings could be seen to play an important role, they projected power and control onto imaginary, human-like beings. Even in situations where creatures or people were clearly involved, there remained a strong tendency to attribute ultimate control to unseen spirits or gods. Furthermore, our ancestors naturally assumed that the same methods of appeal and persuasion that they used in their human relationships could also work in their relationships with other creatures, spirits, and gods. Prayer, the building of temples (homes and palaces for the gods), sacrifices, and systems of cultic offerings (including tithes) are all attempts to communicate with and to curry favor with a god just as one might do with a powerful human leader such as a tribal chief or a king.

With the emergence of science over the past five-hundred years, we have added a screwdriver to our toolbox. Now, we are able to see that many of the things that our ancestors assumed to be nails when their only tool was the hammer of social intelligence are really, in fact, screws that can be handled much better with the screwdriver of disciplined rational intelligence and objective evidence (science). When it comes to understanding and manipulating the material universe, science simply works much better than religion. In fact, science so fully explains the operation of the material world that the idea of a god or gods is no longer needed to explain such things.

The result has been the tremendous clash of worldviews that is a major topic of this book. Traditional worldviews ultimately see the universe as a very personal place. That is, they understand the world primarily in terms of interactions between persons. I use the word *person* here to mean not just humans but also other living beings, both visible and invisible, who are believed to feel and think and make decisions much as humans do. This is a world where other creatures and natural phenomena are personified and which is understood as being ultimately under the willful control of some form of human-like consciousness. In the modern worldview, on the other hand, nature and other creatures have been largely depersonified, and the origins and functioning of the universe are understood without reference to the conscious intention of any sort of divine personal being. The traditional worldview uses a subjective lens and sees the world as an enchanted place; the modern worldview uses an objective lens and sees the world as a disenchanted place.

The great question is whether there is any place at all left for religion. Was there any truth and value in the traditional, enchanted worldview that has been lost in the modern, disenchanted worldview? Does religion offer anything of value that science cannot offer?

If what religion is selling is belief in one or more supernatural beings as the answer to our existential questions and concerns, then it has no future. Human-like supernatural gods simply do not exist and never did. Such gods were psychologically and socially helpful constructs for much of human history when we had nothing better, but they are no longer credible and do not provide a plausible explanation as to why things happen as they do. This is what *Death of God* theology is about. The old idea of God as a distinct, "personal" being just does not work anymore.

The death of supernatural theism, however, does not mean the death of the idea of spirit. That is, the death of the anthropomorphized god or gods does not require the death of the more abstract dimension of God that has always been present in the Judeo-Christian and other religious traditions. In other words, the death of the named gods does not mean the death of the nameless God. The god who strolled with Adam and Eve in the Garden of Eden is a myth that must be understood as such, but the God who is spirit and who must be worshiped "in spirit and truth" (John 4:24 NRSV) and in whom "we live and move and have our being" (Acts 17:28 NRSV) is not really mythical but rather philosophical.

Science is simply forcing us to realize that our traditional, anthropomorphized version of God was too small. The best social intelligence could do was imagine God as a bigger version of us. Rational intelligence, informed by spiritual awareness, has long pushed for a larger, deeper, more awesome understanding. It is only recently that we have matured enough in our application of rational intelligence to loosen the stranglehold the old, socially-rooted perspectives of traditional religion have held on our culture. If the hole left by the death of the gods of supernatural theism is to be filled, it will be by the single, nameless, abstract, generic God toward which philosophy and spiritual theology have long tended.

Religion is such a difficult mess across our culture right now because the newer, emerging understanding of God is precisely that: emerging. It is not very well articulated and certainly not broadly accepted at the popular level. While many theologians and mystics are quite comfortable with this more abstract God, many of the ordinary faithful are very confused and threatened by it. Churches do their members no favor by leaving them to tread water in outmoded, immature understandings of God—but that is pretty much what they have been doing. Supernatural theism remains the mode of belief for the vast majority of ordinary Christians today, even for many in supposedly progressive churches. It has been easier to let the laity believe whatever they believe than to rock the boat and push them to grow. It's time for some serious boat rocking.

Popular, traditional religion thinks of God as the ultimate being, the being who created and has power over all other beings but also stands apart from the creation. However, it is really improper to refer to God as *a* being. God is not *a* being in the same sense that any other being is a being. The indefinite article *a* implies that there are other instances of the same category. For example, "a tree" implies that we are referring to one actual or hypothetical tree of the many actual or hypothetical trees that do or might exist. God is simply not a being in the same sense of anything else we might call "a being". Although ancient peoples conceived of their gods (the gods with names) very much as distinct beings with physical bodies who lived within the physical universe, that is an entirely inadequate understanding for the abstract, nameless God. I am a being, and you are a being, but God is not a being in the sense that we are beings.

In Modernity Paul Tillich has suggested that God is better defined as *the source and ground of being*. I like this definition, which is entirely compatible with Acts 17:28. I see it to mean that everything that exists somehow comes from God and exists within God. This definition of God is fully consistent with traditional theology that sees God as both transcendent (beyond temporal, physical existence) and immanent (present in everything). Such a God is beyond or before being as well as present in everything that has being. When applied to such a God, the concepts of being and existence simply break down. We cannot say that God does or does not exist because existence itself comes from God.

We are forced to recognize that the word *God* is a linguistic placeholder for an abstraction and mystery that is ultimately beyond our comprehension. Our brains have evolved to function within the context of this physical universe, and they simply lack the capacity to comprehend and understand much beyond that context. We can use metaphor and analogy to try to speak of such things, but the results always somehow fall short. God simply cannot be described or defined in the way we describe or define other things because God is not a thing. That is to say, we cannot truly define God in terms of boundaries and qualities and categories. God transcends all boundaries and encompasses all qualities and categories.

This nameless, incomprehensible, paradoxical God belongs not just to Modernity. The traditions of apophatic spirituality and mysticism, versions of which are found in all major religions, have been around a very long time and understand God in exactly this way. That is, apophatic mystics, though they have profound experiences of God, find their experiences of God to be ultimately ineffable and beyond understanding. The God of apophatic spirituality is so profoundly ineffable and paradoxical that whatever is said about that God must finally be negated or unsaid. The term for this act of unsaying is *apophasis*, which derives from the Greek *apo phasis* that means "un-saying" or "speaking-away".[19]

Apophatic spirituality is not so much a distinct school of spiritual theology as a strand that runs through much of mystical expression the world over. A few important figures in the history of Christian apophatic expression include Gregory of Nyssa, Pseudo-Dionysius, John Scotus Erigena, Marguerite Porete, Meister Eckhart, Theresa of Avilla, John of the Cross, Nicholas of Cusa, and the author of *The Cloud of Unknowing*, but this only scratches the surface.

---

[19] Sells, Michael A. *Mystical Languages of Unsaying*. (Chicago: University of Chicago Press, 1994), 2.

Of these, Meister Eckhart (1260-c.1327 C.E.) is my favorite. Here is a sample of apophatic discourse from the end of one of his sermons:

You should love God apart from loveworthiness: not because he is worthy of love, for God is unloveworthy: he is superior to love and loveworthiness.—'How then should I love God?'—You should love God non-spiritually, that is, your soul must be unspiritual and naked of all spirit. For while your soul has form as spirit, she has images; the while she has images, she has neither unity nor union; the while she lacks union, she has never really loved God, for real love lies in union. Therefore your soul should be de-spirited of all spirit and should remain spiritless. If you love God as he is God, as he is spirit, as he is person, or as he is image, that must all go.—'Then how should I love him?'—Love him as he is: One not-God, One not-spirit, One not-person, One not-image; as a bright, pure, clear One, apart from all duality. And in this one let us sink down eternally from nothingness to nothingness.
So help us God. Amen.[20]

This passage illustrates the process of negation behind the term *negative theology* and the transrational move of apophasis. The point is that our ideas about God are not God. Our ideas about God become idols that prevent us from experiencing the reality of God. We become trapped in our conceptual thinking. Apophasis

---

[20] Translation by John Speers working from:
Eckhart, Meister. *Die deutschen Werke*, vol. 3, ed. by Josef Quint. (Stuttgart: Kohlhammer, 1958), 447-448.
Eckhart, Meister. *Deutsche Mystiker des Vierzehnten Jahrhynderts*, vol. 2, ed. by Franz Pfeiffer. (Leipzig: Göschensche, 1857), 320.
Eckhart, Meister. *Meister Eckhart*, trans. by C. de B. Evans with some omissions and additions from *Deutsche Mystiker des Vierzehnten Jahrhynderts* (London, Watkins, 1924), 247-248.
Eckhart, Meister. *Meister Eckhart: The Essential Sermons, Treatises, and Defense, The Classics of Western Spirituality*, trans. and introduction by Edmund Colledge, O.S.A and Bernard McGinn (Mahwah, NJ: Paulist Press, 1981), 208.
Eckhart, Meister. *Breakthrough: Meister Eckhart's Creation Theology in New Translation*, trans., introduction, and commentary by Matthew Fox. (New York: Doubleday, 1980), 180.

pushes us to the edge of reason and invites us to jump off into the Cloud of Unknowing, into the void of nothingness (no-thing-ness) beyond all ideas. In that void, from whence all things arise, we encounter the reality behind what we call God, which is also our own deepest self.

The great question of traditional religious faith in the modern age has been, "Does God really exist?" For the anthropomorphic God of supernatural theism, the answer must be no: God is not a distinct, humanlike being who dwells physically in the sky. But, if we let the great mystical traditions of Christianity, point us toward the ineffable, paradoxical, abstract, nameless God that is the source and ground of being, then the question falls apart. The fact that we exist means that being must have a source and ground, which is our definition of God. But here the paradox sets in. We can say that God exists because everything that exists is of God, but we also have to say that God does not exist because God simultaneously stands outside of existence as the source of existence. This is an example of the unsaying and negation of apophatic spirituality: if we say that God exists, we must also say that God does not exist. It is ultimately a mystery beyond our capacity to understand.

This is not a negation or rejection of reason, for the mystical tradition uses reason as a path to encounter the God that is to be found both in and beyond reason. The nameless, abstract God can never be fully comprehended or understood by the rational mind, but neither can it be intuited and apprehended in isolation from the rational mind. Mature spirituality is transrational (beyond reason), not antirational (against reason). The limits of reason are an important stepping off point for encountering the nameless God.

In the next chapter I shall explore the Christian doctrine of the Trinity as a model of this nameless God and the dynamic of being. It is an important example of how myth can express profound meaning.

The One and the Many

"Hear, O Israel: The LORD our God is one LORD.
Deuteronomy 6:4 (RSV)

One of the central doctrines of Christianity is the doctrine of the Trinity: that God, though absolutely one, exists simultaneously in three persons: Father, Son, and Holy Spirit.

This doctrine seems to have arisen among gentile believers in the Christ during the mid to late first century. Jesus surely never thought or taught such a thing. As a devout Jew he would have regarded as utter blasphemy the idea that any human could be God, and he would have been mortified to think that his followers might someday regard him as such.

After Jesus' death, the first generation of his followers consisted mostly of Jews and was led by Jews. They would have been comfortable calling Jesus the Son of God because that was an established and accepted title for Israel's kings. If Jesus or his followers believed him, as Messiah, to be King of the Jews, then the title *Son of God* would have been entirely appropriate, but no Jew would have understood it to mean that he was divine. Jewish (Ebionite) Christianity, which lasted over six-hundred years until it was swept away by Islam, never accepted that Jesus was divine but rather placed its hope in him as a divinely-anointed but entirely human messiah and prophet. This is the Jesus that was absorbed into Islam.

The Jesus movement and early Christianity seem to have been culturally porous from the beginning, attracting many Hellenized Jews and some gentile God-fearers. In Hellenistic culture the title *Son of God*, which was applied to such figures as the Caesar, did imply divinity. In the Hellenistic mind, any figure who stood at the center of religious devotion and hope ought properly to be a god. It appears that, during the early decades after the crucifixion, a Christ cult that did regard Jesus as divine took root among some Hellenized Jews and gentiles. After the repeated destruction of the Temple and the devastation of Judea by the Romans in 66-73 C.E.,

115-117 C.E., and 132-136 C.E., the first generations of Christian leaders, who were Jews, were replaced by successively more gentile waves of leadership. Christianity became an increasingly gentile movement, and the gentile inclination to see Jesus as divine quickly prevailed.

(Gentile Christians also missed their goddesses and the multiplicity of devotional options once available to them as pagans, hence the eventual elevation of Mary to the status *Mother of God* and the emergence of saint veneration.)

Of course, this was a huge problem because the God of Judaism—the God Jesus believed in—was a staunchly monotheistic God who strictly forbade worship of any other god. How could Jesus the Son also be a god next to God the Father? Enter the paradox of the Trinity: Father and Son are not two gods but one, and let's throw the Holy Spirit in too for good measure. With a lot of philosophical and semantic contortions, the theologians of early Christianity managed to turn what were effectively the three gods of the popular Christian movement into one God in three persons, thus forcing a strained continuity with the movement's Jewish origins. Jews, of course, did not see much continuity there, but they had almost no power to oppose it.

It does not really matter how the doctrine came about or if the steps in its development make sense from our current perspective. The fact is that the doctrine stands. It is one of the core myths of Christianity and, like any good myth, it carries deep meaning that far transcends its origins.

It took Christians three-hundred years to formally agree on how the Trinity should be understood, but the agreement extended to little more than the formal wording of creeds. Even after agreement on the words, there have been vastly different understandings of their meaning. The doctrine of the Trinity is simply a confusingly paradoxical doctrine that has invited widely differing interpretations. This is entirely appropriate because, as I suggested in the previous chapter, God is confoundingly paradoxical.

I shall not attempt to discuss most of the ways the Trinity has been understood, but, rather, I wish to focus on what I see as its deepest meaning. It is meaning that arises from and has profound significance for the path of spiritual awakening. It is also meaning that, if carried into the worship life of local churches, can facilitate the conscious shift in popular Christianity from the perspective of supernatural theism to the perspective of evolutionary panentheism.

As I see it, the validity of the myth of the Trinity is rooted in the spiritual experience of the oneness or interconnectedness of being. Many people—not just a few dedicated mystics—but many people of different cultures and religions, including many who had not previously engaged in disciplined spiritual practice— have had such experiences. Although we live in a world of multiplicity and diversity—a world of many different and apparently quite separate things and beings—intense experiences of a profound unity underlying that diversity are rather common. Such experiences naturally give rise to the idea that the dualistic, material world we experience in our day-to-day lives is somehow a manifestation of an unseen unity that is actually more real than the diversity we normally experience. Although the doctrine of the Trinity was not originally fashioned specifically to express this idea, I suggest that the accidents of history and the collective unconscious of the historical Christian community have produced a myth that wonderfully expresses precisely this idea. In other words, the doctrine of the Trinity can be understood as a mythic model of the metaphysical structure of being.

At the core stands the mysterious One, the Godhead, the God-Beyond-God, that is beyond all qualities and that encompasses everything. This is the *one* part of the one-God-three-persons formula. It is completely nondual, which means that even when it expresses as what might seem to be more than one thing, it remains fundamentally and inseparably one, never two or more.

We can and do say a lot about this mysterious, profoundly paradoxical unity, this oneness at the core of being and beyond all being—but there is nothing we can say about it that is fully accurate. After exhausting the limits of our language, we are ultimately forced into awed silence.

It is important in this discussion to be aware that the term *persons* when used in the context of the Trinity does not carry its normal meaning of *people*. We are not making an analogy of God being like three people who are somehow really one person. In Trinitarian theology, the term *person* comes from the Greek *persona*, which means *mask*. This is a term from Greek theater, where actors would wear different masks to take on the identities of different characters. Thus, the three persons of the Trinity can be thought of as three masks of God; that is, they are three ways that the same God appears to us—three aspects or facets of the mystery that is the subject of faith.

The three persons of the Trinity represent the activity and result of creation. In this model, the three persons—traditionally and patriarchally referred to as the Father, Son, and Holy Spirit—are best understood as Creator, Creation, and the creative dynamic of Love moving in time. The Creator is unmanifest spirit; the Creation is spirit manifest (incarnate) in and as matter, and Love is the relation/process that connects and moves it all.

One of the principles that has emerged from apophatic spirituality is the idea that, as the Creator creates the Creation, the Creation also creates the Creator, both through the action of Love. In other words, there is no Creator (Father) if there is no Creation (Son), and there can be neither of them without the dynamic of transformation (Love/Holy Spirit) and vice versa. This is consistent with the traditional Trinitarian assertion that the Son is eternally begotten by the Father through the Holy Spirit and there was never a time when the Father was without the Son. In other words, the three persons of the Trinity come as a package; there never was and never will be a time when they are not together.

Just as a potter who has not made a pot is not a potter, a Creator who has no Creation is not a Creator, and a parent with no child is not a parent. These labels—potter, creator, parent (father/mother)—each give a name to a producer of a product according to a producer-product relationship. Before the product there is no such relationship and the producer label is inappropriate. Creation does not create the God-Beyond-God (the One), but it does create God as Creator. God wears the three masks (persons) at the same time or none of them.

But there is an even deeper meaning here. Spirit is an all-pervasive unity. Though it may manifest in a vast diversity of seemingly separate beings and things, spirit remains ultimately one. The spirit in each of us and in all things is the same spirit. This means that your spirit and my spirit and the spirit of the Creator are the same spirit. The one spirit is the source of all things and is all things. We have all created each other and ourselves.

It is proper to think of the Trinity as eternal if we understand *eternal* to mean for all time because time is a part of creation. This means there can be no time in which the three persons of the Trinity do not exist, because time comes into being with and from the Trinity. There was no time before it and can be no time after it.

(I will interject here that this is idea of eternity as the entirety of time is not how I normally use the term. There are two senses of eternity: 1) for all time, and 2) beyond time. These could be distinguished as *temporal* eternity and *trans-temporal* eternity, although I don't normally use those terms. The distinction predates modernity but has become especially meaningful with the understanding by modern physics that time is a fourth dimension of the physical universe and came into being with the universe.)

Actually, any reference to or implication of time outside of Creation is meaningless in any literal sense; we are forced to use the language of *before* and *after* metaphorically because it is the best we can do in referring to what lies outside the scope of our created universe. Likewise, spatial references (i.e., *lies, outside, beyond*) for things beyond creation must also be taken metaphorically rather than literally.

Does this mean that the Trinity did not exist before the Big Bang? In theory, if ours is the only created universe and it was created at the Big Bang, then yes, there was no Trinity before the Big Bang. Or, if our universe is one of many in a multiverse, one might wonder if each created universe has its own Trinity that comes into being with the universe and eventually collapses or fades away if and when that universe collapses or fades away. Or, maybe creation is a continuous and endless process, so there was no before or after, either literally or metaphorically. All of this is interesting to think about, but I suspect it is beyond our ability to know in this life. What we do know is that, from our perspective within this created, material, temporal universe, the three persons of the Trinity are temporally eternal.

The dominant interpretation of the doctrine of *Creatio Ex Nihilo* (Creation from Nothing) asserts that material reality was created out of nothing and is, therefore, quite separate from and other than God. My model posits that all of material creation comprises the second person of the Trinity, is created by and from God, and is always a part of God. This means that there is no Trinity without a Creation because the Creation is one of the persons of the Trinity—and, yes, this means that you and I are both a part of God.

I suspect that this inclusion of all things, including ourselves, in the Trinity will seem especially heretical and shocking to many Christians today. However, there is much in the Bible and in the history of Christian theology, especially in the Eastern Orthodox tradition, that asserts precisely that. Eastern theologians understood that all of Creation participates in the Christ. Since the Great Schism of 1054 that drove apart the Greek and Latin Churches, western Christianity has largely lost track of this strand of thought. We need to recover it and build on it.[21] I hope you will read on and give the idea honest consideration.

Actually, I do not deny that God created out of nothing; I have simply concluded that the nothing from which God created is God's self, and I am in good company there. The idea is very prominent in Christian apophatic mystical theology.

Threads of Thought

I have found support for my interpretation of the doctrine of the Trinity from the convergence of numerous strands of thought, seven of which I shall share here. These strands do not prove my perspective, but together they provide a somewhat consistent conceptual framework for regarding all of reality as being God manifest.

The first strand is the discoveries of antimatter and quantum fluctuations by modern physics. Antimatter consists of particles identical to the ordinary matter of our world except that many of their fundamental properties such as electrical charge are opposite. A positron, for example, is the antimatter equivalent of an electron but has a positive charge instead of the electron's negative charge. When an antimatter particle and its ordinary

---

[21] For an excellent explication of the all-inclusivity of Christ, see:
Richard Rohr. *The Universal Christ: How a forgotten reality can change everything we see, hope for and believe.* SPCK Publishing, 2019.

matter equivalent collide, mutual annihilation occurs with the complete conversion of the matter to energy according to Einstein's famous equation $E = MC^2$.

But this process of two somethings combining to make nothing can and does work in the opposite direction, which has been observed in the phenomenon of quantum vacuum fluctuations. In the nothing of empty space, pairs of virtual matter and antimatter particles temporarily pop into being and then collide back together and annihilate each other. In other words, what we take to be nothing somehow separates itself into a matter-antimatter particle pair that then merge back together. This is a proven and widely accepted phenomenon among physicists, and it is anything but rare. Empty space teems with these fluctuations.

The point is that what we think of as nothing (empty space) actually foams with energy and matter at the quantum level, and the Trinity models this activity: empty space (nothing) is the Creator, the particles are the Creation, and the energy that makes it happen is the Holy Spirit. At the level of the One, everything and nothing merge so that everything and nothing and one are different manifestations of the same mystery: $0 = \infty = 1$

The second strand is the doctrine of the dual natures of Jesus Christ: that Jesus is both fully human and fully God. This doctrine is closely related to the doctrine of the Trinity. It is rooted in soteriology, which is the theology of salvation. It was argued that by being both God and human, Jesus served as a connection point between the immortal and the mortal and could thereby be a bridge by which mortal humans could cross into immortality. This idea relied on a lot of confusing Neo-Platonic arguments regarding essence and substance that I don't find very convincing, but I think the myth that Jesus was both God and human carries important meaning.

How can Jesus be fully human and fully God if other humans are not also fully God? If other humans are not fully God, but Jesus is, then Jesus has never had the experience of being fully human like the rest of us. Our mortal limitations and frailty are an essential part of what it means to be human. A Jesus whose divinity gives him power that frees him from those limitations is not really one of us even if he voluntarily limits the use of his divine power. The only way the dual natures of Jesus make sense is if all humans are equally as divine as he. Does not the creation myth in Genesis say that Adam came to life when God breathed God's spirit into him? Has not traditional theology always insisted that all humans carry the image of God? We humans are each enlivened by spirit which was never born and can never die. That spirit is divine and eternal even if our bodies are mortal. I do not deny that Jesus was divine; I simply insist that we must recognize that his divine nature is shared by all of us and, in fact, by all of creation.

The third strand comes from Anselm of Canterbury (d. 1109). Anselm was a very important figure in medieval Christianity.[22] He is best known for his argument for the existence of God that has come to be known as the ontological argument. Anselm famously defined God as *that than which nothing greater can be conceived*. That is, he proposed that God is the greatest imaginable (ultimate) being. In a nutshell, he argued that a being with all the greatest attributes who did not also have the attribute of existence would not be as great as a being that was otherwise identical but did exist, therefore God must exist. Less famously, he later admitted that his proof did not really work and that reason could not prove the existence of God; rather, he suggested, such proof was to be found only in spiritual encounter with God on a level of awareness beyond reason.

While I have always found Anselm's proof a little silly, I find his definition of God profound. I am aware of no meaningful argument as to why it should be accepted as a proper definition of God, but it works for me. My sense is that Anselm had little awareness of where his definition might lead. My argument is that a God who encompasses and includes everything including all of Creation is greater than a God who does not, so God must encompass everything and everything must be a part of God. There is no proof here, but it feels deeply right to me.

The fourth strand is what I call the *field theory of relationship*. I suggest that any two things that can in any way interact or be

---

[22] Anselm's legacy is far from entirely positive. He was a major proponent of the crusades.

known one by the other are connected within at least one context. By *context* I simply mean the shared environment that is the medium for interaction between the two things. In our material world, such contexts would include the space-time continuum and whatever electromagnetic, gravitational, quantum, and other fields permeate that continuum. I further suggest that there are non-material levels of being that interact with our material levels, which means there are one or more relational contexts that include our material universe but extend to levels beyond it. Thus, reality can be thought of as a hierarchy of nested contexts like a series of concentric spheres or nested Russian matryoshka dolls. God is simply the outer context within which all things and all other contexts relate to one another. That greatest field of relationship is Love (Agape) in the broadest sense (1 John 4:8,16). In other words, Love is the glue of being, the ocean in which all things swim.

By *Love* I do not mean just the various human emotions and processes that English lumps together under that single word. Those are certainly very important for us humans, but I use the term to mean something far more. Love is the push and pull of creativity and being. It is the reality of oneness that underlies and connects the multiplicity that is creation, and it is the energy by which the One manifests itself into that apparent multiplicity. Love (Agape/the Holy Spirit) is the lively energy by which the Creator pushes Creation out of undifferentiated oneness into a manifest expression of God's self in which God can experience God's self in the dance of being. Because it is rooted in the oneness of God, the energy of Love also provides the pull of relationship that keeps the multiplicity of creation connected within God. Love is the energy that pushes God apart so that God can dance with God's self; it is the energy that pulls and pushes the partners together and apart in the dance; and it is the energy that pulls them back into oneness when their dance ends.

The fifth strand is how I have come to reconcile theodicy and the implications of evolutionary theory for our understanding of good and evil. Theodicy is the theological attempt to explain why there is evil, sin, and suffering if God is absolutely good, loving, and all-powerful.

The traditional answer places evil in the world through no fault of God and makes that fallen world other than God. It posits that God refrains from intervening to stop evil and to prevent suffering in order to preserve our free will. How lame can you get? There are so many ways a God of supernatural theism could intervene and be helpful without seriously impinging on our free will. Such thinking also contradicts the traditional belief that the God of supernatural theism controls everything that happens in this world and that nothing happens in the world that is not consistent with God's will. The insistence that God is totally other and separate from the creation seems to be based on the desire to see God as only good and as separate from evil. Hence, evil is attributed only to Satan and fallen humanity. This is dualism plain and simple, which has long been considered a serious heresy. And this is the state of traditional Christian theology: a contradictory mess.

Evolutionary theory makes it clear that death, disease, pain, conflict, and competition for survival have always been a part of life on earth. We need pain because it teaches us what to avoid and when something is amiss. Death, far from being the enemy of life, is essential to it. Biological evolution moves forward because of the higher average death rates of those who are less fit for survival in whatever conditions life places them. Without death there would be very little biological change, and we would all at best be slime growing in the shallows or near a thermal vent in an otherwise lifeless sea. As Christians, we must realize that God has created us through an evolutionary process that has gone on for over thirteen billion years and continues today.[23] Death is not a consequence or punishment for Adam's disobedience. The story of the fall of humanity in Genesis is a great, great myth, but we are very mistaken to read it as literal history.

From our perspectives as individuals and from the perspectives of the social groups with which we identify (family, friends, communities, nations), death is often to be feared as a source of painful loss; it is only by seeing the bigger picture that we are able to realize that it is essential and ultimately good. Pain,

---

[23] I highly recommend *The Universe Story: From the Primoridal Flaring Forth to the Ecozoic Era—A Celebration of the Unfolding of the Cosmos* by Brian Swimme & Thomas Berry (HarperSanFrancisco, 1992).

suffering, disease, disaster, conflict, and death are a part of life. That we have evolved to want to avoid and minimize the pain of these things—which is what ethics, politics, economics, and medicine are properly about— is an expression of the divine will. God calls us to manage these things through self-discipline, collective action, and compassion, but we will probably never eliminate them. They are inseparable from the Creation and the creative process and, therefore, from the Creator. The evil we perceive in them is a matter of perspective. Evil is how we characterize the currents of creation and being that we experience as painful and horrifying. This is not to downplay how horrible and seemingly unnecessary those currents can sometimes be and how important it is for us to oppose and mitigate them, but they are part of the package of Creation.

Once we accept that evil fits into the bigger picture and that God painted and continues to paint the picture, there is no need to hold God apart as separate. This does not prove that God is not separate, but it removes the taboo of thinking it. We do not insult God by thinking that God encompasses what we perceive as evil. We need not fear that an angry God will take offense and punish us for daring to think such things.

This has a lot to do with how we tend to project ourselves onto God. That is, we tend to imagine God in our own image. As I have already said in many different ways, this is natural given that human intelligence has evolved in the context of human social groups. It is natural that we would anthropomorphize everything including God and project ourselves onto God. That being the case, one must also wonder if not wanting to see evil in God also has something to do with not wanting to see evil in ourselves. We objectify evil into a container we call sin, but, though we make great show of confessing our guilt and depravity, do we honestly own it? Christian theology has preferred to see sin as a stain of foreign origin, something Satan tricked us into and not an inherent aspect of our created nature. We like to project the worst evil onto special villains—Hitler, the Communists, serial killers, terrorists—those we can classify as quite other and who we can assure ourselves are altogether different from us. But are they really? Where exactly is the line to be drawn? Doesn't God supposedly love them just as much as the rest of us? Did Jesus not condition our own forgiveness on our willingness to forgive even these? To be able to see God as whole, perhaps we need to see and accept our own wholeness, including our own shadow aspects and our own capacity for evil.

The sixth strand is the mystical theology of the state of divine union. The Christian mystical tradition has long posited that a life of self-discipline, purification, prayer, and contemplation can lead to a state of mystical union with God, a state in which the person knows her- or himself to be one with God. This has traditionally been seen as a gift bestowed by God on a few especially saintly individuals in response to great faithfulness and spiritual effort. I think this theology is distorted by the traditional concerns regarding evil and sin discussed in the previous paragraphs and other orthodox doctrines that have made it dangerous for mystics to express their thoughts more freely. My experience is that the unity is always there and that it is simply very difficult for us to be aware of it.

To survive and prosper in a biological and social world where so many things can harm or kill us, we need to pay really good attention to that world. We have evolved egos for that very purpose. The job of the ego is to keep us alive and to push us to act in our own best interest. This is pretty much a 24/7 job, but occasionally the ego relaxes enough to let us become aware of what is underneath it, and then we have one of those experiences of oneness that I mentioned at the beginning of this chapter. In the myth of the Fall in Genesis, the garden represents this state of awareness of our oneness with God, and the fall is the overshadowing of that awareness by minds focused on survival. In this regard, we can think of our egos (our preoccupation with our self and our quality of life in the material world) as original sin—something we are born with that makes us feel separate from one another and from God. Nonetheless, we are not really separate, and it is possible to be aware of that fact—not constantly and not exclusively, because we really do need to pay a lot of attention to the concerns of the ego if we want to survive well— but getting in touch with the underlying unity can be a life changing and enriching experience. While this can happen unexpectedly like a bolt from the blue, the intention of spiritual practice is to invite it to happen more often and more deeply.

The seventh strand is the neurological understanding of this experience of unity. Research indicates that our sense of the physical boundaries of our body and of our location and physical orientation within our environment depend on the flow of sensory input to what is called the orientation area of the brain. When this area of the brain is deprived of adequate neurological input, a process called *deafferentation*, we lose our sense of the boundary between our self and the world, and we lose our sense of physical orientation in the world. The result is a feeling of the self merging into a state of unity with a boundless reality. This can result from a variety of causes including illness, certain drugs, extreme relaxation, fatigue, or intense mental focus.[24]

This phenomenon is open to two interpretations: 1) The mystical experience is simply a neurologically induced illusion; or 2) the sense that our self as bounded is an illusion needed for survival in the material world and the mystical experience is actually a more primal and transcendentally accurate level of consciousness. In other words the question is, when we experience the state of mystical union, are we simply neurologically confused or are we enjoying a moment when the illusion collapses and we experience a deeper level of reality? The answer depends on what consciousness actually is and its relationship to biological nervous systems. If consciousness happens only as a product of biology, the first interpretation is likely accurate. If, however, consciousness is more fundamental than matter and exists as spirit apart from biology, the second interpretation makes sense. Again, I have no proof, but my point here is that the neurological explanation does not rule out the possibility that the experience of mystical unity is an authentic perception of a more fundamental level of consciousness.

These are the major strands of thought that have contributed to or supported my interpretation of the Trinity. I am sure that there are other strands that would also support it. Again, none of this proves that my concept of the Trinity is correct. I simply offer

---

[24] Andrew Newberg, Eugene d'Aquili, and Vince Rause, *Why God Won't Go Away: Brain Science and the Biology of Belief.* (New York: Ballantine, 2002), 98-127. You may find other books on the topic of neurotheology of interest.

it as an understanding that adapts the traditional doctrine to our contemporary, scientifically-aware worldview.

What I feel is most important about my understanding of the Trinity is that it makes us—humanity; you, me, everyone—and everything a part of God. This is, I believe, the deepest meaning of the great Christian sacrament, the Holy Eucharist. When the Jesus of the myth says that "this" is his body and blood, he is using metaphor to express that the material world, represented by the bread and the wine, is the physical matrix that holds and supports the incarnation of spirit. It means that all of Creation is the body and blood of the one spirit that unites and enlivens us all. There is no transubstantiation here; it is the body and blood (the physical abode of spirit) exactly as it is.

In this chapter I have offered what I see to be the most important meaning of the core myth of Christianity—the myth of Jesus as God incarnate. It must be said that the tradition bears much more mythic material that is rich with spiritual meaning. This would include all of Genesis, the exodus story, the judges and heroes and prophets, the birth narratives and ministry of Jesus, the Easter stories, the apocalyptic material including the Book of Revelation, and church legend and hagiography. In this work I shall interpret little of this material. My intention is to offer a few important examples and leave the broader activity of interpretation for other settings. Progressive Christianity would do well to take on such interpretation as a major emphasis for both personal and communal practice. The rewards to be reaped are immense, and the process of discovery can actually be fun.

The Subjective Jesus

He asked them, "But who do you say that I am?"
Mark 8:29 (NRSV)

I have already asserted that the Jesus of faith is not the historical Jesus. We do not have much specific knowledge of who Jesus of Nazareth really was and what evidence we do have suggests that he did not believe himself to be the savior of the world. Yet, many millions of Christians believe him to be precisely that. This is what the Christian myth teaches, and it is valid as a myth. The meaning of the myth is the subjective response—the symbolic understandings, insights, feelings, values, concerns, hopes, and inspirations—it evokes in the minds and hearts of those who seriously consider the myth both as individuals and as groups.

The word *subjective* refers to the inward, private, personal experience of the individual. Subjectivity is what we perceive and think and feel inside ourselves. Subjectivity is ultimately an individual experience even in group contexts; groups can strongly influence the subjective experience of individuals in the group, but the subjective experience is always finally personal. Because subjective response is private and unique to each person, the subjective meaning of Jesus and the role such meaning plays in each of our inner lives will be different for each of us. In other words, all of us for whom Jesus is an important figure carry around within us a unique perspective on Jesus—our own personal Jesus.

This phenomenon of subjective perception is not at all limited to Jesus but applies to everyone and everything we think we know. We never fully know anyone as they truly are—not even the people to whom we are closest. We know people only in the context of our relationships with them, but their lives extend into other contexts and areas that we don't see. Everyone has private parts of themselves that only they know, so even the people we know the best and love the most are not exactly the people we think they are. Furthermore, everyone has subconscious parts of themselves of which not even they are fully aware, so it is not even possible to fully know ourselves.

We know the world only through our senses, and we build our understanding of everything from what we perceive. We carry that understanding around in our brains. The sum of all the memories and understandings we carry around is our worldview, and it is always an imperfect picture. Life is a continuous learning experience. We like to think we see and understand the world exactly as it is, but over and over again we realize that we were mistaken about something—maybe a very small thing or maybe a big thing—and we have to revise our mental picture. Over time we learn to understand things better, but we never see them wholly as they are. Our perceptions and our brains are limited. Even if our perceptions and understandings are accurate as far as they go, they can only go so far, so our understanding can never be complete. We all know from experience that we often misperceive or fail to understand. Our worldview is only our best take at the present moment, and our interactions with the world are always mediated through our imperfect worldview.

Even if you knew Jesus when he was alive, you would know him only partially. The fact that he lived two-thousand years ago and that virtually everything we know about him comes to us through the Christian narrative all but guarantees that the personal Jesus carried by any of us will be considerably different from the historical, flesh-and-blood Jesus. The flesh-and-blood Jesus set the narrative in motion, but it has since been shaped according to the understandings and interpretations of many, many people.

Culturally transmitted understandings are the raw material from which we subjectively build our personal Jesuses. In western culture especially, but ever more broadly in our increasingly global culture, Jesus has come to represent the ideal human—the one who did it right and is worthy of divinity. Thus, the personal Jesus many of us carry around is an embodiment of what we regard as ideal—an idealized reflection of what we each most value or want. Possible personal Jesuses include the great moral teacher and example, the paragon of self-mastery, the gentle and caring friend, the healer and comforter, the powerful Lord and King, the suffering servant, the grantor of blessing and prosperity, the advocate for the oppressed, the spiritual master, the Cosmic Christ, and the judge who will mete out well deserved punishment and reward in due time. And more than a few people carry around a negative Jesus, a Jesus who accuses or condemns or rejects or who represents intolerance, superstition, or servile conformity. How much of your personal Jesus do you recognize in this list?

If you are of a born-again or evangelical bent, you may reject all of this as not applying to your relationship with Jesus. It may all be true enough for ordinary human relationships but, you say, my relationship with Jesus is different; he lives inside me, so I know him from within. But do you really? I totally affirm the experience at the root of such belief, but I question the accuracy of the understanding that some Christians seem to impose on it. I think it is a mistake to label it "Jesus".

My fundamental point in this book is that we are all connected to God and that awareness of that connection comes from deep within the self, from a level deeper than the ego. I believe that this divine presence, this image of God, is present in every person— not just in those who have had a born-again experience. We are all influenced by this presence in the course of our lives. Some are affected dramatically and quite consciously; others are not really aware of it; but it is always there. Life as a spiritual journey is about becoming more aware of this divine presence, learning to work with it instead of against it, and letting it shine through us. This is not just about overtly religious or spiritual activity, but about the fullness of life and all the drives and interests that propel us through it and feed our ambition and creativity.

True conversion experiences are moments when the divine presence becomes more conscious for us, when we see ourselves and our relationship to everything else a little clearer. Sometimes this happens suddenly and dramatically, but often it is a gradual process. Such experiences are transformative in and of themselves, and they also open us to further growth. We become aware that there are things that need to change and we find that we want to change them. It is an opening of the heart, soul, and mind—an awakening to a deeper level of meaning— often coupled with a willingness and desire to serve something greater than our self. The spiritual journey can be seen as a series of such experiences, a few very big ones, perhaps, and many little ones.

The born-again experience is one of these moments of spiritual opening. Just as birth frees us from the constriction of the womb and opens our awareness to the much larger outside world, so spiritual rebirth frees us from the constriction of existential self-absorption and opens our awareness to eternity, spiritual interconnection, and the ultimacy of love.

It is important to note that one can have such an opening without identifying it as spiritual rebirth. The label "born-again" is a cultural fixture of evangelical Christianity, and not at all required to validate the experience. The experience is what it is regardless of label. For some it comes suddenly; for others it sneaks in slowly. It is a huge mistake to look for or expect a particular experience. Just be open to how the Spirit moves in you.

When we first experience such an opening, it may feel so different from what we are used to that we suspect that something has brought it into us from outside. This makes it easy to believe that the Holy Spirit or the spirit of Jesus as something separate from us has come into us. This interpretation is reflected in Bible passages like John 14:23: "Those who love me will keep my word, and my Father will love them, and we will come to them and make our home with them" (NRSV). This is how the Johannine community—the community that gave us the Gospel and Epistles of John—understood their experience of spiritual opening at the time the gospel was written. Such passages are not entirely incorrect. There is really only one spirit, so the Holy Spirit and the spirit of Jesus and your spirit and my spirit and all spirits are ultimately inseparable facets of God as Spirit. I would simply argue that, despite how it may seem initially, it does not come from outside but from deep within. God does not invade and possess us. Rather, being born again is a process of opening and integration. It does not establish a new connection or a new relationship; instead, it is about becoming more aware of the relationship that has always been. It is about getting in touch with who we really are and recognizing our deep connection to God and to everyone and everything.

Evangelical Christianity wants to label the result of this opening a "personal relationship with Jesus Christ". That goes too far. It is not possible for hundreds of millions of Christians to all have a personal relationship with Jesus in the sense we normally use the term "personal relationship". Yes, we all have a spiritual connection to everyone and everything, including Jesus, but a personal relationship is more than just a connection. A personal relationship requires real, regular, 2-way conversation—not just the imagined conversation that is contained only in the mind of one person in the relationship. Such imaginary conversations can be a valid form of prayer if understood as such, but can become delusional if not kept in realistic perspective. Being sensitive to the presence and promptings of spirit in one's life is not the same as knowing Jesus as a personal friend. A personal relationship takes time and attention. No one can maintain more than maybe several dozen personal relationships, and only a few of those can possibly be close relationships. All the hocus-pocus hoopla about Jesus' divine nature freeing him from such limitations is just so much silliness. Yes, we all absolutely do have a close personal connection to God, but it is misleading to call it a personal relationship with Jesus.

In this regard it is worth noting how St. Paul famously expressed his own experience of transformation: "… it is no longer I who live, but it is Christ who lives in me." (Galatians 2:20 NRSV). He does not say that Jesus lives in him but that Christ lives in him. *Christ* is not a name but a title; it is the Greek word for *messiah*, and both words mean *anointed*. It seems to me that Paul was deliberate in how he used the terms *Jesus* and *Christ* separately and in combination. In passages where he speaks of his own internal mystical experience he seems to be careful not to name it *Jesus* but to refer to it as *Christ*. It is as though he recognizes Jesus to be a separate person—the human side of the second person of the Trinity, if you will—who was and remains an individual, but he sees Jesus' state of being anointed, his Christhood, as the spiritual/divine side of the second person that he and all Christians can share in. Of course, the doctrines of the Trinity were in the earliest stages of formation in Paul's time, so he would not have said it in these terms, but it seems like this sort of distinction may have been present in his mind.

Paul expresses similar thoughts in this passage:

From now on, therefore, we regard no one from a human point of view; even though we once regarded Christ from a human point of view, we regard him thus no longer. Therefore, if any one is in

Christ, he is a new creation; the old has passed away, behold, the new has come. All this is from God, who through Christ reconciled us to himself and gave us the ministry of reconciliation; that is, in Christ God was reconciling the world to himself, not counting their trespasses against them, and entrusting to us the message of reconciliation. 2 Corinthians 5:16-19 (RSV)

Here Paul recognizes that Jesus had a human side like all of us, but the human side is not what concerns Paul. It is what Paul labels *Christ*—this anointing, this state of relationship between Jesus and God—that Paul thinks is important. It is important for him because he sees it as something we can all enter into. To enter consciously into this state is to be spiritually opened and drawn into deeper awareness of God and to take on the concern to reconcile ourselves and the entire world to God.

Reconciliation is the overcoming of discord and alienation. It is overcoming the barriers of separation and otherness between us and God. Social intelligence in the ancient world tended to understand our alienation from God as a matter of God having chosen to pull away because of our sinfulness. My own spiritual experience has convinced me that the alienation happens entirely on our side of the relationship, not God's. It arises from the limitations of our awareness and attention. God is not distant at all, but in our incarnate state we have inwardly lost touch with the presence of God. Our egos are so busy taking care of our little selves that we lose sight of our larger Self. This difficulty is inherent in the structure of Creation and can be properly labeled *original sin*.

Reconciliation is necessary both as an inward process and as an outward process. We must awaken to the presence of God in ourselves, but we must also awaken to the presence of God in other people and in all things. There is no set order in which this must happen. Some people may first awaken to God through their experience of the natural world. For others it may come through their relationships with other people. For some, ideas passed from other people through reading or teaching may open the door. Yet others may have spontaneous spiritual experiences. For many, deliberate spiritual practice may lead to the opening. It does not matter how it gets started, but, given enough time, it will expand into all these dimensions.

But then, what subjective perspectives can we validly hold regarding Jesus? By now you have figured out that I depart from traditional Christianity in that I assert a strong distinction between the historical, real Jesus and the imaginary Jesus of faith, which is the Jesus of the Christian myth. This gives us two Jesuses to draw from in forming our own personal Jesus. The historical Jesus was an apocalyptic preacher, religious teacher, leader of a social and political movement, and erstwhile revolutionary who believed himself to be chosen by God to be a Messiah for the Jewish people. The Jesus of the myth is a deity who entered a virgin's womb to be born as a human in order to enlighten us and to die to save us. Both Jesuses were crucified by the Romans, but only the Jesus of faith rose from death. The historical Jesus was his own, separate person; the Jesus of the myth is all of us.

It is crucial that we objectively understand the difference between these two Jesuses, and that can require wrestling with the understandings and feelings about Jesus that long ago took root within us. The spiritual journey is, among other things, a journey toward honesty and clarity. It is about seeing reality as it truly is. Subjectivity is by no means entirely rational; it involves the heart every bit as much if not more than the mind. How you feel about Jesus and how you relate to Jesus from within yourself at any given moment is what it is. If you have everything worked out, great!—but if not, that's okay too. The Jesus you carry inside you is the Jesus that fits where you are in your spiritual journey. It may well be complicated, and it will surely change over time. There is a lot to be sorted out, but it also does not have to make any more sense at a particular moment than you need it to make.

The Bottom Line

"I came that they may have life, and have it abundantly."
John 10:10b (NRSV)

It is time to get to the heart of the matter: What is Christianity ultimately about? What does Christianity offer the "believer"? What's the bottom line? For most traditional Christians today, the answer is simple:

> *"For God so loved the world, that he gave his only begotten Son, that whosoever believeth in him should not perish, but have everlasting life."* John 3:16 (KJV)

This has come to be understood in terms of substitutionary atonement: that Jesus, being without sin, took the punishment for our sin upon himself and thereby made our salvation possible. We need only accept this salvation by believing it to be true.

Really?

For one thing, I am very confident that Jesus did not believe this and never said these words. As I have explained elsewhere, what authentic words we have from Jesus are found mostly in the Synoptic Gospels (Mark, Matthew, and Luke) and in the recently discovered Gospel of Thomas. The Gospel of John seems to have been written later than the Synoptics, as much as 50 to 70 years after the crucifixion. Apart from the story of the crucifixion, the Jesus of the Gospel of John is almost unrecognizable as the same Jesus we find in the Synoptics. That does not mean we should reject the fourth gospel. It just means that we need to be careful about how we understand it. It contains almost no history but rather reflects the opinion and emerging faith of the community in which it was written. It is a theological and spiritual reflection on the meaning of Jesus and his life, death, and resurrection from the perspective of that particular group many decades later. It appears to have been assembled in part from sermons and teachings based on the theology that developed within the group and that the gospel writer has placed on Jesus' own lips. This results in some awkward passages like this one where Jesus speaks of himself in the third person. If Jesus had wanted to express the idea stated in John 3:16, would he not have said, "For my Father so loved the world that he gave *me* ...""? Instead we have what appears to be a carefully crafted creedal statement that reflects, not Jesus' own thinking, but the beliefs of a later Christ cult.

The opinions expressed in the Gospel of John were by no means widely accepted within the larger Christian movement at the time it was written, but they were soon to become extremely popular among gentile Christians. They are the basis of the myth of the Christ that eventually prevailed in orthodox Christianity. I dare say that without the Gospel of John there would be no Christianity anything like we know today.

It is important to see the disconnect here. Jesus was concerned with bringing God's rule to this life ("Thy will be done on earth as it is in heaven") but the Gospel of John and traditional Christianity are concerned with securing salvation in an afterlife. This shift is, I think, a major misstep on the part of the Church. It is an entirely understandable misstep considering the historical development and cultures involved, but a misstep nonetheless that needs to be recognized and corrected if Christianity is to speak helpfully to future generations.

A Solution in Need of a Problem

The Church's offer of "pie in the sky by and by" is a solution to a problem that early Christians adapted from the Judaism of the day and developed into something of their own. Earlier Hebrew religion assumed the human soul to be eternal. It was believed that after death all human souls descended into Sheol, which was not a place of eternal reward or punishment but a sort of cold storage for souls whose earthly lives had run their course. Life happened only on earth, but what people experienced and became during their life—their identity—was not erased or forgotten; it remained in the netherworld as a part of collective human experience.

Over time and with exposure to the afterlife beliefs of other cultures, especially the Persians, the idea of punishment after death began to appear around the edges of Jewish religion. It is not present in the Hebrew Bible (Old Testament), but the idea became associated with a place that is mentioned there. Gehinnom (the valley of Hinnom) was a valley outside of Jerusalem associated with burning, including Pagan fire rituals and burnt sacrifice. It was also prophesied to be a place where Israel's enemies would be destroyed by fire. The name eventually became associated with punishment after death, although not necessarily eternal punishment. *Gehinnom* came into koine Greek as *Gehenna*, which is the primary word translated as Hell in most versions of the New Testament.

Jews had good reason to be attracted to the idea of the afterlife as a place of reward or punishment. The Jews of Jesus' day and many earlier generations struggled with a crisis of faith triggered by their experience of suffering under the domination of other cultures. Jewish faith centered on the Covenant, which promised earthly prosperity and security for those who obeyed God's laws and corrective punishment for those who did not. In other words, the Covenant promised reward and punishment in this life, not in an afterlife. The problem was that the Covenant did not seem to work as promised: Jews who were faithful often suffered and those who paid little heed to the Covenant often prospered. In Jesus day, faithful Jews suffered under Greek and Roman rule, and those who prospered tended to be those who compromised on the Covenant. This was not at all how it was supposed to work. It was simply not just, and Jews believed deeply that their god was a just god.

At least two possible solutions to this problem emerged in Jewish thought. One was resurrection, which was understood to be a return to earthly life in which the dead literally rose from their graves. The other possible solution was a non-earthly afterlife in which appropriate reward was enjoyed or appropriate punishment was suffered. Both options were naturally associated with the idea of eternal life. The Judaism of Jesus' day had not arrived at a consensus on these issues.[25]

---

[25] For a more in-depth discussion of this history, see Bruce Chilton. *Abraham's Curse: The Roots of Violence in Judaism, Christianity, and Islam.* (New York: Doubleday, 2008), pp. 43-64.

Nascent Christianity then entered the picture with an additional concern: the crucifixion. The fact that Jesus had been crucified was a huge impediment to placing religious faith in him for both Jews and gentiles. In the Torah it is written, "a hanged man is accursed by God" (Deuteronomy 21:23 RSV), so the rabbinic Judaism that emerged in the first century took the position that Jesus, having been crucified (hung on a cross), had actually been cursed by God and could not be a/the messiah. For pagans it was simply too unseemly to think that any god would ever allow himself to suffer such a demeaning and humiliating fate at the hands of humans, not even if it was followed by resurrection. This meant that Christianity's initial appeal was not to the mainstream of either culture but to the poor and to women who could identify with being demeaned and humiliated. The problem facing the Christian movement was how to make a crucified lord acceptable to the broader society.

The solution to the problem of the crucifixion was to reframe it as central to God's plan for salvation, to paint it as something that God had intended all along, even if that was not really evident to Jesus and his followers while he was alive.

This reframing went through several versions. For earliest Christianity, as expressed in the Synoptic Gospels and some of the letters of Paul, the crucifixion seems to have functioned primarily as a test of Jesus' faithfulness to God and God's will, establishing his worthiness to be adopted as God's Son and Messiah. As such, Jesus was the first to be resurrected and was expected to return very soon to establish God's kingdom on earth and to call forth the rest of the dead to resurrection and judgment. It seems that by the time the Gospel of John was written, the scandal of the crucified savior had caught quite a lot of public attention and fascination. For the Gospel of John, this attention and fascination became the purpose of the crucifixion: to draw the attention of the entire world to God's eternally divine (rather than adopted) Son. The Book of Hebrews, apparently written even later, expressly stated the idea that Jesus death was a final sacrifice to reconcile humanity to God. All of these New Testament perspectives saw the crucifixion as playing an important role in God's plan of salvation, and the trend was to understand that salvation increasingly in terms of an afterlife.

A key factor in the shift of emphasis from God's kingdom on earth to God's kingdom in heaven was the simple fact that Jesus did not return in the expected timeframe. The Jesus of the Synoptics had promised that some of those who witnessed his ministry would also witness his return and the day of resurrection, but by the time the fourth gospel was written, the first generation of believers had all but passed away. The Gospel of John dealt with this problem by beginning to disconnect the promise of salvation from the messianic return of Jesus. It offered a two-fold form of salvation. It offered salvation in the present as a close inward relationship with Jesus and, through Jesus, with God the "Father" (John 14:23). It also offered salvation after death in the "many mansions" of the "Father's house" (John 14:2). The idea that Jesus would return was not entirely abandoned, but the Gospel of John is rather vague and ambiguous about it. This provided an opening for the dominant understanding of salvation in Christianity to focus on the afterlife.

But salvation from what? Throughout the history of the Hebrew people the focus of salvation changed. For Abraham, it was salvation from dying childless and without a legacy. For Moses, it was salvation from cruel slavery by deliverance into a homeland flowing with milk and honey. In the period of the Judges, it was salvation from invading kings and adversarial tribes. In the period of the Israelite monarchies, it was salvation from corrupt monarchs and foreign empires. During the Babylonian exile it was being allowed to return to Judea. In the wisdom literature it was salvation from ignorance and error. In many of the Psalms, it was deliverance from disease and misfortune or from scheming and treacherous adversaries both foreign and domestic. In the Greek and Roman periods, it was the hope that God's Messiah would arise to throw off foreign domination and establish just and harmonious rule under God's law. All of these were salvations here on earth; the idea of what might happen to one's soul after death did not enter into any of them.

This began to change during the Hellenistic period, which began a few hundred years before Jesus. In particular, the persecution early in that period of devout Jews by the Greeks was horrific. For many Jews it seemed that God had abandoned God's people. The book of Daniel, the last book written of what became the Hebrew Bible (Old Testament), was composed at that time to encourage the Jewish people to hold fast to their faith. Its story was set during an earlier time of crisis, the Babylonian exile, to remind the people that God had not forgotten their ancestors then and would not forget them now. The book of Daniel introduced into Hebrew scripture both the idea of resurrection and the idea that "one like a son of man" would be sent from heaven to establish God's rule on earth.

During the intertestamental period—the time between the writing of the last book of the Hebrew Scriptures and the first book of the New Testament—the idea of reward or punishment after death crept into Jewish thought. The idea of heaven had always been present, but it was the dwelling place of God, not the normal destination of the dead. God had chosen to take a few special people to be with "him" there, but all other deceased humans went to Sheol. Although never mentioned in the Old Testament, the idea of Hell becomes important in the Apocrypha and New Testament.

The appeal of the idea of Heaven and Hell to Jews under Greek and Roman domination is entirely understandable. They suffered much, and it seemed that true justice rarely happened. Believing that reward and punishment would be meted out in the afterlife was comforting. It made a harsh, precarious life a little more bearable. That applied not just for Jews but for the vast majority of the poor, powerless, and exploited in the Roman Empire. The idea had appeal even to some among the privileged classes who valued fairness and aspired to righteousness and justice. So, by the time the Gospel of John was written in the late first century, the Christian idea of salvation was well on its way to shifting from an earthly kingdom of liberation and justice to eternal reward or punishment in an afterlife.

The new concept of salvation required something further: divine judgment. It would be up to God to separate the goats (bad people) from the sheep (good people) and send each to their appropriate destination. Originally this duty fell to God the Son to perform on his return to Earth at the end of the age, but today the popular belief is that it happens when we die.

This idea of final divine judgment had a profound impact on how people regarded death, justice, and salvation. No longer was everyone headed to the same place of eternal rest. No longer was it believed that punishment was suffered on Earth and that it should be proportional to the offense. Instead, eternity became a matter of absolute binary fate, either all good or all bad. No longer was salvation about deliverance and protection from suffering in this life; it was now about avoiding the wrath of God in the next.

God's wrath in the context of eternal judgment was the problem that Christianity settled on to be solved by the crucifixion. The basic idea, which eventually developed into the full-blown doctrine of substitutionary atonement, was that God's wrath toward human sin had to be satisfied; someone had to bear the punishment. Jesus' torturous death became the punishment for our sins; God could forgive us because Jesus suffered our punishment. Such forgiveness is secured simply by believing this to be true and by trying to live in faithful obedience to God.

Problems in the Solution

There are at least three major problems with this scheme. First, eternal suffering is disproportionate and unfair punishment, no matter how much suffering a person has inflicted on others. Forever is simply a very long time, and eternal punishment is inconsistent with the contention that God is just. Second, Jesus absolutely never taught that punishment was necessary for forgiveness. Rather, he taught that in order to be forgiven we must forgive—period—end of story. This is arguably the clearest and most authentic of his teachings. Third, this theology turns God into a hypocritical monster. God's own son, who is also supposedly fully God, teaches us that we must forgive, yet substitutionary atonement implies that God cannot forgive but can be satisfied only by the retribution of painful, bloody suffering and death. There is, in fact, no forgiveness at all if Jesus suffered the punishment. The traditional perspective on the crucifixion reduces the Kosmos to a crude economy of crime and punishment and elevates divine anger rather than love to be the ultimate driving principle of reality.

The very premise that all the guilt for sin should rest on humanity has been shattered by the modern, evolutionary perspective. As I discussed in the chapter on the Trinity, what we call sin arises from the very nature of creation. The process of biological evolution that has given rise to all life places every living thing in competition with other living things. Conflict, disease, pain, aging, and death are inevitable and necessary aspects of the created order, not the corruption of creation by evil. Yes, we humans could better exercise our free will to avoid much of the most egregious sin we commit, but the sources of suffering and conflict—including us--are ultimately part of the fabric of material being. They arise from the inherently and unavoidably conflicting interests of the different beings within the created realm. In this sense original sin is very real, but it is not the fault of humanity. There is no justice in punishing us eternally for what we cannot ultimately avoid. Our fallibility has been created into us, and our evolutionary task is to push against it, to strive to do the right thing in a reality where the choices are not simple. We need God to help us learn to minimize suffering and conflict, not to heap on more suffering as punishment for what we are incapable of entirely preventing.

The doctrine of substitutionary atonement is, thus, quite grotesque if taken literally as it is commonly understood. Yet, wrath, punishment, and suffering were major aspects of life in Jesus' world and, if we are honest about it, throughout the world for all of human history. That this negative side of life should show up in the Christian myth is entirely understandable and appropriate—necessary, really. If we see substitutionary atonement as part of the larger Christian myth, then we can interpret it quite differently if we are willing to let go of its literal meaning.

In the myth, Jesus represents both God and all of creation, including all of humanity. This dual symbolism requires dual interpretations. First, as God, Jesus takes the punishment for sin on himself because God is responsible for Creation and all that comes with it, including sin. This is not a guiltless God magnanimously accepting someone else's punishment but a God taking responsibility and fully experiencing the consequences of Creation. This God is fully present in the Creation and suffers in and with all who suffer.

Second, as a symbol of creation, Jesus on the cross teaches us the very nature of being: Everything ultimately gives its life for everything else. Whether we know it or not, we all live and die for each other in the context of the divine love that gives us being and binds us together. That is the way being and evolution work.

Although suffering is sometimes genuinely a matter of punishment, mostly it is not. Suffering is a part of life and, in a very real sense, the price of life. The Law of the Jungle applies: eat and be eaten. I have most often heard the Law of the Jungle stated as, "Eat *or* be eaten", but in reality everything that eats is eventually also eaten. We all sometimes benefit from the misfortune of others, and others sometimes benefit from our misfortune. While it is also true that we can benefit with others when they prosper, that's not a problem; it is the negative side of the equation that is hard to accept—that one being's detriment can be another being's benefit.

Life can never be purely win-win. Win-win is the ideal we strive for as represented in the Judeo-Christian tradition by the dream of the Kingdom of God, but it is an ideal, a goal, a telos, that draws us forward but that can never be fully achieved as a static goal. We must seek win-win relations whenever we can recognize the option to do so, but we must also expect win-lose, lose-win, and lose-lose situations. From the perspective of the unmanifest One from which all being arises, it is all WIN, but from the perspective of individual beings, shit happens.

When the Jesus of the myth invites us to take up our cross and follow him, he is inviting us to recognize the full nature of life and love and to bravely accept its negative side along with the positive. Suffering is not to be sought out, but it does come to us all. The myth calls us to not let existential fear dissuade us from striving for righteousness and justice; to forgive those who may inflict our suffering; to know that our spirit, as part of the eternal spirit that is God, will survive the suffering; and to be compassionate and responsive to others when they suffer.

Resurrection

But what about resurrection? The myth of Jesus' bodily resurrection is just that, a myth. Reports that Jesus' resurrection appearances included his physical body seem to have emerged somewhat late in the formation of early Christianity along with the story of the Ascension, which became necessary to explain how his physical body got from Earth to Heaven. The earliest theology of the resurrection seems to have been that Jesus was "raised up" spiritually, not bodily, directly into Heaven. It seems likely that some of his followers had visions and dreams of Jesus as being alive after the crucifixion, but that is just a variation on the widely held belief in ghosts. That is not the same as the idea that Jesus' dead body came back to life. The reports that people saw and touched the living body of Jesus after Easter are just not very credible. None are first-hand reports in a witness's own words. Some, such as Luke's story of the appearance of Jesus on the road to Emmaus, seem to have been composed by their authors to be lessons about faith. Others seem to be responses to theological controversies in early Christianity regarding the nature of the resurrection.

The earliest gospel, the Gospel of Mark, seems originally to have included no reports of anyone witnessing Jesus' resurrected body. It merely states that women found the tomb empty and that a young man in a white robe (usually interpreted to have been an angel) told them that Jesus had risen and would meet his followers in Galilee. However, it also says that they told this to no one. So how did Mark know? This could be another nod and wink from the author of the first gospel to indicate a passage that need not be taken literally. A young man in a robe is mentioned at several critical points in Mark's gospel, and more than one commentator has suggested that he is a symbolic figure inserted by the author to represent catechumens (new Christians undergoing instruction in preparation for baptism). If that is so, then Mark's passage about the empty tomb may be saying that belief in the resurrection is a matter of faith, not direct, physical experience.

In any case, passages regarding resurrection, the Ascension, the Millennium, and the afterlife in the New Testament, when taken together, are mushy at best. Resurrection was a controversial idea in first-century Judaism. In Christianity it became central and closely tied to the idea that Jesus would return soon to end the age. However, Jesus did not return soon, and it is time that we recognize that these ideas belong to the realm of myth and are best understood metaphorically.

What Comes After Death?

What, then, is the eternal disposition of our souls?

Let me begin by making a semantic distinction between *spirit* and *soul*. These words are used to mean a variety of things and often interchangeably. I use them here with specific meanings. I have already associated spirit with consciousness and identified it with God as the mysterious source and ground of being. In this sense there is only one spirit; the spirit that is present in you and me and everything is one. A soul is the one spirit as it incarnates in a particular sentient being. Such beings do not so much *have* souls as they *are* souls. Souls are mortal because they are inseparable from bodies, which are mortal. Soul includes ego and body-bound personality.

I don't know exactly what happens to our consciousness when we die, and neither does any other living person—not for sure. Some who have had near-death experiences offer amazing—and conflicting—reports of a possible afterlife; others report having experienced nothing at all. But, near-death is not death. Near-death experiences may be glimpses into what lies on the other side, or they may be nothing more than hallucinations triggered by near-death conditions in the brain. We simply cannot know for sure what death holds for us until we fully die and then, perhaps, see for ourselves.

The topic of life after death is rife with wishful thinking, self-deception, and outright chicanery. This is a matter where certainty is elusive and where skepticism is justified.

It seems entirely possible to me that there are dimensions within Creation where some aspect of our individual consciousness survives physical death for a time or even continues the spiritual journey on a different level, perhaps even to the end of time. It is also possible that individual consciousness ends completely with death. I simply don't know, and I am very comfortable not knowing.

It seems to me that, in the religious context, this issue is almost always addressed with more than a little wishful thinking. Our egos cherry-pick the evidence and available options and choose the scenario they like best, which, not so surprisingly, always seems to involve the eternal and blissful existence of that same ego. I call BS on that. I can't rule it out, but I think the more honest approach is to work from what is usually considered the worst-case scenario, which I suggest is not really so bad: Maybe who we are in this life simply ends with death.

The differentiation that comes with being—the existence of multiplicity, variety, and difference that is necessary for life and individual identity—is a feature of Creation (manifest, temporal being), not of eternity beyond Creation. Although the word *eternity* is often used to mean endless time, that is an incorrect understanding. Eternity is outside of time. Eternity encompasses time and cannot be measured in terms of time. It seems very likely to me that the separation between us that makes us individuals must eventually collapse or fade back into the primal oneness of eternity.

I am quite sure that the traditional concepts of Heaven and Hell are not literally true. As I have discussed, we can see their development in the history of the Judeo-Christian tradition. They have rich metaphorical meaning, but they are products of human hope, imagination, and desire for justice. They are not literally real. They suggest a bifurcation of reality, an ultimate separation of good and evil, which is inconsistent with the unity of God. This duality, this polarity between good and evil, is meaningful only within the created order. It is for we who live within that order that Heaven and Hell have meaning as metaphors, but they are not a literal picture of eternity beyond Creation. They warn us that the choices we make effect the quality of this life for ourselves and for others; they do not tell us what awaits us after death.

The psychological and neurological sciences have accumulated much evidence that human self-awareness and personality are grounded in the physical brain. It makes a lot of sense that the death of the brain would bring them to an end. Furthermore, I have experienced in meditation that I, as this physical person with my particular body and personality, am mortal. I have seen that my egoic personality is a function of my brain, and I expect it will die with my brain.

But what else should I expect? Non-existence is the flipside of existence. All things are impermanent. Everything changes. Being dances on the surface of nonbeing. Our egos are misguided to hope to live endlessly. Even if some aspect of individual human consciousness continues on after death, I am quite sure that preserving my egoic self for all eternity is not the purpose of Creation.

Do you *really* want to live forever? The knee-jerk reaction of the ego tends to be, "Hell yes," but would that really be so wonderful? Forever is a very, very, very long time. For an extended and fun consideration of this topic, I highly recommend the Michael Schur series *The Good Place* (NBC, Netflix).

I am blessed to be a part of this messy dance we call life for whatever brief lifespan I may enjoy. I, as an individual human being, am blessed to play my part as one tiny, fleeting cell in the body of a very big God. It is not nearly so much about me as it is about the Me that is the All. In Creation it moves and it changes like a river flowing to the end of time, and my egoic self is just a ripple on the surface of the much bigger true Self that I share with everyone. I strongly suspect that, when incarnate spirit finishes its dance in Creation—however long that may be—it eventually returns into the oneness of the Godhead beyond all qualities, including the qualities that manifest in personality and ego.

What I don't know is the full nature and duration of the dance, but does it really matter? What is clear to me is that full-blown incarnate life happens only in Creation and that we humans, as physical beings, are ultimately mortal. All I or any of us living human beings can really see with any certainty is the part of the dance we are dancing now—the dance of physical life in this material, temporal universe—and that is where we should focus our concern. We need to worry about loving one another as best we can here and now. We just don't need to worry about what comes after we die.

What Faith Is Really About

The ability to accept without fear that we will sooner or later pass from life is an aspect of faith. Faith is not literal belief in any sort of mythical story about magic saviors and pie in the sky. Faith is trust in the mystery some of us call God, trust that God's ultimate nature is love, and trust that we share in that nature. Fear of death is rooted in identification with and attachment to the body and the ego (brain-based personality), which are indeed mortal. The remedy for such fear is to see through the ego and, thereby, come to identify with the immortal spirit that is everyone's deepest self. This results in what the New Testament calls the *peace that passes understanding.*

This shift of identity is exactly the spiritual meaning of the crucifixion and resurrection in the Christian myth. The Jesus of the myth, as its hero, represents every person, and he invites us all to follow him on the path he walked. The crucifixion and resurrection are metaphors for detaching from the ego, which can feel like dying, and connecting to one's true identity in eternal spirit, which can feel like rising into eternal life. In traditional terms this is referred to by the Greek words *kenosis* (self-emptying) and *theosis* (deification). There is quite a lot of baggage attached to these two words in the tradition, but, underneath it all, this is what they are about.

It is not necessary or in any way required that anyone do this. It in no way determines the eternal disposition of your soul. It is simply a perspective on ourselves and the journey of life that the Christian myth expresses and invites us to take seriously. There is no punishment if we do not, but taking it seriously can relieve a lot of anxiety and confusion and bring deeper meaning and more balanced intention to life.

By taking it seriously I mean turning one's attention and intention toward following the spiritual path suggested by the Christian myth. In the Greek of the New Testament this was called *metanoia*, which is often translated as repentance but really means turning around or changing course. In the words of the tradition itself, this means turning one's intention toward loving God with all one's heart, soul, and mind and loving one's neighbor as oneself. This is known as the Great Commandment because it distills the essence of Torah and all its commandments. It was taught by Jesus and many other rabbis of his time and since. It requires opening both the heart and the mind. The tradition does not offer a single, explicit, step-by-step how-to manual for doing this, but it is loaded with clues, suggestions, and encouragements from the experience of those who have gone before us. We must each find our own way into it.

The important thing is to realize that perfectly personalized guidance is available—not from any human teacher, although it often works through such teachers—but from the dimension of God that Christians call the Holy Spirit. All you have to do is ask for help and be open to the nudges you feel from within and from without. The journey may often seem slow, so patience is necessary—in fact, patience is one of the big lessons—but it does progress and it is worth the effort. Just remember that you must weigh all the teachings that you encounter outwardly against the promptings of the spirit that you feel from within. Look for what makes sense and feels right to you and what seems especially meaningful or calls to you.

Change and growth will happen on this journey. What does not make sense or feel right at one time may be meaningful at another time. Likewise, what feels correct or reasonable at one time may not feel at all right later on. That's okay. You can only move forward from where you are. Trial and error is part of the journey. Mistakes will happen. Honesty, humility, and sincerity will make the journey faster and easier. You must be willing to let go and be reborn—and more than once.

The change will not always feel comfortable. Giving up old ways and familiar understandings can be difficult and even painful. You may experience moments of deep crisis when it feels like your whole world is coming apart at the seams. Sometimes the old has to die for the new to be born.

People at every stage of psychosocial-spiritual development have contributed to the Christian tradition, as is true for any other religious tradition. This means that there is something in Christianity that will speak to you meaningfully no matter where you are on the journey, and it means that there will be other things in the tradition that seem wrong or confusing or challenging. As with every other sphere of human activity and culture, there is that in any religion that is profoundly true and uplifting, that which is truly pathological, and a lot that falls in the middle somewhere. Learning to discern what is what and the way forward is all part of the journey.

The real point of this chapter is that there is ultimately nothing to fear. If fear of death is a significant motivation for your involvement with Christianity, that is fine because that is where you are in your journey, but such fear is not ultimately valid and must not be allowed ultimate influence over your life and belief systems. Be fully aware of it and face it squarely. The journey goes through the fear and beyond it. Our ultimate destination is the unity of Spirit from which we have come, a Spirit that is love beyond any fear. The meaning of grace in the Christian tradition is that this is not something we must or can earn. It is free. It is simply there—always. Once you know it—really know it—the fear just goes.

The hope of pie in the sky by and by—by which I mean the hope that the persons we are on Earth will enjoy continued life in Heaven—is bogus. It invites us to focus on something we should not be worrying about and distracts us from what really matters: life here and now on Earth. That is what the Kingdom of God preached by Jesus was about. He seems to have believed it would come about supernaturally as promised by the Hebrew scriptures—and that did not happen—but the deeper hope behind his faith was not misguided. The original hope, the hope expressed by the entire Hebrew Bible, was always for a life here on Earth of happiness and prosperity, a life of sisterhood and brotherhood free of unjust suffering and exploitation. That is not a goal we can ever expect to attain completely and permanently— stable perfection is simply not attainable in the complex and ever-changing milieu of our material universe—but this goal expresses values that arise from the deepest source of being (God). It expresses the direction of the evolutionary process that is Creation.

The expectations of how this hope might come about have gone through some literally fantastic permutations over the past few thousand years. Those permutations have become so fantastic, in fact, that the original hope has become tragically distorted. Our egos have grabbed onto the ideas of resurrection and the afterlife—ideas invented to answer problems of injustice in this life—and fully invested them with the hope of endless life for our bodies and our egos themselves. It is not true. Our egos are mortal.

Existential fear happens when our egos mistake themselves for the core of our being. They are not. It is the eternal spirit, the image of God, within us that is the core. Once the ego comprehends its own nature and its relationship to spirit, the fear goes away and the focus of concern shifts. Personal survival remains important—that is the ego's primary job—but when spirit shines through and enlightens the ego, love becomes the moving force of life in a more conscious way. Love is always the moving force, but our egos can lose sight of that fact if they become lost in the concerns of survival and daily living. That is what the myth in Genesis of the fall into sin is about, and the myth of Jesus is about finding our way back. Once that happens, our highest concern becomes exactly what Jesus taught that it should be: love of God, self, and other.

It is a mistake to see life here on Earth as a minor detour on the spiritual journey, as just a brief sojourn in an unpleasant place that is to be waited out on the way to something better, as merely a place of testing that determines our eternal fate. Creation is the main event. It is where God expresses and experiences God's self by dancing into and back out of being. We are here to be part of that dance, and we are always in and of the God who dances. Christianity is not properly about saving us from the outcome of the dance; it is about teaching us how the dance was done in the past and helping us to find even better ways to do it ourselves in the present.

The dance is a flow from the unity of unmanifest, undifferentiated spirit into the experience of differentiation, separation, and individuality (the knowledge of good and evil) within Creation and eventually back again to the unity of unmanifest spirit. In the differentiation and separation of Creation, each of us—and through us, God—experiences relationship in a dynamic way not possible in the unmanifest state. Creation is not a means to some other end. Creation (being) is its own point and purpose. To the extent that Creation (evolution) may have a direction and goal within this or any other created universe, I am quite sure it is a goal about collective spirit and not about preserving anyone's individual ego.

The hardest part of this from the perspective of earthly life is accepting the mortality of those whom we love. It is easier to face our own death than to face the passing of loved ones. This is the most painful part: saying goodbye forever. Relationships in this mortal realm always end in final goodbyes, at least physically. Yes, we are all ultimately united in eternal spirit, but the forms that spirit assumes in this creation are transient. Everything in the physical universe is impermanent; everything eventually passes away. How very hard and very painful this is. It is not so hard to understand, but it can be very, very painful to experience.

As so often seems true of deeply spiritual things, I suspect there may be a paradox at the core all of this: I suspect it to be simultaneously true that all created things are ultimately lost as seen from within time and yet, perhaps, that nothing is finally lost as seen from eternity--but that is beyond what I can claim to know. Although I cannot explain it, somehow it all just really feels okay. IT ALL HAPPENS IN GOD.

The important thing for us here in Creation is to live as fully as possible in the now. For everything there is a time and a season (Ecclesiastes 3:1), and our fulfillment lies in living the life that comes our way—whatever it is, however notable or seemingly insignificant—as fully and sincerely as we can. That is, we must dance our part of the dance with as much love and sincerity as we are able. This includes feeling the grief of loss in its time and season. But loss does not ultimately overcome love, beauty, and goodness. To have lived and loved is a great and beautiful thing, and each beautiful moment is somehow a part of eternity. Pain and suffering may and often do overshadow love and beauty and joy for a time, but the negative does not finally negate the goodness to be found in being and life.

In God We Trust

But I say to you, Love your enemies
and pray for those who persecute you,
so that you may be children of your Father in heaven;
for he makes his sun rise on the evil and on the good,
and sends rain on the righteous and on the unrighteous.
Matthew 5:44-45 (NRSV)

If we accept that Christianity should be about this life rather than paradise in an afterlife, we must then wonder what help we can expect from God in living this life. Can we count on God to take care of us? This is the question of divine providence. Does God deliberately, actively, and continuously provide for the welfare of the faithful?

The Judeo-Christian tradition has traditionally assumed a quid pro quo, a deal between God and the believer: the believer believes in and obeys God, and God takes care of the believer. In the Hebrew Bible this deal was codified as a series of covenants culminating in the Law of Moses, popularly thought of as the Ten Commandments. If Israel obeyed and worshipped God, then the expectation was that God would protect and bless Israel in return. This was a covenant between God and the Hebrew people as a group, but it was also understood to have an individual dimension: that individuals also were rewarded and punished according to their righteousness or lack thereof.

This is pretty much how all ancient peoples understood their relationships with their gods. If you wanted a good life, you had better keep your god or gods happy. For the Israelites this idea was developed and stated most clearly in the book of Deuteronomy and associated books of the Old Testament and can be referred to as Deuteronomic theology. It emerged to prominence during the reign and religious reforms of King Josiah of Judah (640-609 BCE). Just prior to that, during the reign of Josiah's grandfather King Manasseh (697-642 BCE), Judah had been under the thumb of the Assyrian empire, and Manasseh seems to have compromised religiously, engaging in pagan practices and repressing the worship and prophets of the god of Israel. Under Josiah, who was only eight years old at the time he ascended to the throne, the prophets gained the upper hand in Judean politics and restored Judah to what they saw to be proper religious practice. They did this in part by claiming to have found a lost book of the law—which might actually have happened, although it is also clear that they did plenty of their own writing to suit the situation.

It is important to realize the larger historical setting of these developments. The original unified nation of Israel split into two kingdoms, Israel in the north and Judah in the south, after the reign of King Solomon. The northern kingdom of Israel fell to the Assyrians in 722 BCE. The Assyrians permanently erased the northern kingdom as a political entity by exiling much of the population and replacing them with defeated peoples exiled from other regions. Some refugees from Israel, including many of its prophets, fled to Judah, Israel's sister kingdom to the south, which was the political homeland of the Jewish people thereafter.

The destruction of the northern kingdom presented a huge religious crisis for the Hebrew people. Why had their god let them down? Their god had shown "his" power by defeating Pharaoh through Moses and by giving "his" people the Promised Land. Why had "he" allowed nine of the twelve tribes of Israel to be defeated and permanently scattered by the Assyrians? The leaders of the northern kingdom seem to have believed that Yahweh would protect them because Yahweh was their god whom they worshipped. The Deuteronomic prophets provided an answer: It was not enough simply to worship Yahweh; it was necessary to keep the Covenant, and, in their view, the Hebrew people had not done that very well.

Deuteronomic theology became the lens through which the Jews made sense of the destruction of the northern kingdom. It was also the lens through which they would make sense of the coming defeat and exile of the southern kingdom by the Babylonians and of their subsequent return to Judah under the Persians. In the understanding of the Deuteronomists, the defeats were Yahweh's corrective punishments by which "he" was chastising "his" people and calling them back to "him", and the return was permitted because the Jews were once again taking the Covenant seriously. The real history behind all this seems to have been much more complicated, but this is how the Deuteronomists wrote their version. Much of the Hebrew Bible was redacted into more or less its present form during and after the Babylonian exile, and this theology was superimposed onto many of the older writings. It was not necessarily the mainstream understanding of Hebrew religion prior to Josiah. To be sure, being in Yahweh's good graces was always a concern, but, for much of the history of Israel in the Promised Land, it may not have had so much to do with observance of the Covenant as later presented by the Deuteronomists.

The problem, in any case, is that Deuteronomic theology and the basic logic behind it simply do not work—not for Jews, not for any other ancient peoples, not for Christians today, not for anyone. These ideas that God blesses or punishes us based on how well we honor and obey "him" or how good or bad "he" judges us to be are simply false. It is a product of how our social intelligence makes sense of the world. We relate to reality as though it were controlled by an unseen being who watches everything we do and who thinks much as we think. This instinct is generally helpful because we humans do watch each other and judge each other and react to each other according to our judgments: Best to assume someone is watching even if they are not. We simply take things too far when we project this sense of being watched onto all of reality by imagining an all-powerful, divine parent or king. Often such an understanding may appear to be accurate, as with the Babylonian exile and return, but at other times it clearly does not work. Not long after the Persians allowed the Jews to return to Judah, the Greeks under Alexander the Great conquered them all. Under the Greeks it was the most observant Jews who suffered the worst, which was exactly the opposite of what the Covenant had promised.

The fact is that bad things happen to good people all the time. Good things also happen to bad people. What we get is too often not what we deserve—if that even means anything. Exactly what standard should be used to decide what anyone deserves? Sometimes what befalls us is definitely the consequence of our own actions, but very often it is not. I am not going to belabor this point with examples. If you are not sure about this, you need to take a long, hard, honest look at this world. Shit happens!

If it is God's job to protect and care for good people and punish bad people, then God is doing a terrible job of it—but maybe that is not God's job. Maybe our social intelligence has projected this job onto God. It is the job we expect our parents and our social leaders to do, so if we imagine God as the ultimate and supreme social leader—the divine Parent, the King of Kings, the Lord of Lords—then it's a job God ought to be doing. This has everything to do with how we have chosen to see God and nothing to do with the reality of God. God simply does not play favorites. That was the God of supernatural theism; it is not properly the God of evolutionary panentheism.

This is a matter of psychological and spiritual honesty and maturity. The scientific revolution has brought us a new perspective on how the material world, this place where we exist, works, and it has nothing to do with unseen beings deciding or allowing every little thing that occurs. Science has opened the door for us to step beyond superstition, and we need to find the guts to do so.

Sure, the world is a scary place, and there is much appeal in the idea that a supernatural God has our backs. It just ain't so. We come from God, we will return to God, we are always in God, and God is always present in us, but God does not promise us a good, easy, painless life. Again, I call your attention to the Christian myth, to the story of God's son crucified and risen. If God did not spare God's own son, why on earth would you expect God to spare you? We are all God's children, and Jesus' path is our path. The myth reflects the pattern of life and evolution: crisis and suffering (crucifixion) may eventually result in the emergence of something new and better (resurrection), but crisis and suffering there will be, and those who suffer may not be the ones who get to enjoy whatever new and better things follow the suffering.

Once again, the myth points us toward taking responsibility for the welfare of one another. That is what the Jesus of the myth calls us to do: love one another, even our enemies. The belief that everything is in God's hands and that God willfully controls the flow of everyone's life has for too long provided a convenient escape into self-centeredness and indifference to the situations of others. It is just easier to see other people's problems as purely between them and God. But we are not separate from God, and we are all part of the social systems that both help and hurt people. Yes, our safety is in God's hands, but only in the sense that God's hands are the hands of every single person. If we don't love one another, no one else will.

Christianity is not finally about personal salvation. To be sure, the spiritual journey is deeply personal in many ways, but it leads eventually to the awareness of connection and the opening of the heart. Taking responsibility for oneself and allowing others to take responsibility for themselves is absolutely a part of the journey, but that does not justify indifference. Responsibility for oneself must eventually overflow into compassion, mercy, and generosity toward others.

The Kingdom of God that Jesus of Nazareth preached was an expression of hope from within his cultural context for a more fair and compassionate human society. While we can no longer realistically expect it to come about in the manner and form he seems to have expected, the same hope resides in some form in almost every human heart. Waiting for God to make it happen does not make positive change. People of good will and commitment make positive change. We are, in large part, God's hands on Earth. We are all in this together, and the safety and prosperity we enjoy is the safety and prosperity we allow and provide for one another. The real kingdom of God on Earth will not be a sudden gift from Heaven. It will not be supernaturally forced on us from above. It has been evolving for billions of years and will be achieved incrementally as we focus our God-given consciousness and intention on learning how to build social, economic, and technological structures and systems that truly reflect and support respect for human dignity and wellbeing.

The Patterns and Power of Spirit

He said to her, "Daughter, your faith has made you well;
go in peace, and be healed of your disease."
Mark 5:34 (NRSV)

In the preceding chapters I have butchered two of the most sacred cows of traditional popular Christianity—and of the traditional, popular versions of pretty much any religion. By *popular* I mean the way most ordinary people involved in the religion understand it. The two sacred cows are the two major hopes that motivate many people to be religious. The first is the hope of an afterlife for the ego. The second is the hope of divine providence, the hope that one or more divine beings will protect and bless us in this life. These two hopes are responses to two fears: the fear of death and the fear of suffering. I have suggested that the fear of death is unwarranted and immature and that it can and should be outgrown. Further, while I have allowed that fear of suffering has a legitimate place in the material world, I have suggested that we are mistaken to count on God to supernaturally protect us. So, if I am right on these two points, does Christianity really offer its adherents much of practical value? Does God ever help us? Is there any power in prayer? Does faith count for anything in this life?

As I have already discussed, the big thing that Christianity and all religions actually offer is insight into and deep experience of our connection to and identity within our divine source. In the Christian context this leads to the peace that passes understanding. It is the most important thing. It is what is often referred to as enlightenment. It does not change the world to our benefit in any way, nor does it remove death, but experiencing it dramatically changes our orientation to both life and death. In this chapter I shall discuss what I see to be the practical applications of this understanding of spirit and our relationship to it.

The point of the preceding chapters was not to kill God, but only to kill the God of supernatural theism. This is a metaphorical way of saying that religion in Modernity and beyond, if it is to have significant meaning and value, requires a new understanding of the structure and dynamics of reality. We need to kill off the God of supernatural theism to make room for the God of evolutionary panentheism who provides a much truer model for understanding Spirit and its relationship to the material world.

The Shape of God

Traditional religion is a product of social intelligence, and social intelligence views the world in terms of hierarchy, especially with regard to power and authority. This has very much to do with the instincts by which status and breeding rights are determined in many mammalian societies—including our own human species to a greater extent than many of us might like to admit. We can see much of ourselves in the social behaviors of wolves and wild horses and gorillas and chimpanzees. Hierarchies of social status are not just arbitrary social constructs; they are rooted in the way our brains have evolved to organize our groups for survival over millions of years. To be sure, our social instincts involve much more than just the hierarchies of dominance and submission; but worldviews rooted primarily in social intelligence tend to see the world in terms of hierarchy.

Supernatural theism, which is central to traditional religion, sees reality as a pyramid of power and authority organized in levels something like this: God is at the top, followed by archangels, then angels, etc., on down to human religious and secular rulers, then the aristocratic and ecclesiastical classes, blah-blah-blah, down to ordinary people, then slaves, then animals, etc. and so on. Historically this hierarchy was often referred to as the Great Chain of Being. In Christian culture there have been many variations of this scheme, but it has always been a top-down model where everything is ultimately controlled by the will of the deity "on high". It was assumed that the way to avoid suffering was to get on the good side of the supreme "being".

Figure 1: The Great Chain of Being (Rhetorica Christiania, 1579)

Rational intelligence, on the other hand, does not reflexively impose a hierarchical structure or any other structure on its understanding of the world. Rather, it finds the structure through observation. Some things fall into hierarchical patterns, but many others do not. Rational intelligence does not find a personified deity exercising willful control over the world. Rather, it finds a world that operates autonomously according to inherent and immutable structures, patterns, and dynamics that are often referred to as *natural law*. To be sure, we can find hierarchical patterns, by which I mean patterns of ordered levels. In fact, the Great Chain of Being is a substantially valid and helpful model with regard to development and functional capacities. Evolution does indeed evidence a hierarchical order of the emergence of complexity; simpler structures and organisms precede and give rise to more complex ones. However, power and authority do not seem to be fundamentally hierarchical. Each person has her or his own share of power and is free, at least inwardly, to recognize authority where she or he finds it. We can and often do choose to organize ourselves hierarchically with regard to power and authority, but that is a choice we or our instincts make and not an inherent structure of reality. From the rational perspective, God is not the almighty king at the top of the chain of command because there is no evidence of an actual functioning chain of supernatural command. That is simply not how reality works.

Rational intelligence cannot see God directly. Through the critical study of religion, honest rational intelligence also sees that the traditionally accepted forms of outward revelation (scriptures and traditions) are products of human cultural activity and not direct, unfiltered channels of divine communication. Thus, honest rational intelligence recognizes that it cannot know God in the way that it can know tangible things. God simply cannot be directly observed or measured.

If we are to know God directly, it cannot be with the rational mind. Reason can free us from the superstitions and anthropomorphisms of social intelligence, and we can use it to examine and refine our understanding, but thinking about God is not the same as encountering God. Rational intelligence plays a major role in conceptualizing (theologizing) God, but it cannot give us the direct experience of God. That must happen at a transrational level of perception beyond the expectations and limitations of both social and rational intelligence. That is where direct spiritual (mystical) experience comes in.

Direct spiritual experience has always been at the root of religion. In the agrarian empires in which the Judeo-Christian traditions developed—cultures dominated by social intelligence and organized hierarchically--spiritual experience also naturally tended to be understood in terms of hierarchy. It was simply assumed that, just as power and authority in those societies flowed down from the top, so also was spiritual experience given from above as God specifically willed it. Spiritual awareness was seen as a special gift granted from above to specially chosen

the chain of being

Figure 2: Another Version of the Great Chain of Being (Source Unknown)

people. If some mystics experienced it differently, social and political pressures tended to discourage them from saying so.

Because church and state justified themselves by presenting the masses with a worldview that was thoroughly hierarchical in terms of power and authority, they kept a tight rein on mystics to be sure they did not undermine that worldview.

In recent centuries, as we have broken free of such socially and politically-imposed constraints, a different model of spiritual experience is emerging. We can each see that our own spiritual experience arises from a spiritual connection deep within the self. This experience leads to an understanding of the dynamics of spirit very different from the hierarchical understanding that social intelligence tends to impose. Rational intelligence, informed by the apprehension of spirit at our deepest core, sees spirit not as a hierarchy but as a network. Each conscious being is a node, a connection point, in this network. Every node is connected to every other node directly rather than hierarchically. Power and control does not flow in only one direction from a single point, but emanates from the choices and actions of each node and flows through the network in complex and dynamic currents. Spirit, as the field of consciousness and the ground of being, is the connector. In other words, God is not at the top of the network; rather, God is the network.

Christian tradition has long held that one of the ways we can know about God is through the "Book of Nature". In other words, it has long been accepted that Creation tells us about the Creator. If we read the Book of Nature only with our social intelligence, then we see a world of separate beings who interact socially and often in terms of hierarchical power relationships, and that becomes our model for understanding everything, including God and our relationship to God. God sits at the top with all the power, and whatever God decides happens. However, the Scientific Revolution has opened up a new and deeper picture. We see a vast, vast universe connected within the space-time continuum. Every bit of matter exerts a gravitational pull on every other bit of matter. Electrical and magnetic forces exert influence across distance. We have even discovered the phenomenon of quantum entanglement in which paired sub-atomic particles remain in perfect, instantaneous synchrony at any distance—not at the speed of light or at any speed, but immediately—no time lag at all no matter how far apart they are. From all of these and many other discoveries, we have come to realize that ours is a fundamentally connected universe. If we read the Book of Nature with our scientific understanding, we have to conclude that connectedness is a fundamental attribute of God.

The common idea of God as a distinct and separate supreme being who is the center of concentrated power and will at the top or center of some sort of hierarchy must give way to the idea of God as the omnipresent source, unifying ground, and substance of all things. God, as Spirit, is the ultimate field of connection. God is present in everything that is connected by spirit—which is everything. God does not exert God's power and will upon the universe; the universe is the flow of God's power and will. The spirit in us that makes us living, conscious beings is of God. Thus, each of us, as nodes in this divine-material network, are nodes of God's consciousness, power, and will.

This emerging perspective has profound implications. To begin with, it decentralizes God. God's consciousness does not sit on a throne somewhere, controlling everything at a distance. Rather, God's consciousness is present everywhere and encompasses the consciousness of every being in Creation. In other words, our human consciousnesses are not separate from God's consciousness. To be sure, our minds are stupefyingly tiny in comparison to the whole mind of God, but they are a part of it.

This perspective also calls into question the language of monarchy used so prominently in traditional Christianity: such words as *Lord, king,* and *prince.* It made sense to speak of God and Jesus in such terms for people immersed in the monarchical societies of the past, but the politics of the world has largely left that behind. Monarchy was a hierarchical model, but democracy is a network model. It is incongruous to attend church today in America—a country that prides itself on having thrown off all lords and kings more than two-hundred years ago—and hear ultimate reality addressed in terms we have otherwise rejected.

Also, *omnipotence* has a very different meaning in evolutionary panentheism than with supernatural theism. In supernatural theism, omnipotence meant that God had the supernatural power to do anything over and against the natural flow of the created order and the ordinary power exercised by creatures. In evolutionary panentheism there is no supernatural power and all natural and creaturely power is God's power.

In my view, God has two fundamental powers: the power of being and the power of change or dynamism. The power of being is the power to create and sustain temporal, material existence. It is the mysterious power to actualize this physical universe we occupy out of the potential of unmanifest spirit. The power of change is the power of evolution by which the undifferentiated matter of the Big Bang has become the awesome variety of all that exists, including us. These powers are interdependent; they are the two strokes of the ongoing process of creation.

Prayer?

The question for this chapter is whether our faith and spirituality can have any influence on the ongoing process of creation. It is the question of prayer. Traditional Christianity simply assumed that God could hear our prayers and that God had the power to answer them. How that actually worked was not questioned. Because we created the idea of God to explain why things happen as they do, it was axiomatic that whatever happened was within God's power. The limits of that power were unknown and assumed to be unlimited. If, however, God is not a distinct and separate divine being manipulating the universe from the outside, how can prayer have any impact?

At this point I need to be clear about what I mean by *prayer* in the context of this chapter. I divide prayer into three types: The first is utilitarian or practical prayer, which seeks a particular outcome in one's life or in the world. This is a prayer of asking (petition) or visualization for something like food or healing or success or safety. The second type is reflective or thinking prayer, which seeks insight or guidance. This is prayer as meditation on a specific concern, question, or object of thought. The third type of prayer is contemplative prayer, also called resting in God. Pure contemplation is the experience of divine presence in the absence of active thinking; it is meditation without an object of thought. In actual practice, these forms of prayer can flow into and out of one another, but what is happening in each type of prayer is distinct. The first seeks to direct the flow of events, the second seeks insight and guidance, and the third seeks to suspend seeking. There is also a distinction to be made between group (corporate) and individual (personal) prayer. Contemplative prayer is always personal. Utilitarian and reflective prayer can be done as a group with petitions or intentions spoken by a leader or by members of the group. Such group prayer can have strong effects on group cohesion, but even in a group setting the process of prayer really happens within the individual. That is, "God listens to our prayers" through each of our inner spirits.

In this chapter I am concerned almost entirely with utilitarian prayer. Reflective and contemplative prayer happen entirely within the realm of consciousness and spirit, so the connectedness of spirit pretty much explains how they might happen. The question of this chapter is whether prayer can really have any utility (usefulness or influence) in the material world.

To answer this we must look a little closer at utilitarian or practical prayer. It consists of two movements: the request and the response, the ask and the answer. It begins with the conscious expression of a want by the person praying. It is completed by the unfolding of events in which the want may be fully, partially, or not at all satisfied.

The ask is a problem neither for tradition nor for progressive spirituality. Both see consciousness as an aspect of spirit and assume that God as spirit in some way "knows" our thoughts. The difference is at the level of the answer. The social intelligence of prerational culture assumed that God could do anything. There was no understanding of any mechanism by which this might happen; it was accepted as supernatural magic. Science, which is the application of rational intelligence, has found no credible evidence of supernatural power—no evidence of magic—but only natural mechanisms. At first blush this would seem to rule out any possibility that prayer can change anything. Once the natural mechanisms are set on a particular course, how can prayer change that course? While I don't think that it can change the course of events in any way that violates the natural operation of the mechanisms involved, I see two ways that prayer can have an effect.

The first way that I believe prayer can alter a situation is through psychic influence on the conscious beings involved in the situation. If all consciousness is connected within the same field of spirit, then perhaps earnest prayer can sometimes somehow touch one or more important actors in a situation—be they human, animal or even plant—and influence them to change their behavior or choices. This mechanism—as with reflective and contemplative prayer—happens in the realm of consciousness and does not directly affect the material world. Any impact on the flow of events comes about indirectly through choices made by the beings involved.

The second way that prayer might be able to influence events—and I absolutely admit that this is speculation—is at the quantum level, and this does involve direct influence on the material world. At the smallest scales, the scales studied by quantum mechanics, science finds that it must concern itself, not with just a single path of movement, but with the set of all possible paths, and that which of those possibilities becomes the observable result may be influenced by the consciousness of the observer. Furthermore, chaos theory has found that minute differences in initial conditions of complex systems can result in extremely different outcomes. Hence, if all things are in fact connected by the field of spirit, and if that spirit is in fact the medium of consciousness, perhaps the application of our consciousness through prayer or in other ways can really influence how events unfold at the point where they cross from random possibility to specific actuality. This would not change the established trajectories of macro components in the natural system, but it may be able to nudge the randomness of quantum phenomena to be just a little less random and thereby nudge the chaotic natural system in a particular direction consistent with the conscious intention of prayer.

This is truly a mind-over-matter mechanism. It is also unproven in any detail. Quantum physicists are by no means in agreement as to the connection between quantum phenomena and consciousness, and the subject is really far above my pay grade. However, I have gleaned enough on the subject to believe that the mechanism I have suggested in the previous paragraph cannot be ruled out.

From a theological perspective this is a simple theory: If spirit is both the fundamental stuff of the Kosmos from which all being continually arises, if it is also the stuff of consciousness, and if connectedness is a fundamental property of spirit, then it makes perfect sense that human consciousness should be able to influence how spirit unfolds from possibility into actuality from one moment to the next. As I see it, prayer is not about asking a supernaturally powerful being to do our bidding but a way of focusing consciousness to nudge reality in the desired direction.

All of this rests on the idea that the process of creation was not just a onetime event at the Big Bang—when most of the matter of our universe came into being—but that it is also an ongoing process in which the unmanifest oneness of spirit, which encompasses all possibility, continually supports the material world and gives rise to the specific actualities we experience.

Even if I am right, the Kosmos is a very complex system. The consciousness of those praying for a certain outcome may be only a small part of the consciousness that has bearing on what comes to pass. Different people may have conflicting interests and desires in the matter, and even the same person may have conflicting desires. So, the impact of the totality of all consciousness (God) on the outcome is impossible to predict from our perspective. Nevertheless, it may be possible, if most beings are indifferent regarding a particular matter, that clear, deliberate intentionality on the part of a few people may be able to strongly influence an outcome.

Importantly, this is consistent with the way that Jesus gave credit for healings to the faith of those healed. He did not say it was God but their own faith that had healed them.

From this perspective, God's will is not a distinct and separate thing, but the sum of all will. This does not mean that the Kosmos is valueless or that God's will is neutral. The ultimate unity of spirit, from which all things arise, stands eternally. This unity of spirit is the basis of love, which is a value inherent in the Kosmos. If I may riff on a theme Dr. Martin Luther King Jr. adapted from the Transcendentalists: the arc of being, long though it may be and slow though it may seem, bends toward ever fuller expression of love and compassion.

So, what does all of this mean for how we should pray? Should we ask God or saints or our ancestors for help or should we assertively envision the outcome we desire and "send energy" to "manifest" that outcome? The first way is more traditional and indirect; the second is more direct and contemporary. I think that both approaches may be worthwhile. Focusing our own hopes, thoughts, intentions, and desires directly toward a particular concern applies our own consciousness to the situation. The approach of appealing to God or lesser spiritual entities, even though rooted in the perspective of supernatural theism, may also be an effective way to direct one's own consciousness toward the desired outcome. Even if no one is really listening, imagining that they are listening can be an effective way to focus one's own concern.

I would not, however, rule out the possibility that it may also actually invite the help of a broader range of consciousness. While I do not believe that God is a separate, human-like being with an individual consciousness as presented by the model of supernatural theism, I cannot rule out the possibility that other discarnate spiritual entities—saints and angels, for example—exist within the spiritual field of the universe or even beyond it. I have had a few experiences of my own that suggest that this may be the case. I don't pretend to completely understand it, but my sense is that petitioning the spiritual side of reality can have real effect. There is a big space of mystery here, and there is a balance to be sought—a balance between self-assertion and supplication, between confidence and humility, between reason and imagination, between hope and realism, between preference and acceptance.

The most crucial thing in prayer, in my opinion, is sincerity. Prayer must flow from what is truly in one's heart and mind. Prayer must be an exercise in deep personal honesty. Personal dishonesty divides the self and blocks one's access to the deeper self where we connect to broader spirit. Sincerity opens the channels of spirit. In this way, truth is the path to power.

This brings us to another powerful benefit of prayer. Whether or not it actually changes outward reality in any way, prayer can definitely change the one who prays. If done with sincerity and persistence, prayer is always a transformative practice.

If you engage seriously in prayer for any period of time, you will soon find that your ego gets very tangled up in it. Prayer is not properly about fulfilling the ego's desires, and my experience is that prayer directed to that end will generally fail. The purity of intention that makes prayer effective comes from spirit at a deeper level than the ego. The traditional caveat in prayer, "Not my will but Thine be done," speaks directly to this issue. A contemporary restatement would be, "Not what my ego wants, but what my deeper spirit, which is one with all spirit, knows to be best." Such an attitude is critical to effective prayer, but it does not put an end to the struggle with the ego—in utilitarian prayer or any kind of prayer. The ego is not essentially bad, but its natural tendency is to run out of control like a wild and frightened animal. It needs to be tamed and calmed and taught to perform its important and essential duties within proper limits so as to allow deeper spirit to have ultimate sway. Prayer of all types is the major context within which this critical transformation can happen. It takes time and effort to achieve and continuous vigilance to maintain.

One more thing must be said about prayer and sincerity. If we are genuinely sincere, then in many cases prayer cannot be limited to a purely mental process. Action in the world can also be a kind of prayer, especially if it is done with the heart engaged. God does not act magically but rather through the mechanisms of the created order. We are part of those mechanisms. It is utterly irresponsible to ignore the possibility that we may be the mechanisms through which God can fully or in part answer our own prayers. Might we help by reaching out to someone or by giving so as to support the efforts of others to remedy a problem or even by initiating such an effort ourselves? In some situations, it may be appropriate to avoid intruding; sometimes people need space to figure things out for themselves and even to make their own mistakes. However, we must also be sensitive to the possibility that action on our part could make a real difference. To be sure, we all have limited time, energy, and resources, so we cannot fix everything, but we need to be concerned that the way we use our time, energy, and resources reflects the values we express in our prayers.

The Journey and the Myth

For through the law I died to the law, so that I might live to God.
I have been crucified with Christ; and it is no longer I who live,
but it is Christ who lives in me.
Galatians 2:19-20 (NRSV)

The spiritual journey is about growing up into the fullness of reality. It is about leaving behind the illusions in which our egos prefer to dwell and coming to know our own place within the divine nature. The Christian myth, as presented in the Bible, can be seen as a map for this journey.

Many mystics have experienced the spiritual path as consisting of stages. This brings us back to the topic of psychosocial-spiritual development and stage theory as introduced in an earlier chapter. As I stated there, different theorists tend to come up with different sets of stages. So also have different mystics come up with different numbers of stages and names for those stages based on their own experience and cultural perspective. Over time, common patterns have been recognized and the tradition has settled on a relatively simple scheme as broadly descriptive of the Christian mystical process.[26]

This scheme consists of three stages, with the transition from the second to the third stage being regarded almost as another stage in its own right. The first stage is the Purgative Way, traditionally understood to be about self-discipline and purification. The second stage is the Illuminative Way in which the individual gains insight regarding God, the self, and the spiritual journey. This stage is characterized by a sense of divine presence and guidance, the feeling that God is with you and leading you. It may or may not involve visions, vivid dreams, and other psychic phenomena. The third and final stage is the Unitive

---

[26] I have encountered no better overview of the Christian mystical tradition than Evelyn Underhill's classic *Mysticism: The Nature and Development of Spiritual Consciousness*.

Way in which one's spiritual identity merges with the divine. The transition to this stage can be difficult and is often referred to as the Dark Night of the Soul.

Unitive Way

↑ Dark Night of the Soul ↑

Illuminative Way

↑

Purgative Way

How the term *Dark Night of the Soul* is used can be confusing. It is often used somewhat loosely by those unfamiliar with mystical tradition to refer to any sort of especially painful passage in life. In spiritual discourse, however, it has two specific, closely connected meanings. As already explained, it can refer to the difficulty and pain of purification and purgation leading into what was traditionally called mystical union or the unitive way, but it can also refer to the experience of union that results from the transition. In the first sense, the Dark Night is painful; in the second sense, it is a state of bliss. This blissful sense is beautifully expressed in St. John of the Cross's poetic masterpiece *The Dark Night.*

> *On a dark night,*
> *Kindled in love with yearnings—oh, happy chance!—*
> *I went forth without being observed,*
> *My house being now at rest.*
>
> *In darkness and secure,*
> *By the secret ladder, disguised—oh, happy chance!—*
> *In darkness and in concealment,*
> *My house being now at rest.*
>
> *In the happy night,*
> *In secret, when none saw me,*
> *Nor I beheld aught,*
> *Without light or guide, save that which burned in my heart.*

This light guided me
More surely than the light of noonday
To the place where he (well I knew who!) was awaiting me—
A place where none appeared.

Oh, night that guided me,
Oh, night more lovely than the dawn,
Oh, night that joined Beloved with lover,
Lover transformed in the Beloved!

Upon my flowery breast,
Kept wholly for himself alone,
There he stayed sleeping, and I caressed him,
And the fanning of the cedars made a breeze.

The breeze blew from the turret
As I parted his locks;
With his gentle hand he wounded my neck
And caused all my senses to be suspended.

I remained, lost in oblivion;
My face I reclined on the Beloved.
All ceased and I abandoned myself,
Leaving my cares forgotten among the lilies.[27]

The difficulty of the transition into the Unitive Way lies in a shift of how the divine is experienced. In the first two stages God is imagined as a separate being located outside and apart from the self. In the third stage, God is found in the deeper universal Self, the self beneath the ego. As this shift of experience commences, the God that was companion, guide, and beloved seems to withdraw, leaving one feeling empty, alone, and disoriented. Eventually this distress passes as one becomes

---

[27] St. John of the Cross, *The Dark Night of the Soul*, trans. E. Allison Peers (Garden City, NY: Image Books, Doubleday, 1959, Electronic edition by Harry Plantinga, 1994), 16-17. The poem takes its title from the larger prose work in which it first appeared.

profoundly aware of the divine presence within, but the passage can be slow and painful.

So, how does this spectrum of mystical development relate to the Christian myth as presented in the Bible and to the spectrum of three stages—prerational (social intelligence), rational, and transrational—I have emphasized?

The biblical myth is a patchwork of stories connected within the history of the Hebrew people. The historical and social context of the individual bits of the myth provide a broad connection to the stages of the cognitive spectrum. This is because cultural history is a record of collective psychosocial-spiritual development, and that collective development is the sum of individual human development and reflects the stages of individual human development. The brain structures that underly the cognitive spectrum have been present in human beings for a very long time, and they have always found a level and mode of expression in the past appropriate to the cultural context of the time. Even those stages that have yet to fully express in a culture nevertheless find symbolic and prophetic expression in the myths of that culture.

The two sets of stages I have referred to as spectra—the spectrum of mystical development and the spectrum of rational or cognitive development—are different lines of development, but they overlap and interconnect. How we experience and understand spirit cannot be separated from our patterns of thought. In the simplified form presented here, both of these spectra consist of three stages, and those stages correlate nicely to each other and to the broad progression of the Christian myth.

Christianity has always recognized stages within its own development as reflected in its scriptures. The obvious division is between the Old and New Testaments. Tradition sees the Old Testament as presenting the dispensation of the Law, and it sees Jesus and the New Testament as presenting the dispensation of Grace. This understanding goes all the way back to earliest Christianity and the theology of St. Paul.

If we take the Law as the first stage and Grace as the last stage, we still need a middle stage and a traumatic final transition to match the pattern we are looking for. The traumatic transition point into Grace is obviously found in the crucifixion and resurrection of Jesus. The middle stage, which would correspond to the rational stage in the cognitive model, is less obvious, but it is there. It is less obvious because the rational stage would not come to prominent expression in human culture for more than fifteen-hundred years after the last words of the Bible were recorded. However, the rational dimension of human cognition was always present and did find expression within the myth, even if that expression was not as clear cut and evident as the other stages. Specifically, we see expression of reason and mental illumination in the wisdom literature (Proverbs, Ecclesiastes, etc.), in prophetic visions, and in Jesus as teacher. This gives us three nicely parallel lines of development.

This triple model provides a roadmap for the personal spiritual journey. In applying it, we must translate the traditional elements from the conventional sin-salvation paradigm to an incarnation-evolution paradigm. That is, instead of seeing the big picture to be about overcoming sin as invasive evil, we need to see it as being about growth into individual awareness and responsibility.

Cognitive Stages	Mythic/Scriptural Stages	Mystic Stages
Transrational	Grace	Unitive Way
↑ Limits of Reason	Crucifixion & Resurrection	Dark Night of the Soul
↑ Rational	Wisdom	Illuminative Way
↑ Prerational (Social intelligence dominates.)	Law	Purgative Way

Taking guidance from the Christian myth as presented in the Bible, deliberate spiritual growth starts with self-control as represented by the Law. From the traditional perspective of social intelligence, this was about obedience to the god who, it was imagined, exercised dominion over us. Sin was seen as an invading stain that had to be driven out (purged). Moving beyond tradition to the perspective where we realize that sin is part of the fabric of evolutionary reality, we realize that what self-discipline really does is to increase the level of control that the more conscious dimensions of our egos have over our instincts and appetites. The Law requires us to think before we act, thus opening a buffer of rational self-review between impulse and action. The Ten Commandments are not just about law and order; they are about claiming our conscious will out of what would otherwise be mindless, instinctual reaction. The Law functions as a sort of yoga to develop the moral and volitional capacities of the ego.

Understanding what the Law is about is all fine and good, but it is no substitute for doing it. Just as understanding physical fitness does not make you physically fit, so also does understanding self-control not build self-control. Physical fitness requires physical exercise, and the development and maintenance of self-control requires ongoing moral application in real life. The first step in the personal spiritual journey is to establish a solid, healthy morality that is practiced consistently in all aspects of one's life. Temptations will arise, and we must learn to manage them.

This must not become harsh self-denial, masochism, or prudish legalism. True morality is about freedom from genuinely unhealthy or destructive tendencies and compulsions. It is rooted in balanced love of self and other—tough love sometimes perhaps—but always love that can forgive when we miss the mark.

Balanced love is not easily accomplished. Because life is complicated, simply following rules does not always have a good result. The sincere application of self-discipline leads to the need to look below the surface of the rules for the intention behind them and for a better understanding both of the world to which the rules apply and of ourselves as implementors of those rules. This leads into the second stage, which emphasizes understanding as represented in the myth by Wisdom (Sophia).

Understanding, which I define as experience and knowledge organized by reason, lets us step beyond innate social instinct and inherited conceptualizations to see reality more directly and to respond to it with more freedom and flexibility. True understanding requires honesty, humility, and the habit of critical thought. Instead of believing what we want to be true or what we think we are supposed to believe, we must be open to what is actually true and what we actually experience.

Understanding is an endless process. It involves building models of reality in our minds. Such models can never completely capture the reality of what is being modeled. That is just how it is. Our mental equipment is limited, and reality is limitless. We can refine our models to be ever more accurate, but they are always different and separate from the real thing.

Furthermore, Wisdom goes beyond just rational understanding. The opening from social intelligence into disciplined, well-developed rational intelligence is quite important, but it is not the whole story. Social intelligence has its own important modes of emotional understanding. There are also intuitive modes of understanding, like dreams and visions, that emerge from the subconscious. In true wisdom, all these ways of understanding work together and must be respected. Bringing them into alignment is a major challenge.

In the spiritual journey, the journey itself and the self that is making the journey both become objects for understanding. Over time, the traveler becomes increasingly aware of the patterns and rhythms of growth, the challenges presented by the ego, the quiet but deep satisfaction that comes with progress, and the call of mystery. There is simply a pleasure in coming to see oneself and the Kosmos in some new or deeper way, as though the God in us enjoys knowing herself through our minds.

Yet, understanding has its limits. The mental models constructed by our minds are objects of understanding; what we really seek is the subjective experience of what those models simulate. The stage of Grace is the subjective awareness of divine presence. It is free, simple, and already present, but the ego and the active mind obscure it. To find it we must quiet the mind and emotions, which requires the realignment of the ego. In the myth this realignment is represented by the crucifixion and resurrection of Jesus.

The goal is not to destroy the ego; life is impossible without it. Rather, the goal is to tame the ego and put it at the service of the deeper/higher, truer self that Christians call the image of God in us. This is usually not easy.

The ego is a product of biological evolution whose job is to keep us alive and give our offspring an even better chance of survival. The fact that we are alive means that the egos of our ancestors did their jobs well. Our natural fear of death resides in the ego and is simply the ego doing what it is supposed to do. Spiritual growth is not necessary for biological survival; therefore, it is not a priority for the ego and will not happen unless the ego and its monkey mind relax some of their control.

The fear-driven ego does not easily give up its habit of constant vigilance and ambition. The ego can be softened by heeding the deeper but gentler drive to know one's deepest nature and by the teachings of tradition, the guidance of spiritual teachers, and spiritual practices. As the ego softens, the dread of death that is fundamental to the ego tends to rise to the surface. The ego must choose to let go in the face of that dread, and that feels like risking death. This can happen suddenly and traumatically or gradually and more gently. The ego is changed as it comes into awareness of a deeper, eternal self even as it accepts is own mortality. The ego that has let go is a mature ego. The fear of death remains as a matter of practical survival, but it is balanced by a sense of eternal identity apart from the ego, a knowing that the center of I-ness is not the ego and can never die.

This transition is distressing also because it involves a shift in the nature of knowing. The shift is from knowing as the understanding of conceptual models to knowing as direct experience. It is the shift from social and rational intelligence to something much more fundamental, something paradoxical and ultimately ineffable. It is the shift from dualistic consciousness to nondual consciousness. In apophatic terms it is the shift from knowing to unknowing. In the midst of this shift away from the familiar ways of knowing, one can feel disoriented, unmoored, and even desolate. As subjective attention shifts away from the mental objects of long-standing emotional religious attachment, it can feel like God has abandoned you. In other words, if you are used to relating to God as another being who is your companion, friend, and even beloved, it can feel devastating when that other being seems to dissolve away.

My own experience is that this Dark Night of the Soul need not be as excruciating as the older literature suggests. To be sure, it is a challenging transition, but my sense is that those who suffer the most pain are those whose experience of God remains strongly rooted in their social intelligence, who still imagine God substantially along the lines of supernatural theism, as a supernatural version of us, as someone who can be friend and companion. Those who enter the transition with a strong rational perspective on God, already understanding the mythic nature of the God imagined by their social intelligence, have less of an adjustment to make and therefore suffer less.

In medieval culture, the perspectives of modern science were not available, so the God of supernatural theism was taken to be fact. That made the shift to the Unitive Way very difficult, and the Dark Night was experienced to be an ominous trial. Today we can see that version of God to be myth, an imaginary product of social intelligence. That makes the shift to a nondual perspective much less confusing and stressful.

What I have presented here is a very high-level correlation between the progression of the Christian myth and the spiritual journey. A deeper look soon becomes a massive Bible study and is more than I can manage here. I leave that exploration for you. There is a lot of wisdom and inspiration there if you can learn to see below the surface. Finding it is very rewarding.

W(h)ither the Church?

And he has put all things under his feet
and has made him the head over all things
for the church, which is his body,
the fullness of him who fills all in all.
Ephesians 1:22-23 (NRSV)

The Christian Church today languishes in a monumental crisis of identity and conflicting worldviews. It stands, largely in bewilderment and denial, on both sides of the culture wars. Its traditional forms can probably survive and even thrive for quite some time in traditional segments of societies around the world, but those traditional forms are not at all compelling to the growing portion of humanity who see reality through a more rational, scientific lens. Meanwhile, the more progressive churches struggle to find and solidify their theological identities and to develop viable new institutional forms. This makes for a lot of confusion, strain, and mistrust within what tradition regards to be the Body of Christ on Earth. Pushing through this crisis to a positive outcome will require courage, honesty, determination, and good will.

At this point in my own spiritual journey I experience the negatives of traditional and conservative churches to far outweigh their positives. While I appreciate the intentions and attempts of liberal churches to venture in a more honest direction, most of them seem to be floundering—bravely faithful but pretty much lost theologically. The vast majority of churches seem to lack the intention and competence to teach real spirituality. I have little hope that many of our existing religious institutions will be able to survive the transition that is needed. Even the most progressive mainline denominations still carry a lot of traditional baggage and a laity that is not eager for change. Regardless of how liberal the clergy may be, dragging local church members who were happy with the way things used to be into radically new paradigms is a herculean challenge.

This does not mean that I don't think there is a need for some form of church in our future. The church has been and ought to continue to be the keeper of the Christian myth and the Christian mystical tradition. These provide a map for the spiritual journey and a wealth of spiritual experience and insight from the historical perspective of western civilization. Healthy progressive churches have value within society as advocates and teachers of morality, compassion, and personal reflection and as some of the few places where the spectrum of human emotions including sorrow, grief, guilt, fear, hope, awe, gratitude, and joy can be expressed and lived out in a supportive context. Churches play a valuable social role as communities where we can publicly observe life's important passages—including birth, coming of age, marriage, and death. Ideally the Church should be helping people successfully mature through both the human lifecycle and the spiritual journey. Most of today's churches don't do any of this very well, but that in no way lessens the need. There is a lot of hard work to be done for the Church to become what it ought to be.

Traditional churches function on a hierarchical and transactional model of faith. God is seen to be the ultimate power at the top of the heap, and the way to security and prosperity is to get on "his" good side: We do what God wants and God takes care of us. This is a transaction, an exchange of one thing for another. This is despite the fact that the best traditional theology on the matter, which I am convinced arose from transrational consciousness in the early proto-Christian community, is that salvation is actually a free gift. This free gift is traditionally called *grace*. Unfortunately, the social intelligence that drives traditional religion cannot resist placing conditions on grace that work to maintain the social cohesion and survival of the church. Social intelligence insists that, at the very least, we must accept grace by having "faith": If we believe that Jesus died for us, then and only then are we saved. We espouse this form of faith, which is assent to a set of religious propositions, in exchange for salvation. We also like to believe that God throws in providence as well, that God takes special care of believers in this life. The traditional church is, in the final analysis, an expression of such transactional faith. We build beautiful churches as homes for God and worship God in them and support them financially to prove our faith and to please God.

Social intelligence gets a lot more from this bargain than just the assurance of salvation. It gets the group identity and reassuring worldview that it craves and the feeling of superiority for being on the right side.

It is true that in the past churches served many other functions—including the founding and support of social welfare organizations and as local centers of social and even intellectual life—but in our secularized culture most of those other functions have shifted substantially to other institutions and social groups. What remains is mostly the conventional understanding that being in church puts us in a good relationship with the big guy in the sky.

The truth, as seen by rational intelligence informed by spiritual experience, is that grace really is totally free. Faith is not something we have to do to secure grace. Faith is an optional response to grace. The grace is always there and is entirely unaffected by the presence or absence of faith. Faith is simply trust in the grace regardless of assent to any proposition. The grace is not withdrawn in the absence of faith; it is simply unrecognized. Despite two-thousand years of literal belief in reward and punishment in the afterlife, grace is not a salvation from anything; it is simply another name for the love that is the ultimate reality western religion calls God. Grace/God is always and everywhere present in and available to everyone. The spiritual journey is properly a quest, not to secure and possess grace/God as something otherwise lacking, but to come to recognize it as already and always present, especially in oneself, and to give it truer expression in one's life.

Just as the forms of traditional church reflected the traditional transactional understanding of our relationship with God, so the church of the future must take on forms that reflect the incarnational and evolutionary understandings of spirit as seen from rational and transrational perspectives. The church of the future will not be about mediating the transactions of salvation but about helping people to grow in the depth and breadth of their awareness of spirit and to make the love at the heart of spirit the driving principle in all aspects of human life, individual and collective. This is a developmental and evolutionary orientation based on seeing the created universe as a manifestation of spirit. It sees not just the Church but all of creation as the body of Christ. It is not about making a deal to secure a comfortable existence in an imagined life to come; rather, it is about growing and loving in the very real and entirely spiritual world where we live right now.

This shift will require the church of the future to focus on spiritual formation and its integration with real life. Such ministry must stand on three pillars: experience, education, and relationship. These correspond to the mystical, rational, and social dimensions of human consciousness and encompass the transrational, rational, and prerational stages of psychosocial-spiritual development.

As we progress in psychosocial-spiritual development, the lower stages don't go away because the brain structures that gave rise to them don't go away. New levels always stand on old levels. Each new stage of spiritual growth necessarily includes the older stages, realigning and refining them perhaps, but never eliminating them. Growing into more rational consciousness does not mean we stop being social animals, and becoming more spiritually aware does not mean we stop thinking. We must strive to harmonize all levels of our body, mind, and spirit with each other and with our best experience and understanding of reality. We must also remember that every person grows upward from the lowest levels, so an effective church must be able to speak to people at every level.

Experience

Experience must be the core. The root of all religion is mystical experience, which historically in western spirituality meant experience of union with the divine. This is the experience that the mystery we call God (an empty name for what is beyond naming) is the nothing from which all things flow and the everything, including us, that flows from the nothing. This sort of experience of unity with the divine is reflected in the words of the Jesus of the Christian myth: "The Father and I are one" (John 10:30 NRSV). Good religion is nothing more than unpacking this experience and letting it fully inform how we live. Thus, inviting people to share in the experience must be a central concern if we want the church to remain authentically energized.

The church can do this most importantly by teaching spiritual practices and especially contemplative prayer. Mystical insight can also be evoked by worship and ritual, especially the Eucharist, by activities of service to others, by intense experiences of nature, by art, and by absorption in activities like singing and dancing. The church must provide deliberate opportunities for a range of such things that will assist the whole spectrum of personality types to find their own mystical knowing. Furthermore, experiences of great joy and great suffering that happen in our broader lives can open us to deeper spiritual awareness. The church must help people engage such experiences and own the meaning found in them. All experience is ultimately spiritual experience.

Mystical knowing, which the apophatic tradition calls *unknowing* (How I do love the paradox!), is just another name for *faith*. It is not faith in any specific expectation but simple trust in spirit/God as ultimate reality. Christianity must ultimately be grounded in the experience of faith—not in the Bible, not in the authority of the Church, not in any person—but in the ultimate unity of spirit that the tradition calls both God and divine love.

This love is far, far more than the human emotions to which we usually apply the term. It is the moving force of life and evolution which only sometimes finds its expression in sweet emotions. It is the third person of the Trinity, the Holy Ghost, that connects everything and is the dynamic principle (will of God) that manifests the created material universe (the Child) from unmanifest spirit (the Parent). It is the driving force behind all we experience as good and pleasant but also behind the pain and suffering that are inherent in evolutionary being. Faith in this spirit is not a hope that God will save us but a knowing—not just a mental concept, but a deep knowing—that we are that same eternal spirit.

You may object that genuine mystical experience is rare and limited to a few special people. You may be concerned that such an emphasis on mystical knowing puts institutional Christianity in the precarious position of tying its ultimate validity to the subjective experiences of a few individuals who might soon become a privileged class.

I would argue that mystical experience is actually not so rare and that, in any case, it is not finally the experiences that validate faith. There are a variety of types of mystical experience. In some—like visions, voices, dreams, and visitations—the perceived content would seem to be important. In others—like nature mysticism, peak experiences, and other altered states of consciousness such as can emerge from spiritual practice—perception and cognition recede to expose a deeper sense of universal identity. We tend to associate the word *mystical* with the content of the first type of experience, but the second type is actually more properly mystical. The deepest levels of contemplation have no conceptual content, only an experience of what might be called emptiness and unity at the same time. The surface content of any spiritual experience is not what finally matters and need not be trusted except for the insights it may bring and the ineffable knowing it leaves in its wake. The experience is a guide that points to what has always been present but unrecognized.

Mystical experience, when understood from this broader perspective, happens a lot. Experiences of intense love or great beauty or suffering or simple deep clarity of awareness in an unexpected moment can all evoke powerful spiritual awareness. The point is not to be able to say you have had a certain special kind of experience; the point is to awaken to the spiritual nature of everything, including yourself. What matters is not the experience but the knowing to which the experience only provides an opening.

As for mystics becoming a privileged class, genuine mystics would not tolerate such a thing. To realize that you are a manifestation of universal spirit and one with all things is to realize that you are very special indeed but absolutely no more special than anyone else. It is a source of simple humility that does not crave recognition. Real mystics don't make a show of it; rather, they tend to hide it. The point is not to find a few charismatic mystics to idolize—that is immature, prerational-stage, ego-driven stuff—but to help everyone come to know the deeper truth in their own way. Anyone purveying prophecies and visions to claim status or authority is not to be trusted.

The ultimate ineffability of spiritual experience seems not to prevent anyone from trying to put it into words. Such attempts can take very different forms, none of which are finally adequate. These might include statements like "God is love," or "I am eternal spirit." Another example is my own concise summary of the meaning of Christianity: *God is incarnate in all of creation and calls us to recognize and love the divine nature in ourselves, in other human beings, and in all things.* This statement is informed by my knowledge of the Bible and Christian doctrine and theology, but the focus comes from a deeper knowing that finally stands on its own. Yes, I had some "spiritual" experiences that helped me find that knowing, but the knowing did not come entirely from those experiences nor is it finally dependent on any of them. It was like discovering something I already knew. The experiences simply brought to the surface what was always there. Mysticism is simply about finding the place in ourselves where we truly know that we are all spiritual beings and that spirit is one. Such awareness is elusive in our ordinary state of consciousness because our egos keep us focused outward on the concerns of life, but deeper knowing is not that hard to find if we look for it with an open mind, a sincere heart, and patience.

Education

The second pillar, education, is about the broadening of understanding and is crucial for relating subjective mystical knowing to the objective, "real" world and vice versa. Spiritual experiences can be wonderful gifts, but they can also send us spinning off on fantastic mental detours. Mystical knowing is not about venturing into other unseen worlds; it is about this very spiritual but ordinary world that we know through our senses. Spiritual experience may open us to levels that go beyond the senses, but it all connects to this world.

To apply mystical knowing to the real world we need to understand and be grounded in the real world. Even putting spirituality aside, life simply works better if we see things clearly. Over the past few hundred years, science has given us a far better understanding of the material world and of how our bodies and minds function than Jesus or the ancient prophets or the medieval church ever knew. The church must enthusiastically embrace science as a source of verifiable, objective understanding. Science is nothing less than a window into the workings of God, and philosophy, as rational reflection on the nature of the Kosmos, can be pretty darn insightful as well. For Christianity to be relevant, it must acknowledge reality as we know it and engage with the cutting edges of human intellectual culture.

The truth is that most of the people who fill the pews of local churches as well as many of their clergy have a very poor grasp of the sciences and philosophy, and many also have poorly developed skills of critical thinking and self-reflection. This is a formula for spiritual immaturity and stagnation. Popular Christianity increasingly barricades itself into a ghetto of shallow religiosity and conservative cultural identity, blocking out anything that might put cracks in traditional understanding and lead to real growth. Time to get crackin'! It is scary at first to watch what once seemed authoritative and reassuring leak out through those cracks, but those cracks are also where the Holy Spirit can leak in.

Christianity was not always so uncomfortable with real education as it is today. Our modern university system is directly descended from the church-founded schools and universities of Europe in the late middle ages and Renaissance. Most private American colleges and universities were founded by Christian denominations. Many of the best of these institutions of higher learning have severed their formal ties with religion for the sake of academic freedom; they found it impossible to be rigorously loyal both to the truth and to traditional religious correctness. It is sad, after investing so much in the belief that pursuing truth could only lead to better understanding of God and better service to humanity, that institutional Christianity has lost courage in this conviction. The faith and hope of the churches in higher education was not misplaced, they were simply overwhelmed by the magnitude and speed of the changes that ensued. It is time to reclaim the conviction and begin bridging the gap between religion and honest scientific and intellectual perspectives.

Understanding is essential to psychosocial-spiritual growth. To a certain point such growth is driven by hard-wired instinct, but instinct is relatively fixed and inflexible. Critical reason—the ability to analyze and understand things based on objective evidence—can respond more flexibly to specific situations and thereby enable greater competence in interactions with the world. In other words, clear thinking aids survival. The rub is that, whereas instincts are inborn and automatic, disciplined reason and intellectual skills require substantial effort over a long period of time. This effort is called learning.

The Church of the future must provide opportunities and encouragement for whatever learning is needed to support spiritual growth and fulfilling life. Churches must be centers of education that accept people where they are and help them grow into greater understanding, competence, and love. The obvious place to start is with Christianity itself—with honest education about Jesus, the Bible, and the history and development of Christianity. These subjects should be taught from the perspective of the best available scholarship distilled to a level the students can understand while also challenging them a bit. Churches should also be educating people on topics that have been troublesome to traditional faith—things like the theories of evolution, relativity, quantum physics, and other religions. Introductory-level classes on these topics can be mind-opening experiences that expose and break through barriers of fear.

Churches should, in fact, seek to stimulate learning in almost every area that can give people understanding and skills for a more aware and fulfilling life. What is appropriate and most needed will vary from one congregation to another. Possibilities include everything from remedial reading or English as a second language to physical fitness, nutrition and cooking, parenting skills, or personal finance and retirement planning.

The overarching theme in all this education must be developmental growth and evolution, which are two names for the same underlying phenomenon as it expresses in individuals and systems. The material and biological worlds have evolved from the moment of the Big Bang. Religion, science, and all of human culture have evolved over time and continue to evolve. People grow and develop as individuals, ideally for their whole lives. Everything evolves, and that evolution is the expression of the divine creative principle; it is the action of God. The goal is to recognize and appreciate it as such in a deep way.

Relationship

The third pillar is relationship, which includes community. This is where the rubber meets the road, where experience and understanding are translated into action in the world. It is in relationship that we have the opportunity to love our neighbor as our self. The heart of relationship is ethics. To apply mystical knowing (faith) in real life is to seek to act in the greatest possible accordance with divine love.

How divine love really operates in our evolutionary reality is not always straightforward. Empathy, compassion, generosity, gentleness, and cooperation would seem to be expressions of love while anger, competitiveness, self-interest, and violence would not—but the evolutionary perspective calls such assumptions into question. There is no life and joy without pain and death. Ethical action is not always sweet and pleasant. Yes, I believe that the evolution of humanity is toward the reduction of suffering and violence, but the negative currents at play in evolution have a valid place and cannot be entirely suppressed or dismissed. Because the inhabitants of our world have conflicting interests, ethical decisions are rarely black and white. It is also difficult to balance immediate concerns with later consequences. There can be a big difference between doing what might be judged as good in the short term and what results in evolutionary progress and broader benefit in the long term. The simplistic moral positions that supernatural theism bases on what it believes to be direct commandments from the deity are inadequate to the complexities of life as we understand it today. The world needs a more mature ethics.

The role of moral advocate is one the Church has performed throughout its history, sometimes admirably and sometimes shamefully, but it is a role where a progressive, intellectually honest, spiritually rooted Christianity can offer much. The Church must not simply stick to traditional positions just because they are traditional, nor should it take seemingly progressive stances just to be progressive. The world needs a Christianity that will do two things. First, it needs a Christianity that will grapple deeply and honestly with contemporary moral issues, seek a convergence of subjective and objective truth, and then strongly declare its positions *and the reasons for them*. Second, the world needs a Christianity that will lead the way by practicing what it preaches, by showing how to live out the positions it advocates in the real world. This cannot be an ethics of impractical ideals; it must be livable.

Many of the issues that warrant such treatment are obvious: overpopulation, war, environmental degradation, resource allocation and conservation, racism, abortion and biomedical ethics, the right to die, sexuality, LGBTQ issues, human rights, economic justice, criminal justice, political ethics, and refugee policies. It is no longer adequate to address these issues in isolation from one another. They all arise from the social and competitive nature of biological evolution which is rooted in the very nature of material existence. Growing populations of physical beings occupying the same finite environment and depending on the same finite resources must inevitably come into competition that will end in violent conflict—unless those tensions are somehow managed to a different result. The point of progressive Christian ethics is to propose what the different result might be and what must happen to bring it about.

Science is a great source of facts for making ethical choices, but facts do not make choices. People make choices. Ethical choices can never be purely objective; the subjective, emotional dimension always comes into play. The default mechanisms of subjective choice in matters of relationship are the instincts of social intelligence. History and experience teach us that these instincts often lead to unnecessary violence and suffering. Our challenge, if we are to evolve beyond the box of instinct, is to expand into a broader subjectivity rooted in the mystical knowing of our deepest connection to one another.

This is very serious business. We are, of course, fools if we think we have ultimate control and that we will be able to keep the car entirely out of the ditch. Evolution (God's will active in the world) is complex and will have its way with us when we fail to understand it and even sometimes when we do understand (global warming?). We can, nevertheless, learn from our mistakes, keep the car on the road more of the time, and maybe avoid the deepest ditches. The alternatives are passive fatalism or aggressive selfishness, both betrayals of mystical knowing. We are neither fully in control nor completely helpless, and we must live as best we can on this middle ground. There is no supernatural God waiting in the wings to save us; if God saves us, it will be through each other.

Surely the biggest challenge with all of this is coming up with institutional structures that can effectively support such ministry and finding ways to transition into them from the existing structures. Local churches as we have known them are expressions of the transactional model of faith. Exposing the transaction for the illusion (Christian snake oil) that it is changes the incentives. Why tithe if you realize that grace is free and that tithing was thought up eons ago by priests to provide for their own livelihood? Churches based on the incarnational/evolutionary model, if they actually come into being, will be supported based on loving concern to share mystical knowing and to improve life for everyone. This is a mentality of giving rather than exchange. There is, of course, a lot of this giving mentality present in most of today's churches, but I doubt there is enough to keep them going if the transactional motivation collapses.

The old model stood on prerational/social consciousness; the new model will stand on transrational/spiritual awareness. These mindsets comprise two mostly different sets of people. The first set dominates the laity of today's churches, though dwindling in the mainline denominations. The second set probably exists more outside the Church than in it. Those transrational folks who are present in the Church lack a shared identity, theology, and vision.

I propose that what is needed is an activist clergy that will try to keep the healthiest existing churches alive while deliberately building a new base of rational and transrational folks who can support the new model. This will require working the problem from both ends. The goal with traditional church folks is to move them forward from traditional theology into incarnational/evolutionary theology and transrational awareness. At the rational/transrational end, the task is to publicly and assertively reframe traditional Christianity in a way that makes sense to non-traditional folks, most of whom are not church people, and invites them to join in a community that affirms, seeks, shares, and supports transrational spiritual awareness and its expression in life using the Christian myth as the conceptual framework. This may not be so difficult in the most progressive churches, but my experience of most mainline congregations is that the majority of their members remain rather traditional and will not find such change to be easy.

I know that there are activist clergy trying to do such things. I know some of them personally, and I was one of them myself for a brief time. I also know that they often give up, as I did. The task is more than any lone pastor can hope to accomplish. I am convinced that the only way for such clergy to succeed is to join together—within the same denomination or even across denominations—to form teams for the purpose of supporting one another, shaping and giving expression to incarnational evolutionary theology, developing joint strategies for church transformation and growth, and conducting shared programs. Ideally, this will be done in close partnership with progressive schools of theology.

Worthwhile innovation has already occurred in many areas of ministry, but I am convinced that the progressive Christian movement will not come together until it agrees on its core theology, on what it really stands for, on its Gospel. This is the crucial point on which clergy must stand up and lead, as gently as possible, but as firmly as necessary. Clarity of understanding is what will unleash the power of spirit to propel the Church of the future.

Meta-Christianity

No one sews a piece of unshrunk cloth on an old cloak;
otherwise, the patch pulls away from it, the new from the old,
and a worse tear is made.
And no one puts new wine into old wineskins;
otherwise, the wine will burst the skins,
and the wine is lost, and so are the skins;
but one puts new wine into fresh wineskins.
Mark 2:21-22 (NRSV)

According to Ken Wilber, the great work or achievement of Modernity has been the differentiation and reintegration of the objective and subjective dimensions of human experience. This differentiation entails fully recognizing the difference between outwardly observed truth and inwardly imputed meaning. Christianity today remains a premodern social beast in that it has yet to fully differentiate these dimensions within itself. Specifically, Christianity has yet openly, explicitly, and honestly to separate the objective truth about its myths—that they are not literally true—from the deep meaning that can be found in those same myths.

This differentiation and reintegration can happen only when rational intelligence is ascendant over social (pre-rational) intelligence. Social intelligence lives inside the myth and cannot view the myth from the outside. It is rational intelligence that can support the process of self-reflection, the process of mentally taking a step back to examine oneself and one's understanding of reality.

What I have found as I have made this differentiation in my own spiritual journey is that it reintegrates into a very different looking Christianity from the conventional version in which I was raised. It is so different, in fact, that the question arises as to whether it can any longer even be called Christianity. I think it can. In fact, I think it is more true to reality and to the deepest meanings and values of the tradition than the currently dominant versions. But it is different, and, as the passage at the beginning of this chapter suggests, failing to be realistic about the differences between old and new can be problematic.

While I definitely think the label *Christian* applies to such radically reconstructed versions of the tradition as I propose in this book, I also think it appropriate and necessary to be able to distinguish them from the traditional versions so that the differences are apparent in public discourse. What I am proposing could be called *transmythic, evolutionary, existential, apophatic, transformative, mystical, panentheistic Christianity*, but that is quite the mouth full. I suggest the label *meta-Christianity*, not as a formal name, but as a classification for my own and similarly reconstructed versions of the faith.

Meta- as a prefix can be used to indicate a successive form of something, especially a discipline, that is aware of itself as a successive form and that deals critically with the older forms.[28]

The meta-Christianity I have begun to sketch in this book fits this and other aspects of the dictionary definition of *meta-*. It is a later and transformed version of traditional Christianity that deals critically with the older version. It holds traditional Christianity within itself and reframes it to be more real and honest than its prior versions. It is concerned to recognize how it has arisen from the older forms and how it is both the same and different from them. Meta-Christianity emphasizes change and transformation, both of the individual and of the human community. Meta-Christianity is not so much self-referential as self-reflective and self-critical.

Meta-Christianity can also be seen as self-performative in the sense that its emergence is a performance or acting out of one of the deep messages of the Christian tradition. At the very core of the Christian narrative is death and resurrection. Meta-Christianity can be seen as a resurrected modern version of Christianity that emerges when the premodern traditional version is allowed to die. The resurrected form is more and different than the old form, and yet the old form is present in the resurrected form.

The following table contrasts traditional popular Christianity and meta-Christianity as I see it.

---

[28] https://www.merriam-webster.com/dictionary/meta, 08/21/2019.

Traditional Christianity	Meta-Christianity
Ultimately concerned with salvation in the afterlife	Ultimately concerned with transformation: spiritual growth and the ever-fuller expression of love in this life
Hopes for immortality of the "soul"	Accepts mortal nature of the body and the eternal nature of spirit present in all beings
Transactional – Belief and good behavior are offered in exchange for "salvation".	Graceful – Our eternal identity with divine spirit is free, needing only to be discovered and respected.
Faith as belief	Faith as trust in and identity with the mystery of spirit
Authority resides externally in powerful beings and institutions.	Authority resides inwardly in discerned truth and value.
Doctrinal/creedal	Experiential
Expects reward or safety for faith and righteousness	Faith and righteousness are their own reward
Scripture is literally true.	Scripture is recorded myth that is important for the deeper meaning it carries.
God understood from the perspective of supernatural theism: God is a magically powerful, human-like being	God understood from the perspective of evolutionary panentheism: God is the mysterious source and ground of being, fully immanent and fully transcendent
Jesus is divine, magical superhero.	Jesus is fellow human being whose story became the seed of an enlightening and inspiring myth.
Sacred and profane are distinct and separate.	Everything is sacred if we can but see it for what it really is.
Fear based	Love (Agape) based
Group/Ethno-centric	Human/World-centric
Obedience is expected of the follower.	Freedom is found by the follower.
Doubt is suppressed.	Doubt is pursued.

Traditional Christianity	Meta-Christianity
Suspicious of and hostile toward science	Regards science as an important path to truth
Threatened by evolutionary perspective	Enthusiastically embraces evolutionary perspective
Sees evil as a foreign influence; projects evil onto devils, demons, and enemies outside the self: avoids responsibility.	Sees evil as resulting from choices inherent in the created order; locates evil in human choice and weakness: takes responsibility.
Dualistic	Nondual

Meta-Christianity is what emerges when the best of traditional Christianity is taken seriously, when its highest values, developmental trajectory, and mystical insights are recognized and applied to understanding it and to living it. Meta-Christianity is what Christianity becomes when it has resolved to be honest with itself in the wake of the scientific revolution and centuries of sincere critical scholarship, when it is allowed to be thoroughly examined and reworked by rational intelligence informed by both science and transrational spiritual experience. This reworking makes possible the healing of the rift between heart and head that has afflicted sincere and thoughtful Christians in the modern age.

I do not claim ownership of the term *meta-Christianity* specifically for my own version of the faith. I hope my thinking will contribute to a robust movement of more honest and revitalized Christianity, but that result will require far more than I alone can offer. While I do feel that such a meta-Christianity—or whatever such a movement might come to be called—should largely embrace the characteristics laid out in the table above, it can become viable only if it emerges from a broad community of like-minded Christians.

After I wrote this chapter, Facebook's parent corporation took the name *Meta*. It is not clear to me how Meta is meta. I guess the word had a cachet and edginess their PR people were looking for. In any case, this muddies the waters. Meta's new major product area, virtual reality, is about creating convincing illusions whereas meta-Christianity is about breaking though illusion to deeper, truer reality. If all of this should cause the label *meta-*

Christianity to become too confusing, misleading, or silly, I suggest *transmythic Christianity* as a fallback.

The Christian Task

"But I say to you that listen,
Love your enemies,
do good to those who hate you,
bless those who curse you,
pray for those who abuse you.
Luke 6:27-28 (NRSV)

This chapter is repetition to emphasize a point that has emerged at numerous places in the previous chapters but that warrants being laid out clearly and more fully one last time.

Christianity is not about getting into Heaven in the afterlife. The deepest part of who we are is already eternal, so once we really connect with that reality we can get on with what really matters: Loving God and loving our neighbor as ourselves. Because God is present in all things—including our neighbor and our enemies—this means striving to relate to all of Creation with as much respect, responsibility, and compassion as we can muster. This is what it means to truly be a member of Christ and Christ's Church in today's world.

This requires a huge shift in consciousness and worldview from what comes naturally. God has created us as biological beings through the process of evolution that relies on natural selection: the survival of the fittest. This means that we naturally compete with one another for survival and prosperity. It has been natural (divinely ordained) that we should have enemies and fight against them for dominance and security. That is how we have become what we are. However, Christianity has been calling us for two-thousand years to step up to the next level, to move on to the next stage of consciousness and human evolution, to work toward the goal that the myth calls *the Kingdom of God* or what could also be translated *the Reign of Love*. This means moving beyond our natural social instincts by using our reason, informed by mystical perception of our underlying spiritual oneness, to develop strategies and adequate self-control toward the goals of minimizing suffering, maximizing joy, and caring responsibly for our world.

The history of Christian culture, horribly brutal though much of it has been, shows significant progress toward the goal. This change has not come in the form of sudden, supernaturally imposed divine rule, as Jesus and his followers seem to have expected, but in our slow progress in such things as human rights, reduction of violence, and the spread of representative democracy over the past few millennia. The progress has been uneven, there has been a lot of failure and backsliding, and the results are fragile, but it has been progress. Such progress is evidence that divine love is the ultimate driver of evolution.

This struggle to realize ever greater levels of love within the created order is what Christianity as a group endeavor is really about: "Thy kingdom come; thy will be done on earth as it is in heaven!" How else can God's will be done within the Creation except by the inhabitants of that Creation? Doing the right thing cannot be forced from the outside; it must come from within. That is one message of the myth of Noah and his ark: killing all the bad people did not change human nature. Human behavior is meaningfully changed by first understanding ourselves and then learning to manage ourselves. This is the stage of human evolution in which we live today and that Christianity invites us to take seriously.

Pain and suffering have not always been part of evolution. Most of the thirteen-plus-billion-year story of our universe has been about chemical and astrophysical evolution: the raw energy of the Big Bang condensed into subatomic particles that then formed atoms of the lightest elements (hydrogen and helium). These atoms globbed together to form stars and planets. Generations of stars and supernovas were the nuclear furnaces in which the lighter elements were fused into heavier elements. Planets that can support life as we know it have come into being only in the last five billion years or so. None of this involved pain.

It is only with the evolution of sentient life that there have been conscious beings with the capacity to suffer. It is hard to say how far back that goes. The first multi-celled creatures emerged on our planet no earlier than 700 million years ago, the first vertebrates no more than 510 million years, the first reptiles 313 million years, the first dinosaurs 235 million years, the first mammals 216 million years, the first primates 70 million, archaic Homo Sapiens 200,000 years ago, and modern Homo Sapiens only 100,000 years ago.[29] Where in this progression did sentience first emerge? When did creatures first became aware of their suffering? Even if we grant some level of sentience to the first single-celled organisms, that was only 700 million years ago or just over 5% of the existence of the universe. If suffering was not necessary for past phases of evolution, is it possible that pain and death need not play as central a role in future phases?

It would seem that pain and suffering have, in fact, been necessary for the evolution of consciousness. Pain and pleasure are what move our behavior. Pain helps us recognize and avoid bad choices; pleasure helps us recognize and seek good choices. We will always have choices, so the possibility of pain and suffering will always be with us, but does suffering and death have to remain the cutting edge driver of evolution? While progress of our present phase of biological evolution clearly requires pain and death, is it possible that evolution could enter into a new phase in which intelligence, compassion, and realistic, self-disciplined morality can significantly contain and moderate pain and suffering?

One of the most important roles of religion is to help us face pain and to help us recognize how we inflict suffering on ourselves and others. The ideal state envisioned in the mythology of all the great religions is a state—call it Heaven, Paradise, Nirvana, Moksha, or whatever—in which there is no suffering. This mythical state points to the serenity of transcendent eternal spirit beyond the physical universe, the state from which our spirits come and to which our spirits may eventually return. It also symbolically expresses the direction, the goal (telos), toward which immanent spirit seeks to bend the evolving cosmos. We cannot hope to eliminate suffering in this world, but we have much power to limit and mitigate it. All great religions call us to the committed pursuit of justice and mercy, both of which are

---

[29] Swimme, Brian and Thomas Berry. *The Universe Story: From the Primordial Flaring Forth to the Ecozoic Era—A Celebration of the Unfolding of the Cosmos.* New York: HarperCollins, 1992.

about the reduction of suffering and the improving of human relationships.

If we want to see positive change, we must be the change we want to see. This means that we must learn to work together in sincere cooperation and good will, not just in a circumscribed religious community, but across all of humanity. This is not easy. In fact, it is very, very difficult. We naturally want to control and limit everyone else so that we can enjoy unlimited freedom and prosperity for ourselves. Because everyone else naturally wants the same thing, unbridled pursuit of such instinctual goals is a recipe for endless conflict, injustice, violence, fear, and a lot of suffering.

Christianity and all the other great religions have long recognized this problem and its solution: Do unto others as you would have others do unto you! So simple and yet so hard! It is only through spiritual consciousness of our own eternal nature and our deep oneness with everyone and everything that we can hope to live in this way.

We must take the log from our own eye before we can credibly ask our neighbors and enemies to deal with whatever is in their eyes. This means that we must personally recognize and admit our own flaws, weaknesses, and shortcomings. We can and should correct some of these things through self-control, but we must admit that we can never make ourselves perfect by act of personal will. Rather, we must find the collective will to structure and manage our systems—technological, economic, political, medical, educational, social, ecological, religious—in ways that support and develop our better natures and best potential and that minimize our worse tendencies.

This is hard, hard work. Kum-bah-yah moments have their place, but nice sentiments alone won't accomplish much. We need innovative, real-world solutions based on clear-headed thinking, and we need the willingness to bear our share of whatever sacrifice is needed to make those solutions work. Are we willing to limit our own prosperity and freedom in order to address the problems that cause unnecessary suffering or threaten human survival? For example, are we willing to limit the size of our families or pay more for renewable fuels or eat less meat or pay more taxes if any of these things appear to be effective ways to reduce crisis, conflict, and suffering?

I cannot overemphasize the collective nature of this task. The only way we can ever succeed is by honestly and sincerely processing the difficult issues with everyone involved. What systems of political representation and discourse do we need to make this possible? What standards of fairness and justice should be followed? How do we make sure that the poor and most vulnerable are treated equitably? How do we deal with those who refuse to engage in the process or who reject the best agreements we are able to make?

These are not issues that the Christian Church should believe it can solve on its own. The fantasy that all such problems would magically vanish if only all of humanity would convert to Christianity is pure nonsense. Other traditions and cultures are just as valid as ours.

The needed deliberations must occur between people as represented by political institutions rather than between religions. Religion or lack thereof will naturally and properly shape the perspectives from which people of different nations and cultures negotiate, but it is the people and not their religious institutions that must have the power to finally decide.

Christianity can support this process, first and foremost, by helping the people it touches to connect deeply to their own spiritual identity, second, by working to identify and promote solutions to humanity's problems that are consistent with our collective spiritual identity, and third, by setting an example of self-control and compliance rooted in goodwill. This is what the Christian myth calls us to if only we let it speak to us authentically.

Christianity that emphasizes belief as a path to eternal salvation is false Christianity. It does not matter what we believe; it matters what we do—here and now—for ourselves, our neighbors, and our enemies.

Epilogue

My hope is that this book will contribute significantly to the demystification of religion in general and Christianity in particular. By demystification I do not mean the elimination of mystery, for such is impossible; mystery lies at the heart of all things. I mean, rather, the honest differentiation of the different types and layers of truth and mystery found in any religious tradition. If we let myth be myth, we merely free it to point us to the deeper, truer mysteries. Such mysteries are portals into awe and joy. Giving up hope in magical gods and pie in the sky gives us an opening to become aware of the profound wonder and sacredness of this Creation and the life we have in it—right here, right now. This brings with it the realization that we must accept responsibility for manifesting the love that traditional religion has projected onto its magical gods. The love that is God has created us and sustains us and calls us into compassionate relationship with one another, but it leaves the work and joy of love on earth to us.

I must end by simply saying that *the journey is the thing*. You can't just think about it or "believe in" it; you have to walk it. Everything else comes if you just keep walking. Spiritual practice is the compass. If you have a meditative/contemplative practice, stick with it; if not, I urge you to take one up.

Appendix A: My Journey

Ask, and it will be given you;
search, and you will find;
knock, and the door will be opened for you.
Matthew 7:7 (NRSV)

I include this autobiographical sketch in case you want to know something more about the yokel who wrote what precedes it. I hope that the important things I have to say stand on their own regardless of who delivers the message.

I was born in Des Moines, Iowa, in 1952 into an American Protestant Christian family. My mother in particular took her religious faith seriously, as had her mother and several of her aunts before her. Hers was a German-American, Midwestern farm family whose home life was dominated by strong women of faith. As far back as I can remember, our family attended church regularly, including Sunday school. Choice rarely entered into it: It was just what we did—what people were supposed to do.

The traditional, premodern Christian worldview as interpreted through the modern Evangelical movement became a major component of my own developing worldview. The other major component was the modern, secular, scientific worldview. These were substantially incompatible perspectives, but they resided together within me in my youth. Science made a lot of sense. Christianity also had its own internal logic, but by the end of my youth I could see that Christianity really did not make much sense if viewed from outside its own cultural box. Still, Christianity spoke of things like spirit and soul and morality and eternity that I could not ignore even though I occasionally tried. Even after I thought I had rejected traditional Christianity, significant parts of the traditional worldview stayed with me— not so much specific beliefs as underlying assumptions, values, and ways of thinking about things. This conflict of worldviews was for me a prolonged and, at times, maddening exercise of being stuck in the middle.

This same conflict presented itself to many of my generation of Americans. Few in our parents' and grandparents' generations seem to have been seriously challenged by these choices, but we boomers had to face them more squarely. A good many of my contemporaries simply chose one side or the other and went with it. For some the choosing was quite conscious. Some chose a traditional religious worldview and resolutely ignored and suppressed any science or reason that challenged their chosen belief system. Others staunchly rejected religion. For still others the choice seems to have been taken less seriously. These folks were able to accept the modern, secular perspective but also leave a little space for religion at the edges where it did not have to make complete sense, where it was more a nod to tradition and a preserving of options than a matter of deep personal commitment.

I took the choice very seriously. The need to sort out the conflict between the worldviews within me became a major focus of my life. I will spare you a detailed autobiography, but here is a quick tour of some significant points.

I was a good Christian child. I received the core of my Christian education in a Missouri Synod Lutheran Church in Phoenix, Arizona, where we had moved because of my father's job. The Missouri Synod is a very doctrinally oriented and conservative denomination. In 1966 I was confirmed after two years of four-hour-per-week instruction. I took what I was taught seriously. This education in traditional theology has been very valuable, but I was also very aware at the time of how at least some parts of that tradition conflicted with the science and critical reason I was learning in school. In other words, I had doubts. I dared not fully embrace them as doubts at that time because doubting was frowned upon, but they were doubts.

The occasion of the confirmation ceremony brought the first of several spiritual experiences that would be pivotal in my life. A confirmation ceremony is in essence very simple: the confirmands declare their faith in the presence of the congregation, and the congregation accepts the confirmands as members. There was an appropriate amount of ceremony with hymns and scripture readings and words from the pastor, but it all came down to the moment when we were asked to affirm that we really did believe the faith as summarized in the Apostles' Creed—or was it the Nicene Creed—I don't remember.

Whichever it was, I of course answered, "I do," but something strange happened in that moment. It was just a moment, just one second, but, looking back on it, it also seemed like time stood still. It was like I was somehow transported out of that church into another dimension without ever leaving the church. I remember the experience as being tinged with golden light. While I was aware of my intention to be true to the tradition, I was also aware of the conflicting modern perspective that was also very real to me. In that moment as I was saying "I do," it was followed silently by *but not exactly in the way you (the pastor/congregation) mean*. This was my soul needing to preserve its integrity, but it also felt like something beyond me was blessing or even giving me the insight and the honesty to start to let God out of the box of tradition. At the time I did not categorize this as a spiritual experience or as anything else really, but it left a strong impression and I knew it came from something other than my ordinary, day-to-day consciousness. I now understand that there are neurological explanations for the experience of time seeming to stand still, but that does not diminish the subjective meaning I found in it.

Fast forward four years, and my family was living in Cedar Rapids, Iowa, and attending a different Lutheran denomination. It was supposedly a less conservative denomination, but honestly the difference escaped me. As I prepared to leave home for college, my doubts reached a crisis point. I decided to reject Christianity. It demanded that I be fully committed to ideas that made no sense. I hated the dishonesty. Yet I valued the tradition's commitments to love and hope and decency, and I still wanted to believe that there might be a power and intelligence behind—well—everything. So, I entered agnosticism with a prayer. I asked God to help me find God if there really is a God.

I fancied myself an atheist for a good while, but all along the way I was driven by a hunger for God, by what Blaise Pascal called "a God-shaped vacuum in the heart of every person" (*Pensees*). It was the 1970's, and the counterculture movement was just peaking. It challenged me to question the direction of my life, and my spiritual hunger drove me to investigate many different religious and spiritual groups and teachings.

The first thing to stick was Transcendental Meditation. I was skeptical of the conceptual framework that came with it, but the technique stuck with me. It seemed to gently clear and energize my mind and deepen my awareness.

The second important thing was Primal Therapy. A friend suggested that I read *The Primal Scream* by Arthur Janov, and it captured my attention. In retrospect I think that what attracted me to PT was the same thing that was attractive about the counterculture and that draws people to apocalyptic religion: the promise of a radically new and better reality for those who are brave enough to believe in and endure a process of transition.

"Primal Theory" suggests that, as we grow up, intensely painful emotions are often suppressed by our brains so as to prevent the pain from incapacitating and even killing us. The suppressed pain builds up in us and causes neurosis and even psychosis, which rob us of our vitality and our capacity to live authentically. The way to healing and personal wholeness is to release and empty this pool of pain by feeling it. Primal Therapy involves intensely paying attention to one's feelings and amplifying them so that they can be fully felt to bring about the release of suppressed experiences. It is done by "going with the feeling" and letting it fully express itself.

In the early 1970s I moved to Pennsylvania to undergo intensive therapy for several weeks. I remained involved in group therapy for many months after that. I also became socially connected with the community of other patients and therapists.

I cannot legally call what I underwent "Primal Therapy" because that term was trademarked by Dr. Janov, and the center I attended was not authorized by him. It was, however, run by licensed psychologists who had experienced Primal Therapy and training under Dr. Janov's direction. I am confident that what I experienced there was for all practical purposes the same thing.

In retrospect it is clear to me that the Primal Therapy movement was quite cultish and that the theory was flawed. While emotional pain and its repression definitely play a big role in emotional pathology, simply reliving pain is not in and of itself sufficient to achieve healing. The idea of a pool of pain that must be emptied to regain psychological health—an idea held almost religiously by many in the "primal community"—is at best a crude metaphor. Psychological repression and pathology arise when the nervous system changes the neural pathways that express and manage emotional energy in response to actual or potential trauma. That is to say, the brain changes how it handles feelings in order to help it cope better with experienced pain and to avoid the experience of more pain. This rerouted energy can manifest as neurotic symptoms. Psychological healing requires changing what the psyche has learned to do with emotional energy. The reliving and release of feelings is an important step, but healing requires that what is released be integrated in a way that again rewires neural pathways into a more healthy pattern. Simply feeling the pain is not sufficient; you have to do something different with it. That last bit, while not entirely missing from Dr. Janov's writings, did not get enough emphasis in at least some parts of the Primal movement.

Still, in a culture that tends to repress feelings, Dr. Janov's work opened a path to deep emotional experience that many people found very beneficial. It was an important part of my own spiritual development. I no longer completely accept the theory, but I very much value the experience. I found that deep feeling could lead to some of the same deep places as meditation.

It is interesting that practices based in an antireligious ideology like Primal theory could open people to spirituality, but they seem to have done so for many. A surprising number of people involved with me in this therapy reported what they regarded to be genuine spiritual awakenings. Others found themselves warming more slowly to the possibility of the spiritual. I and many of my friends were attracted to spiritual subjects, groups, and teachers. We took particular interest in the sort of New Age spirituality typified by the Findhorn Community in Scotland. We explored past-life regression through hypnosis, and we had some experiences with spirit guides and channeling. Although I remained hostile to institutionalized religion for quite some time, I warmed to the possibility that there might be something real underlying religious tradition. This set me on a deliberate quest to know what that might be.

While I remained open to and interested in other religious traditions, I found my interest being drawn back to Jesus and Christianity. I knew this was a cultural thing, a matter of my upbringing. I did not believe Christianity was superior, but it was *my* tradition. It was what I had been raised on, and it had gotten pretty deep into me. I had a strong sense that on some level it related very much to the "deeper places" I touched in meditation and therapy. I needed to sort it out and make sense of it. I started by reading through the entire Bible with as open a mind as possible. I tried not to interpret it as I had been taught, but to let it speak for itself.

To this point in my adult life I had been very skeptical about spiritual experience. I liked the idea that there might be unseen realities beyond what science could detect, but I had no real basis for genuinely believing that there were. It seemed to me that religion was just so much myth and wishful thinking with no reliable proof. The "spiritual" interests and experiences happening among my friends reopened for me the possibility that such things might be real, but I was also aware that it could all be explained away psychologically. I wanted to believe it, but there still was no proof. I had no clear spiritual experience of my own, and I was not sure that the others were not somehow deluding themselves.

Then, early one afternoon, I was praying and found myself falling into a pattern of deep breathing. My prayer was to know what is real regarding spirit. There were so many possibilities, so many confusing choices, and I had nothing solid to go on, nothing to which I could anchor belief. I felt at the same time both stuck and adrift. I wanted to "believe", but I had no basis for making a choice I could trust—and I was a little desperate about it. Then something happened that I was not expecting. It felt like another intelligence, another mind, was entering my consciousness. It seemed to pushed in like a bubble expanding from the back of my skull. It felt like someone else was in a portion of my brain. For the briefest of moments I considered that maybe I should fear and resist what was happening to me, but my curiosity and amazement quickly prevailed. I chose to follow the experience wherever it might lead. Then I realized that this being had something to tell me. It did not use words, but it told me that everything is alright—absolutely EVERYTHING in the broadest sense of the term. It was not referring specifically to what was happening to me in that moment—to it's being in my head—but to the totality of reality. Everything is okay because everything is in God. I don't need to ultimately fear anything or to ultimately worry about anything. Whatever fears and worries might arise at the existential level, they are never of an ultimate nature. At the ultimate level, IT IS ALL GOOD!

The message was delivered in just a few moments, but the experience continued on for what seemed like at least several minutes. I don't really know how long because I was not aware of the passage of time. It could have been as long as 15-30 minutes or much more. At some point the messenger faded from my awareness and I was left in a state of ecstasy. I let myself be carried away by it. Eventually I realized that I had to let it go and return to the "real" world. It was only then that I began to realize how far from the "real" world I had gone. It was a definite and deliberate effort of some minutes to return. I was literally dumbstruck: I could not speak until I pulled myself almost all the way back to normal consciousness. The joy stayed with me for hours.

I was totally absorbed in the experience while it was happening. It was only later that I tried to make sense of it. It seemed to me that I had experienced the sort of thing that could have given rise to accounts of angelic visitations like those found in the Bible. The impressions I had of the messenger were of joyfulness, smallness, and purposeful activeness. It was quite some time later that I connected these impressions to images of cherubs. Classical artistic images of cherubs—chubby, joyful, winged, childlike angels—perfectly fit the "personality" of my "visitor".

This experience created as many questions as it answered, but it felt like real progress. Before it happened I had nothing to go on but wishful thinking based on the words of other people, and I could not let myself fully trust the interpretations those people placed on their experiences. After this I had an experience of my own, I had a reference point of my own to work from. I did not completely understand it—still don't in some ways—but I had the experience. It moved spirituality for me from the realm of hope, conjecture, and fantasy to being grounded in the reality of my own life and consciousness. I know that I had the experience and that it felt deeply real and trustworthy even if it did not fit neatly into how I had come to make sense of the world.

A few years later, in the late 1970s, I had what has been to date the most important spiritual experience of my life. I was meditating late one morning alone in my room and again something new happened: Something opened up. I experienced an overpowering feeling of being flooded with love. I felt a current of love streaming down from above and flowing through me. It did not come to rest in me but flowed through me—and flowed and flowed and flowed—its character was to move, and everything was permeated by it. It was a current of love flowing through the entire universe, a normally unseen current that underlies and drives all being. It was overwhelming. I felt so loved and, at the same time, I felt so much love for all things and all beings. The love flowing into me and the love flowing out of me were inseparably one. It was not like this love was a special gift given to me in that special moment. I somehow knew that this love had always been there and would always be there. The gift given to me in that moment was to become aware of it. I thought my heart would explode. I wept with joy, and I laughed out loud. Though the intensity of this experience faded, the awareness has never gone very far away. It is always there, if less intense, if I only turn my attention to it. It is in this awareness that I have truly found a peace that passes understanding and a sense of being in eternity and of being one with the mystery from which we all come.

There was one other important thing that happened to me in the 70's, between the two experiences I have just related: I gave up on finding true religion. That is to say, I gave up the hope that there might be a religious group or teacher out there in the world somewhere with all the answers. After years of seeking, it became quite clear to me that none of the groups that claim to have ultimate truth actually do. Not churches. Not scientists. Not gurus. Not mediums. Not holy books. Not secret societies. Nobody! This almost made me crazy, but it was a very, very important step in my journey. You see, the problem was less in the groups and teachers than in me. Spiritual truth does not finally reside in ideas and teachings. Ideas can be very helpful, but spiritual truth is encountered in experiences of growth and enlightenment that transcend ideas. Spiritual truth does not contradict reason, but it does transcend reason. As long as one expects to encounter ultimate truth in ideas, one is doomed to frustration. This is the curse of modernity: We are obsessed with reason; we are stuck in our heads. It is not that reason is bad—quite the contrary, it is a very, very important dimension of spiritual growth—but it is not the whole deal. I had to learn to recognize and trust my own inner, subjective experience of being as distinct from my understanding of that experience. I had to learn that my experience and my understanding are two different things. When they line up, it is great; when they don't, it can be painful; but it is crucial to be able to separate them. Love and peace are not the same as the idea of love and the idea of peace.

My quest to find true religion had been a search for someone or something to put my deepest trust in. I was looking for someone or something to tell me what is true and what is right and what I should do. The world, however, refused to cooperate. It kept throwing the search back in my face. I finally just had to give up. It was very, very painful. I felt deeply defeated. All it left me with was the pain and the fear of that moment, but that was real, and that was the shift I needed: What I have ultimately is my own experience of being. That is the basis of spirituality—not ideas—but direct experience apart from whatever sense I might make of the experience. What I sought was not to be found in trusting ideas from someone or something outside myself; I needed to start putting more trust in what came from within. True spirituality is not found in compliantly following a path defined by someone else; it is found only when one travels the path for oneself.

In the early 1980's I moved to Woodstock, NY, at the invitation of friends. I soon found a job as a teacher's assistant in a special education school and there met my wife-to-be, Louise. Having dropped in and out of college for more than ten years, I finally earned a bachelor's degree in Psychology from SUNY New Paltz in 1983. In August of that same year Louise and I married and moved to nearby Saugerties, NY.

At this stage of my life I chose to reengage with the Christian Church. Through my years of seeking I had come to see Christianity differently from how it was generally expressed, at least in Protestant and Roman Catholic culture. The popular understanding of Christianity was that it is about securing "salvation"" by some combination of believing and doing the right things. I had started to see it as being much more about the growth of spiritual consciousness and compassion. I found the idea that God required Jesus to die for my sins both abhorrent and senseless. Instead, I increasingly saw Jesus' story as a pattern of the spiritual journey to which we are all called. I had a sense that I had been led to this understanding not just for my own benefit but also so that I could share it with others. I had a sense that the next stage of my life would be about learning the practicalities of how to do that.

Louise had begun attending the Methodist church in Woodstock before we met. I began joining her there on Sunday mornings, and that is where we were married. We continued our connection there after we moved to Saugerties, about twelve miles away. I eventually became involved in congregational leadership, and I became a certified lay speaker. At the same time, I pursued a career as a computer programmer, and we started a family. Eventually I was able to work less than full-time as an independent contractor, and I used the freed-up time to further pursue my interests in spirituality and ministry. This involved a lot of reading and writing. Louise and I discovered the writings of M. Scott Peck. I stumbled onto the writings of Father Thomas Keating and realized that his Centering Prayer method was exactly what my practice of Transcendental Meditation had become. I did some intense writing of my own to try to sort out my own theological perspectives. I become involved in a prison ministry of theological education founded by Bill Webber, which was the most rewarding ministry experience of my life, so far at least. I became interested in the Emerging Church movement through the writings of Brian McLaren. Eventually I also discovered the writings of Ken Wilber, which blew my mind and finally really helped me start to pull all these various strands together.

Over a period of twenty years I became intimately familiar with how dysfunctional the traditional church has become, and I felt called to somehow get involved in putting it back on track. It seemed like only ordination would give me the standing to take a strong leadership role, so I decided to buckle down and get the necessary credentials. In 2005 I entered the Master of Divinity program at Drew University Theology School.

There was much that I liked about the United Methodist Church, but I could not abide its system of clergy appointment. My uncle and godfather had been a minister in the United Church of Christ, so I looked into that denomination and found it even more to my liking. It was theologically and socially very progressive, and its congregational polity meant that pastors are called by the local congregation rather than being appointed by denominational leadership. Over a period of about two years I unwound my involvement in the UMC and joined the UCC, entering the ordination process in that denomination at about the time I began my studies at Drew.

My plan was not to serve as the pastor of an existing church but to start a new church. It was clear to me that the Christian church, broadly speaking, was stuck in an old worldview that was very much at odds with the worldview shared by most well-educated people of today. The Church is dying because it has failed to adjust fast enough as science and technology have changed the way we understand reality. I think leadership in the mainline churches in America were keeping up pretty well until the mid-twentieth century, but the conservative-vs.-liberal strain got to be too great, and things snapped before the needed changes could mature. There was a conservative backlash at the same time that most modern and post-modern folks left institutional religion altogether. At one time I had thought it possible to work from within the traditional church to help it transform into the new thing that is needed, but I came to see that this is simply too much of a stretch for the traditional stalwarts who sustain most churches. It seemed to me that the Emerging Church movement had the right idea: Start what feels right at the local, grassroots level and see where it goes. Hopefully the surviving traditional churches would learn from these experiments. I thought it worth a try.

I LOVED theology school: good, sincere people grappling with things that matter as though they matter. Sure, there were weak classes, but I found I could learn even in those. There were also many very good classes that pushed me to learn and grow in big ways. It was one of the great things of my life. Thank you, Drew!

Most important of all my experiences at Drew was a course on apophatic spirituality titled *Luminous Darkness* artfully led by Catherine Keller. I had known for quite some time that my own spirituality was of the apophatic sort, but I had little specific awareness of that kind of spirituality in the Christian tradition beyond a smattering of Meister Eckhart. The course helped me connect my own experience to the broad history of the Christian apophatic perspective from the Cappadocian fathers to Nicholas of Cusa, from Marguerite Porete to Howard Thurman. It was wonderful.

By the time I graduated in 2008 I was not so hopeful about my plan to plant a progressive, postmodern church. I had begun to realize that the organizational structure and funding mechanisms of traditional churches arose from and were dependent on the traditional worldview and the pre-technological social context. I have discussed that in a bit more detail elsewhere. My point here is that I began to doubt that truly postmodern people would commit in sufficient numbers to financially support a full-time pastor in a small, local, traditionally-structured church. Nevertheless, I wanted to give it a try, hoping to learn from the experience.

I began inviting people into a faith community I called *Project Hodos* under the auspices of the United Church of Christ. *Hodos* is the Greek word for road, path, or way. It is the word early Christians used before they were called Christians when they referred to themselves as followers of the Way. I wanted the name to convey both the experimental nature of the endeavor and my intention to connect to the earliest and deepest dimensions of the faith.

It was slow going. Even though I had read quite a bit about church planting, attended trainings, and even taken a course on it at Drew, I had no experience and really did not know what I was doing. There is a saying in the Emerging Church movement: If you have seen one emergent church, you have seen one emergent church. Each such community is different, and each new effort has to find its own way. I started with a study group and managed to gather about a dozen people. My plan was to attract a critical mass of committed people and let them help shape what the community would become.

On January 31, 2010, I was approved for ordination by the Hudson-Mohawk Association of the New York Conference of the United Church of Christ. My intention was to be ordained if and when Project Hodos showed promise of long-term viability. Until then I planned to function as a licensed minister, which meant I could perform sacraments only within authorized settings within the association.

Just as it seemed like Project Hodos was getting somewhere, some of those involved moved out of the area, some personality conflicts emerged, and my inexperience resulted in some poor leadership moves. The group shrank back again to a handful. These were definitely learning experiences—and definitely of the painful sort. I regrouped and pushed on. I rented a storefront space and began holding Sunday worship. I also returned to working part-time as a programmer to supplement Louise's income.

Then, in the summer of 2010, I suffered a serious heart attack. I don't think the stress of trying to launch Project Hodos had much to do with triggering the attack, but I did come to feel like it might interfere with my recovery. I was also increasingly skeptical about the long-term prospects for Project Hodos. Based on my own experience, my growing understanding of why conventional churches are dwindling, and from seeing similar efforts struggle and fail, I doubted that my little experiment would ever become self-sustaining. At that point my commitment had to be to my family and my health, so I chose to shut down Project Hodos. I put any further involvement in ministry on hold and returned to employment as a computer programmer.

My health has now fully recovered, and I have retired. Ordination no longer feels like an appropriate goal, but I still care about the Christian community in its current struggles. More than forty-five years into what has been for me a conscious spiritual journey, I want to share some of what I have come to. I wish someone could have shared these understandings with me early in my own journey. I hope that expressing them now will be helpful.

There is one more thing I must try to say about my journey: I have just expended a lot of words—probably too many words—to tell you about it from the perspective of events and experiences—and I guess that's okay—except, somehow, it does not tell the most important thing. There is something much deeper that happened along the way. The experiences and events I have told you about all had something to do with it, yet it somehow depended on none of them. This deeper thing was the dawning in my awareness of the realization that God is the only reality, that God is all there is. This can be referred to as non-dual consciousness. I am not able to spend much of my time in that state of awareness, but I at least touch it occasionally. I recognize this to be what Christian mystics of the past have referred to as the unitive state, what has been considered the culminating stage of the spiritual journey in which the self, after having been appropriately purged and purified, is absorbed into divinity.

While I am grateful for this traditional understanding, I actually see it somewhat differently. For me the key transition came in seeing through my ego. Through meditation, psychotherapy, and life experience I came to see that my ego—this thing that is so concerned with survival and well-being—is just that: a thing—a function of my physical, mortal brain whose job it is to keep my body alive and my needs met. Although it identifies with and is closely connected to the core of my consciousness, it is not that core, it is not the ultimate me. The core is spirit, which is a word for something that I am at a loss to fully define or describe. The ego, the small self, the personality, is transient, mortal, and very much dependent on physical biology; the spirit, the larger Self, is eternal and one with all spirit.

Whereas many in the mystical tradition saw union with God as a gift bestowed on only a few who had struggled long and hard to become holy, I see it as the ultimate fact that always has been and always will be true. God creates by an outpouring or overflowing of Gods own self, so all of creation is simply God incarnate. Creation is a dance of divine stuff. Some of that stuff may not be aware of its divinity—stuff like us humans who become so caught up in our self-consciousness that we lose touch with our spirit-consciousness and our deepest identity. The first major destination of the spiritual journey for such beings is to recover that awareness, to realize that we—each of us—is a little bit of God swimming in a vast ocean of God.

Blasphemy? The shallower parts of the tradition might see it as such, but I think not. This is the root of the experience of grace and the basis of true humility.

About the Author

John Speers has spent most of his life trying to make sense of Christianity in relation to science, spirituality, and everything else. In his 50's he took time out from his career as a computer programmer to complete a Master of Divinity degree at Drew University Theology School. He lives in upstate New York with his wife Louise. They have two daughters.

Made in United States
North Haven, CT
19 April 2024

51530298R00134